"Some of my friends say strange things and hold strange views, but because they are my friends I can't just dismiss what they say. Having friends who think differently from me helps expand my thinking and rescue me from the limitations of my current perspective. I give my friends the benefit of the doubt when they say things that are outrageous. Matthew Schlimm invites us to do the same with the Old Testament, helps us to listen to many of its notoriously outrageous statements, and also shares with us worthwhile insights from other people who are friends with the Old Testament (and from yet other people who would not see themselves as its friends)."

—**John Goldingay**, Fuller Theological Seminary

"At a time when many critique and marginalize the Old Testament, Schlimm argues that we need to appreciate it as a friend—a friend who is at once odd, insightful, complicated, controversial, and realistic. He is not willing to give up on the Old Testament or its God. *This Strange and Sacred Scripture* creatively engages the difficulties that trouble interpreters. While some may disagree with the author at points, this book's tone and presentation invite readers to join the conversation about and with this unique friend we call the Bible."

—**M. Daniel Carroll R. (Rodas)**, Denver Seminary

THIS STRANGE
and
SACRED SCRIPTURE

THIS STRANGE
and
SACRED SCRIPTURE

Wrestling with the Old Testament
and Its Oddities

Matthew Richard Schlimm

Baker Academic

a division of Baker Publishing Group
Grand Rapids, Michigan

Published by Baker Academic
a division of Baker Publishing Group
P.O. Box 6287, Grand Rapids, MI 49516-6287
www.bakeracademic.com

Printed in the United States of America

Library of Congress Cataloging-in-Publication Data
Schlimm, Matthew Richard.
    This strange and sacred scripture : wrestling with the Old Testament and its oddities / Matthew Richard Schlimm.
        pages cm
    Includes bibliographical references and index.
    ISBN 978-0-8010-3979-9 (pbk.)
    1. Bible. Old Testament—Introductions. 2. Bible. Old Testament—Theology. I. Title.
BS1140.3.S35 2015
221.6—dc23   2014030699

15   16   17   18   19   20   21   8   7   6   5   4   3   2

To
Stephanie Lind Schlimm

In Loving Memory of
Catherine Ann Schlimm

Contents

Figures

Preface and Acknowledgments

S TAYING ON MIDDLE GROUND IS DIFFICULT, like trying to walk along the jagged ridge of a mountain.

In this book, I try to find and remain on middle ground when approaching the Old Testament's problems. It's not easy. I have sought, on the one hand, to affirm the sacred status of the Old Testament, as the church has done for centuries. I refuse to give up on the Bible, no matter how problematic it may be. The Old Testament has been my friend since childhood, and as with any good friendship, there are commitments that persist amid difficulties.

On the other hand, I have also sought to be completely honest about the disturbing things readers find in the Old Testament. I refuse easy solutions that disrespect readers' honest reactions to the Bible. I will not abandon my God-given sense of what's right and wrong to endorse things like violence or sexism in God's name.

It's easy to lose one's footing on the top of a mountain, falling off one side or the other to injury or death. Similarly, it's easy either to give up on the Old Testament or to insist that people accept whatever the Bible says as an act of blind faith. But either option is hazardous: If we reject the Old Testament, our faith is harmed by abandoning all the riches there. If we accept it blindly and simplistically, our conscience is injured.

It's only on the summit that we see beauty in every direction. This book tries to find the Old Testament's beauty even while dealing with difficult issues.

This book is written for Christians by a Christian. There are times when a scholar needs to address a broader audience. But there are also times when a scholar has important words for her or his own faith community.

I try to write in an engaging and accessible style that makes this book readable by college students and educated laity. At the same time, I also aim to address issues intelligently so that this book is useful to seminary students and perhaps even some scholars.

This book tries to answer questions that naturally arise when Christians today open the Old Testament. I don't address certain questions that result from academic study (e.g., how many layers of editing there are in different books of the Bible). At the same time, biblical scholarship has resources that can answer questions Christians find themselves asking about the Old Testament. I draw on these resources throughout. Readers wanting to dig deeper are invited to study the footnotes and the "For Further Study" sections at the end of chapters. The website www.MatthewSchlimm.com has additional resources.

Even with these limitations, this book is far from exhaustive. I don't focus on bizarre onetime happenings in the Bible, like the frightening events of Exodus 4:24–26 or the account of the *nephilim* of Genesis 6:1–4 (though I have used "Nephilim" as a name for one of my fantasy football teams). I don't have the space to explore issues like election (why God appears to have favorites) or how the Old Testament relates to the New. More could also be said about matters I deal with briefly, like imprecatory psalms. Perhaps future volumes will take up these issues.

A Word about the Words "Old Testament"

It may seem odd that in a book affirming the Old Testament's value, I have chosen to call it the *Old Testament*. This title has problems, and some have suggested that we instead talk about the first thirty-nine books of the Protestant Bible as either the *Hebrew Bible* or the *First Testament*.[1]

There are good reasons for preferring these alternate titles. Today, "old" often means "inferior." No one boasts, "I get to do all my work on a really old computer!" Look up "old" in a thesaurus, and you're bound to find words with highly negative connotations: *outdated, obsolete, archaic, senile, decrepit, dilapidated, faded, dull, feeble, weak, remote, bygone, extinct, passé, replaceable*, and *on the way out*.[2] Hardly an attractive portrait.

Unfortunately, substitutes like *Hebrew Bible* and *First Testament* have problems as well. Some parts of the Old Testament were originally written in Aramaic, not Hebrew, so calling it the *Hebrew Bible* is inexact at best. Furthermore, this title isn't particularly relevant for the vast majority of Christians

---

1. For essays on this and related topics, see Brooks and Collins, eds., *Hebrew Bible or Old Testament?*; Knowles et al., eds., *Contesting Texts*; Bellis and Kaminsky, eds., *Jews, Christians, and the Theology of the Hebrew Scriptures*.

2. Rodale, *Synonym Finder*, 805.

A Jewish Perspective on the Term "Old Testament"

"At least for Christian seminaries and churches, the term *Old Testament* is not only appropriate but also desirable. I further contend that terms like *Hebrew Bible* . . . serve ultimately either to erase Judaism (since 'Jews' are not 'Hebrews' . . .) or to deny Christians part of their own canon. . . . The so-called 'neutral' term is actually one of Protestant hegemony."

Amy-Jill Levine, "Jewish-Christian Relations," 297

---

today, who read a translation rather than the original Hebrew. Some Jewish interpreters have even found the term *Hebrew Bible* to be more problematic than *Old Testament*. (See "A Jewish Perspective on the Term 'Old Testament.'")

The title *First Testament*, meanwhile, lacks currency. It has a biblical precedent (Heb. 8–9), but with so few people using it, it creates confusion. Those who have never heard the term before might even assume that it refers to something outside of Protestant and Catholic Bibles, like the *Book of Mormon*, which is subtitled *Another Testament of Jesus Christ*.

In the end, I have chosen to keep using the term *Old Testament*, because, despite its problems, Christians tend to know what I mean when I use the term. This name doesn't match what it describes especially well. (While the Old Testament is old, it speaks in new ways to faith communities today.) It's important to remember that names rarely do justice to the complexities of what they describe. My last name, for example, is a German word that means *bad, nasty, awful,* and *naughty*.[3] I have no idea what my ancestors did to earn that name! Nevertheless, I hope that when German-speakers meet me, they recognize that my name's meaning may not be the best description of who I am. In a similar way, the term "the Old Testament" doesn't describe the contents of its books especially well. Yet we can still use that term for convenience's sake, just as people can use my last name.

Acknowledgments

I couldn't write this book without a community of support. First and foremost, I thank the president and trustees of the University of Dubuque. Their generous support of me as a scholar has allowed me to complete this book expeditiously. I am especially grateful for the sabbatical they granted me in

---

3. Fortey, *Collins German-English, English-German Dictionary*.

the spring of 2012 and for the Joseph and Linda Chlapaty Research Chair in Church Renewal that they awarded me for the 2012–13 academic year. The University of Dubuque Theological Seminary is a wonderful place, where we do a great job preparing pastors for ministry.

Furthermore, I am deeply grateful for the many people who read drafts of this book (or parts thereof) and offered vital feedback: John Goldingay, Amy Frykholm, Caleb Schultz, Elmer Colyer, Jacob Stromberg, Amanda Benckhuysen, Margaret Jumonville, Stephanie Schlimm, David McNitzky, David Stark, and Christian education classes at Alamo Heights United Methodist Church (San Antonio, Texas) and Highland United Methodist Church (Raleigh, North Carolina). Thanks are also due to my trusty research assistants, John Emery, Stephen Cort, and Julius Sheppard.

Last of all, I thank my family: Roger, Ruth Ann, John, David, G & G, Gram, Amanda, Mom, and Dad. I give special thanks for my wonderful wife, Stephanie, and our children, Isaiah and Anna. They make me smile more than I had ever dreamed possible.

Abbreviations

General

ABD — *Anchor Bible Dictionary.* Edited by D. N. Freedman. 6 vols. New York: Doubleday, 1992

AEL² — *Ancient Egyptian Literature.* Edited by Miriam Lichtheim. 2nd ed. 3 vols. Berkeley: University of California Press, 2006.

alt. — altered

ANF — *The Ante-Nicene Fathers.* Edited by Alexander Roberts and James Donaldson. 1885–87. 10 vols. Repr. Peabody, MA: Hendrickson, 1994

BCE — before the Common Era

BDAG — Bauer, W., F. W. Danker, W. F. Arndt, and F. W. Gingrich. *Greek-English Lexicon of the New Testament and Other Early Christian Literature.* 3rd ed. Chicago: University of Chicago Press, 2000

chap(s). — chapter(s)

CE — Common Era

CEB — Common English Bible

cf. — *confer*, compare

COS — *The Context of Scripture.* Edited by W. W. Hallo. 3 vols. Leiden: Brill, 1997–2003.

ed(s). — editor(s), edited by; edition

e.g. — *exempli gratia*, for example

esp. — especially

et al. — *et alii*, and others

exp. — expanded

Gen. litt. — *De Genesi ad litteram,* On Genesis Literally Interpreted

ibid. — *ibidem*, in the same place

i.e. — *id est*, that is

KJV — King James Version

LCL — Loeb Classical Library

n. — note, footnote, endnote

NASB — New American Standard Bible

NIV — New International Version

NJPS — *The Tanakh: The Holy Scriptures; The New JPS Translation according to the Traditional Hebrew Text*

NLT — New Living Translation

NRSV — New Revised Standard Version

NT — New Testament

OT — Old Testament

OTP	*Old Testament Pseudepigrapha*. Edited by J. H. Charlesworth. 2 vols. Peabody, MA: Hendrickson, 1983–85	TDOT	*Theological Dictionary of the Old Testament*. Edited by G. J. Botterweck and H. Ringgren. Translated by J. T. Willis, G. W. Bromiley, and D. E. Green. 15 vols. Grand Rapids: Eerdmans, 1974–95
pt(s).	part(s)		
repr.	reprinted		
rev.	revised	trans.	translator, translated by, translation
TDNT	*Theological Dictionary of the New Testament*. Edited by G. Kittel and G. Friedrich. Translated by G. W. Bromiley. 10 vols. Grand Rapids: Eerdmans, 1964–76	vol(s).	volume(s)
		x	(number of) times (a term occurs)

Old Testament

Genesis	Gen.	Nehemiah	Neh.	Hosea	Hosea
Exodus	Exod.	Esther	Esther	Joel	Joel
Leviticus	Lev.	Job	Job	Amos	Amos
Numbers	Num.	Psalms	Ps. (Pss.)	Obadiah	Obad.
Deuteronomy	Deut.	Proverbs	Prov.	Jonah	Jon.
Joshua	Josh.	Ecclesiastes	Eccles.	Micah	Mic.
Judges	Judg.	Song of Songs	Song	Nahum	Nah.
Ruth	Ruth	Isaiah	Isa.	Habakkuk	Hab.
1–2 Samuel	1–2 Sam.	Jeremiah	Jer.	Zephaniah	Zeph.
1–2 Kings	1–2 Kings	Lamentations	Lam.	Haggai	Hag.
1–2 Chronicles	1–2 Chron.	Ezekiel	Ezek.	Zechariah	Zech.
Ezra	Ezra	Daniel	Dan.	Malachi	Mal.

New Testament

Matthew	Matt.	1–2 Thessalonians	1–2 Thess.
Mark	Mark	1–2 Timothy	1–2 Tim.
Luke	Luke	Titus	Titus
John	John	Philemon	Philem.
Acts	Acts	Hebrews	Heb.
Romans	Rom.	James	James
1–2 Corinthians	1–2 Cor.	1–2 Peter	1–2 Pet.
Galatians	Gal.	1–3 John	1–3 John
Ephesians	Eph.	Jude	Jude
Philippians	Phil.	Revelation	Rev.
Colossians	Col.		

1

Is the Old Testament an Enemy, Stranger, or Friend to the Christian Faith?

A DEEP TENSION EXISTS at the heart of the Christian faith. On the one hand, the church affirms the sacred nature of the Old Testament. We claim it as God's word. It forms three-quarters of our Bibles.

Yet the Old Testament is utterly strange. It's the last thing we would expect God's word to say. It remains foreign, even when translated into English. It's filled with bizarre stories, laws, and poetry. (See "Strange, Unfamiliar, and Surprising.")

Right at the outset, readers find talk of the world's origins, and it has nothing to do with what modern scientists have found.

As if this stumbling block weren't bad enough, the chapters that follow depict the legendary figures of our faith engaging in all sorts of sordid behavior. Abraham has multiple wives. The first thing Moses does as an adult is kill someone. David, supposedly the greatest king of Israel, is actually the sleaziest of politicians—someone who has his own friend killed after sleeping with the friend's wife.

Even if we can stomach the debauchery of Old Testament characters, we face a new set of challenges when confronted with the Old Testament's violence. Warfare appears in nearly every book of Old Testament. We cannot escape it. Perhaps most disturbing of all, God sometimes commands the Israelites to kill everything that breathes. Why has the church kept such writings in its Bibles?

Or, to turn to an equally pervasive problem, why does the Old Testament give so little attention to women? Why do some texts devalue women? Obviously the Old Testament came from an ancient culture that was biased in favor of men, but can we say anything positive about the Bible and women?

The Old Testament's strangeness takes center stage in its law codes. What do we do with these never-ending lists of rules and regulations? How could anyone possibly keep them all straight? Why would anyone want to? Why do these laws command people to do weird things like sacrifice animals at the place of worship? Why does the Old Testament forbid pork (including bacon!), but then allow people to eat locusts?

If readers stick with the Old Testament long enough, they begin to notice that one text will say something completely contrary to what's said elsewhere. To name one of many possible examples, some passages say that people get what they deserve in this lifetime (e.g., Deut. 28), while other texts are certain that the wicked prosper while the righteous suffer (e.g., Eccles. 8:14). Which one is it? How do we handle the contradictions of the Old Testament?

Prayers are another oddity in the Old Testament. Rather than being calm and collected, people praying in the Old Testament display their fiercest anger toward God. They scream with rage at the Creator, hurl insults at God, question God's ways, and demand that God get back to work. Who dares to talk to their Maker with such animosity?

Even more bothersome are texts where God speaks with animosity toward Israel. The God of the Old Testament strikes many readers as cruel, vindictive,

---

Strange, Unfamiliar, and Surprising

"There is something very strange about the biblical story—something that we cannot reduce to the categories of our experience, something that cannot be domesticated within our world. There is a 'scandalous,' offensive dimension to the biblical story."

Bernhard W. Anderson, *Living Word of the Bible*, 82

"Because the Bible is, as we confess, 'the live word of the living God,' it will not submit in any compliant way to the accounts we prefer to give of it. There is something intrinsically unfamiliar about the book, and when we seek to override that unfamiliarity we are on the hazardous ground of idolatry."

Walter Brueggemann, in Brueggemann, Placher, and Blount, *Struggling with Scripture*, 5

"The Bible is *essentially surprising* in all its parts."

Ellen F. Davis, *Wondrous Depth*, 4

If We Wrote the Bible

If God had put any of us in charge of writing Scripture for billions of believers in future generations, surely we would have come up with something quite different. Our account of the world's beginnings would match the latest scientific findings. The characters in our Scripture would avoid evil in fun ways that inspire others to do the same. Violence would recede to the background while blessings of peace showered down on everyone. Women and men would be treated as equals without inequalities that make no sense. Laws wouldn't ramble for very long, and they certainly wouldn't command strange behaviors. Every contradiction would be ironed out before things went to print. The prayers would be beautiful, and God's love would always be self-evident.

However, God didn't charge us with writing Scripture. So what do we do with the Old Testament, which is so different from what we expect God's word to be?

---

vengeful, and destructive. They see little resemblance between this wrathful deity and the forgiving God of the New Testament.

The Old Testament is seriously strange Scripture. (See "If We Wrote the Bible.")

The Old Testament as Enemy: Marcion and His Children

Faced with so many troubling features, many people have rejected the Old Testament's sacred status. About a hundred years after the death of Jesus, an influential leader named Marcion did just that. He firmly believed that the wrathful God of the Old Testament couldn't also be the loving God revealed by Jesus Christ.[1]

Although the church in Rome kicked Marcion out in 144 CE, his ideas spread quickly. Some historians estimate that around 170 CE, the followers of Marcion outnumbered those opposed to him.[2]

In time, church leaders like Irenaeus and Tertullian mounted attacks against Marcion's thinking. Among other things, they showed that Jesus himself did not come to destroy the Old Testament (cf. Matt. 5:17).[3] Marcion's movement

---

1. Cf. Tertullian, *Against Marcion* 1.25–26 (*ANF* 3:290–93); Moll, *Arch-Heretic Marcion*, 47–64, esp. 54, 59, 62–64. I use the term "Old Testament [OT]" for convenience's sake, not because Marcion used it.

2. Clabeaux, "Marcion," *ABD* 4:514–15.

3. Irenaeus deals with Marcion in *Against Heresies*, e.g., 1.27; 3.4; 3.12.12; 3.25.3; 4.27–32 (*ANF* 1:309–567, e.g., 352, 417, 434–35, 459, 498–506). Tertullian deals with Marcion in *Against*

Paving the Way for Nazism

In the late nineteenth and early twentieth centuries, many prominent thinkers in Germany devalued the Old Testament. Both the theologian Friedrich Schleiermacher and the church historian Adolf von Harnack expressed deep sympathy for Marcion.[a] In biblical studies, the famous Old Testament scholar Friedrich Delitzsch emphasized, "The Old Testament is full of deceptions of all kinds."[b] Meanwhile, the world-renowned New Testament scholar Rudolf Bultmann wrote, "To the Christian faith the Old Testament is not in the true sense God's word."[c] It's not difficult to imagine how such assessments contributed to a society willing to persecute Jews.

a. Schleiermacher, *Christian Faith*, 608–11; Harnack, *Marcion*, esp. 134, 137–38, 142–43.
b. Delitzsch, *Die grosse Täuschung*, 2:52 (trans. Kraeling in *Old Testament*, 158).
c. Bultmann, "Significance of the Old Testament," 32; see also 34–35. For more on this topic, see S. Heschel, *Aryan Jesus*.

eventually lost popularity. However, even while many details of his thinking have faded away, his basic impulse to devalue the Old Testament persists across time.

To name an extreme example, in the eighteenth century the British philosopher Thomas Morgan spoke with vehement hatred about the Old Testament, saying its authors were a "miraculously stupid People [who] were always inspired and prepossessed with the Spirit of the Devil."[4]

Similar examples can be found, especially in the decades leading up to the Holocaust, when many German scholars spoke comparably. They called for a return to Marcion's ideals while ridiculing the Old Testament's contents. (See "Paving the Way for Nazism.")

The Old Testament as Stranger: The Church Today

Today, few Christians want to go as far as Marcion or the Nazis. Yet the Old Testament is *so* strange that Christians have a much easier time ignoring it than wrestling with all the issues it presents.

In other words, we don't openly oppose the Old Testament, but then again, we don't go to great lengths to emphasize its importance either. We may recognize it as useful background for understanding Jesus and Paul, but we tend to stick to the New Testament. We treat the Old Testament less as an enemy and more as a stranger, a mere acquaintance, or a superficial friend. (See "The Situation Today.")

Marcion (ANF 3:269–475); see esp. 7.7 (*ANF* 3:352). See the useful discussion of these and other ancient works in Moll, *Arch-Heretic Marcion*, 48–54.
    4. Morgan, *Moral Philosopher*, 2:71.

The Situation Today

"It would be more correct to speak not of a rejection of the Old Testament but of an apathy towards it, a feeling that it does not matter greatly, a sense that, while no doubt theoretical arguments for its importance can be advanced, the whole matter remains remote and lacking in immediacy."

James Barr, "New Crisis," 29

"Few Christians today would take as extreme a negative view of the Old Testament as Marcion, Harnack, or the Nazis, but one need not officially and explicitly decanonize the Old Testament in order to achieve practically the same effect."

J. J. M. Roberts, "Old Testament for the Church," 18

Thus many churches do very little with the Old Testament during Sunday morning worship. Some congregations avoid reading the Old Testament altogether. Others read from it but then focus on the New Testament in preaching.[5]

My sense is *not* that these churches hate the Old Testament. Instead, people in these congregations are painfully aware of all the difficult issues the Old Testament raises. They recognize that these issues are too complex to address in the middle of a worship service. They realize that people often feel stupid when the Bible doesn't make sense—as though there's something wrong with them for not knowing what's going on. And so, it simply becomes easier to lay the Old Testament aside, to treat it as a stranger, rather than fix our attention on it.

The Old Testament as Friend in Faith

The problem with ignoring the Old Testament is that we make ourselves deaf to all the incredible things that God has to say to us through it. For thousands of years, Jewish and Christian readers have cherished the words of these Scriptures. People from across the world in different ages have made the audacious claim that they experience the one true God as they read and study the incredibly odd Old Testament.

In this book I argue that, even in the face of perplexing questions, we can still see the Old Testament as our friend in faith.[6] This idea needs some unpacking. How can the Old Testament, or any other book, serve as a friend?

5. R. Hays, "Can the Gospels Teach Us?," 405.
6. Many books exist that wrestle with questions raised by the OT. Two recent examples are Lamb, *God Behaving Badly*; Copan, *Is God a Moral Monster?* A key difference between these other books and mine is my emphasis on seeing the OT as a friend in faith.

In a *Calvin and Hobbes* comic strip, Calvin waits for the school bus alongside his do-gooder neighbor and classmate Susie Derkins. Holding up a textbook, she remarks, "I love my schoolbooks. Just think! Pretty soon we'll have

Caring for Books

"People care for the books they read; and they are changed by what they care for—both during the time of reading and in countless later ways more difficult to discern."

Martha Nussbaum,
Love's Knowledge, 231

read *all* this!" In the next frame, she continues: "I like to read ahead and see what we're going to learn next. It's so exciting to know stuff. Having a book is like having a good friend with you."

Calvin then lifts his own textbook, which he has obviously spent considerable time doodling in. He replies, "If you flip the pages of *my* book, an animated T. Rex drives the Batmobile and explodes!"

The strip ends with Susie staring blankly into space while remarking, "Sometimes I think books are the only friends worth having."[7]

This idea of *literary friendships* has been around for centuries. In the Italian Renaissance, Niccolò Machiavelli described his friendship with books. After facing imprisonment and torture, Machiavelli went into exile. He spent his days as a farmer and his nights reading great books. He writes:

> I take off my work-day clothes, filled with dust and mud, and don royal and curial garments. Worthily dressed, I enter into the antique courts of men of antiquity, where, warmly received, I feed upon that which is my only food and which was meant for me. I am not ashamed to speak with them and ask them the reasons of their actions, and they, because of their humanity, answer me. Four hours can pass, and I feel no weariness; my troubles forgotten, I neither fear poverty nor dread death. I give myself over entirely to them.[8]

Machiavelli's sense that books could be companions has become increasingly common in our own day. The great literary critic Wayne Booth says that literary friendships offer "loves of a kind that make life together worth having."[9] (See "Caring for Books.")

At the heart of this book is the basic idea that THE OLD TESTAMENT IS OUR FRIEND IN FAITH.[10] As we get to know its characters and authors, we are drawn into their worlds. They teach us about the difficulty of the moral life,

7. Watterson, *There's Treasure Everywhere*, 25.
8. Quoted in Marriott, "Biographical Note: Nicolò Machiavelli," in *The Prince*, x.
9. Booth, *Company We Keep*, chap. 6, esp. 174.
10. My mentor Ellen F. Davis describes how the OT can be our friend in faith in "Losing a Friend," 83–94; cf. Lancaster, *Women and the Authority of Scripture*, 169.

the wonder of worship, and the longings of the God who created the universe. As we embrace the Old Testament, we embrace its God. As we become close to the Old Testament, we also become close to the God who showed up at Abraham and Sarah's tent, the God who heard Hannah's desperate prayers, the God who stood beside Daniel in a foreign land.

"Without friends," Aristotle observed, "individuals would not choose to live, even if they possessed all other goods."[11] There are many reasons why Aristotle thought so highly of friendship, and each reason can help us see the value of the Old Testament as our friend in faith.

First, friendship dispels loneliness. Many Christians today feel very alone. Our secular culture teaches us to act as though God doesn't exist. And so, we need people in our lives who tell us we aren't crazy for believing in God. We need friends who admire rather than question self-sacrifice. The Old Testament does precisely this. It reminds us that people of faith are not alone. We are joined by a great cloud of witnesses— as the author of Hebrews puts it (12:1)—a community of Old Testament heroes who cheer for us even when the world tries to shoot us down. (See "Breaking Down Isolation.")

Second, friends are fun to be around. While some parts of the Old Testament are certainly difficult and require discipline to read, other parts are a joy to spend time with. For example, the story of Joseph and his brothers (Gen. 37–50) has been recognized as one of the great stories of world literature.[12] While it has much to teach us about God and ourselves, this learning is an innately pleasurable activity: we travel with Joseph amid his reversals of fortune and watch in suspense as he encounters his brothers later in life. Other parts of the Old Testament are similarly a joy to read, whether we think of the dazzling visions of hope in Isaiah 40–55, the intimate sexual imagery in Song of Songs, or the thrilling moments as Esther saves her people. When we read the Old Testament, it's like we're listening to a friend who knows how to capture our imaginations, whisper juicy secrets, and tell great stories.

> **Breaking Down Isolation**
>
> "Reading the Old Testament will lead us to community. The Old Testament breaks down our isolation and teaches us that we enter into the life of promise by joining ourselves to God's people."
>
> Michael Duggan,
> *Consuming Fire*, xiv

---

11. Aristotle, *Nicomachean Ethics* 8.1 (trans. Rackham, LCL 73:450–51, alt. for gender inclusivity).

12. As Speiser (*Genesis*, 292) puts it, "For sustained dramatic effect the narrative is unsurpassed in the whole Pentateuch."

Third, in addition to bringing us happiness, friends are also useful to have around. They provide valuable information and ideas that allow us to navigate life more easily. The Old Testament provides us with equipment for faithful living (cf. 2 Tim. 3:16–17). Readers of the Old Testament receive prayers for crying out to God, stories that speak to our hearts, and prophetic speeches that challenge our ways of living. Ultimately, reading the Old Testament brings us into the presence of God.

Finally, the best of friends make us better people. Friends shape our attitudes, desires, and character. We become like our friends. When the Old Testament is our friend, we become more holy, more aware of God's presence in the world, and more concerned with justice and righteousness.

Many of us do things we wouldn't otherwise simply because a trustworthy friend recommends them. The Old Testament, similarly, inspires us to try new things. It gives us new ways of being and acting—ways of life that we never would have considered otherwise. (See "The World Anew.")

> **The World Anew**
>
> "Friends create the world anew each day. Without their loving care, courage would not suffice to keep hearts strong for life."
>
> Helen Keller, via Seymour, *Treasure of Friendship*, 8

Even while inspiring us to try new things, good friends know who we truly are. At times, they even know us better than we know ourselves. We need these sorts of close friends in our lives because all of us are prone to self-deception. Sometimes we fail to see sin as harmful to ourselves and all we love. Other times, we suffer from low self-esteem, feeling worthless and unlovable. Like a good friend, the Old Testament reminds us of the dangers of sin, as well as how we are made in the very image of God (Gen. 1:26–28). It artfully holds in tension the worst of human nature and our worth in God's eyes. The Old Testament reminds us of all that really matters.

Being a Good Friend to the Old Testament

Lasting friendship doesn't just happen. Certain elements must be present, like trust, respect, and vulnerability. We won't develop a deep friendship with the Old Testament if we are suspicious of it or somehow biased against it.[13] Similarly, we won't get very far if we assume we know what it will say before we've listened carefully. (See "Reading with Trust.")

13. Davis, "Losing a Friend," 86, 88.

Because the Old Testament is such a quirky friend, it requires extra work. We cannot relate to the Old Testament on the basis of a shared culture or common age. The cultural, geographic, and temporal barriers are too great. Our friendship with the Old Testament is like a long-distance relationship.

Communication mishaps are bound to happen. We will need a peaceful persistence as we deal with all the differences between our world and the world of the Old Testament.

Unfortunately, patience doesn't come easily for most of us. Our culture teaches us to read things as quickly as possible. With the Old Testament, we instead need to slow down. (See "Looking Closely.") Sometimes, passages make sense only if we're willing to read, reread, and read yet again, dwelling on particular words and phrases with much reflection. Talking about Scripture, an early rabbi said, "Turn it this way, turn it that way, everything is in it; keep your eye on it, grow old and aged over it, and from it do not stir—for you have no better portion than it."[14] These words apply as much to us today as they did centuries ago.

Good friendships require not only patience but also ways of dealing with differences fruitfully. In the course of any friendship, unanticipated challenges arise. Even close friends are bound to have fundamentally different perspectives on some matters. An aspect of authentic friendship is that the relationship does not cease amid such differences. Instead, good friends are willing to be humble, to consider different perspectives, and to be open to new ways of living.

At times, friends say upsetting things. However, friendship means that these challenges

> **Reading with Trust**
>
> "I must subordinate my mind and heart to the book if I am to enjoy it to the full."
>
> Wayne Booth,
> *Rhetoric of Fiction*, 137–38
>
> "No poem will give up its secret to a reader who enters it regarding the poet as a potential deceiver, and determined not to be taken in. We must risk being taken in, if we are to get anything."
>
> C. S. Lewis,
> *Experiment in Criticism*, 94

> **Looking Closely**
>
> "Movies and television, even modern novels have taught us to expect dramatic scene painting, psychological probing, explosive exchanges. But the Bible tells a story like Rembrandt etches one. You have to slow down and look closely to see much of anything at all, and then let your heart dwell on what you see."
>
> Ellen F. Davis,
> *Getting Involved with God*, 57

---

14. Goldin, ed., *Living Talmud*, 223, alt. to update the language. Ellen Davis first drew my attention to this quotation.

do not end the relationship. Friends stay committed to others even when they do not understand each other. We may question our friends. We may challenge them. We may playfully engage and entertain our differences, even joking about our contrary perspectives. However, we don't reject friends simply because they aren't what we expected. The Old Testament holds much that's unexpected, and friendship with it requires a willingness to deal with differences between ourselves and the text.[15]

Christians have many friends in faith: not just the Old Testament, but also the New Testament, the church's rich tradition, the church's teachings today, and fellow believers (i.e., literal friends). The Holy Spirit can even use our experiences, reason, and emotions to serve as friends in faith.[16] While this book focuses on reclaiming the Old Testament as our theological companion, I hope that the Old Testament joins a great company of friends who together bring us into God's presence and help us discern to God's will.

Conclusion

Some of the most life-changing friendships are those we develop with people unlike ourselves, people who come from other cultures, people who don't belong to our age or demographic. As our worlds collide, new realities crack open. We are no longer stuck with the same old boring existence. We are transformed by the renewing of our minds. Despite its age, the Old Testament can give the church fresh ways of thinking about God, humanity, and creation.

For Further Study

Other books also foster deep friendship with the Old Testament, whether they use friendship imagery or not. The books below were written by two of the best seminary professors today, and each one offers many ways of growing closer to God's Word.

Davis, Ellen F. *Getting Involved with God: Rediscovering the Old Testament*. Cambridge, MA: Cowley, 2001.

> Ellen Davis does a masterful job while carefully studying a variety of passages from the Old Testament. This book has led many to fall in love with the Old Testament.

15. Davis, "Losing a Friend," 88.
16. The Wesleyan tradition upholds the Bible as the primary source of theological authority, but it also recognizes the importance of tradition, reason, and experience (see Gunter et al., *Wesley and the Quadrilateral*). Additionally, one could make a case for adding emotions and fellow believers to the mix.

Fretheim, Terence E. *About the Bible: Short Answers to Big Questions.* 1999. Rev. and exp. ed. Minneapolis: Augsburg, 2009.

> Terry Fretheim excels at concisely and clearly explaining a host of questions people bring to the Bible, such as: Why do Bible translations differ? How does the Bible relate God to suffering? Do prayers change the future?

The website www.MatthewSchlimm.com has additional resources, including group discussion questions.

2

Our Fleeting Moments in Paradise

ALREADY ON ITS FIRST PAGE, the Old Testament presents us with a problem. How do we read it after Darwin? Scientists claim the earth is billions of years old. Genesis talks about six days. Evolution asserts that humanity descended from animals. The Bible talks about Adam and Eve being fashioned by the hand of God.

Can we take the Bible seriously and also be open to the claims of modern science? Or do we need to choose between the two?

Many people feel particularly uneasy about this question because it seems that their deepest commitments come into conflict. On the one hand, they affirm the Bible as reliable, truthful, and sacred. On the other hand, they wonder whether they can honestly deny the evidence scientists have assembled in favor of evolutionary theory and the earth's old age. How do we balance our firm commitment to Scripture with an honest consideration of scientific evidence? This chapter considers these questions. It begins by turning to the idea of genre.

The Genre Question

Perhaps the most important judgment readers can make concerns *what type of literature*, or *genre*, they are reading. If we make a wrong judgment about the genre before us, we could easily miss the most important points the literature is trying to convey. In fact, things can quickly become comical when mistakes are made about the type of literature at hand.

In a stand-up comedy act, Ricky Gervais provides an interpretation of the popular nursery rhyme "Humpty Dumpty." It's funny precisely because he takes elements of the story much too literally. He begins, "I've never worked out what the moral of Humpty Dumpty is. I can only think of, 'Don't sit on a wall if you're an egg.' How is that applicable to an eight-year-old human?" As he continues, things become more and more ridiculous: "Don't send horses to perform medical procedures. Of course, they couldn't put him back together again. . . . They haven't got the dexterity. . . . They haven't got thumbs, let alone opposable thumbs. . . . If I had to design a perfect egg-crushing device, it would be a hoof."[1]

It would never occur to most of us to take "Humpty Dumpty" so literally. We instinctively know that it's not to be understood in this way. Yet many of us suspect that there's more to this poem than its clever rhyme and rhythm. It has a level of proverbial wisdom, suggesting that placing yourself above others ("on a wall") can lead to disaster ("a great fall") that cannot be fixed ("couldn't put him back together again"), no matter how many resources we have ("all the king's horses and all the king's men").

Drawing on this interpretation, Hollywood has made two movies titled *All the King's Men*, as well as one called *All the President's Men*—each about politics in America. These titles make clear *allusions* (or references) to this nursery rhyme, showing how power can corrupt and lead to irreparable disaster. They illustrate, in different ways, the figurative meaning of "Humpty Dumpty." Ricky Gervais, however, intentionally misses the figurative meaning to show how absurd the literal sense of the poem is.

To consider a more serious example, John Bunyan wrote the classic book *The Pilgrim's Progress* in the seventeenth century. At the beginning of this book, he describes it as an *allegory*: a story filled with symbolic and metaphorical meaning. As one reads it, the symbolic meaning is hard to miss. The main character is named "Christian." He travels to a place called "the Celestial City." Along the way, he talks with people who have names like "Hopeful" and "Hypocrisy." He travels by places like "the Doubting Castle," which is owned by "Giant Despair." Obviously readers are not supposed to see this quest as a historical journey undertaken by an actual individual who once walked the earth. Rather, it symbolically describes the types of things Christians may encounter during their lives.[2] Trying to read this narrative historically would completely miss the point. It would fly in the face of the many signs Bunyan gives the reader that this quest should be understood figuratively. (See "Wolves and Whales.")

1. Gervais, "Humpty Dumpty from Politics."
2. Bunyan, *The Pilgrim's Progress*.

Wolves and Whales

"The story of Little Red Riding Hood may serve to caution mothers not to send their young daughters on dangerous errands as well as to teach little girls not to stray from the straight path, be their intentions ever so laudable. In no circumstances, though, may it be used . . . for instructing zoologists in the anatomy of wolves."

Yehuda T. Radday, "Rivers of Paradise," 29

"When Melville wrote *Moby Dick*, the central concern of his work was not whaling per se so much as the effect of an obsession on Captain Ahab's life. To read *Moby Dick* as if it were a book about whales therefore misconstrues Melville's discourse."

Kenton L. Sparks, *God's Word*, 209

How we read is determined by what we think we are reading. If we misjudge genre, the Bible can become nonsensical.

Christians sometimes assume that reading the Bible faithfully means we must read it literally. However, as these two illustrations show, literal interpretations can actually take us very far from the meaning literature tries to convey.[3] (See "Genres of the Bible.")

Genres of the Bible

"The Bible contains a dizzying array of genres: histories, myths, novellas, tales, parables, legends, biographies, autobiographies, letters, genealogies, king lists, itineraries, theophanies, rituals, treaties, prophecies, apocalypses, proverbs, laments, love poetry, songs, and even a work of philosophical skepticism (Ecclesiastes). None of the biblical books corresponds precisely to any genres of modern literature. So if we approach a book like Genesis as if it were modern science . . . , the results can be very misleading and confusing."

Kenton L. Sparks, *Sacred Word*, 91–92

---

3. The word "literal" means different things to different people. For some people, reading the Bible "literally" simply means taking it seriously, in accord with the grain of the text. Interpretation in this sense is very good, and I'm not out to criticize those who read the Bible this way. However, other people think that reading the Bible literally means we must assume it's always speaking in historical terms and without symbols, exaggerations, metaphors, or figures. This approach is problematic, and it's what I focus on below. This approach reveals more about one's commitment to history than one's commitment to God. See "Literal, adj. and n.," *OED Online*; G. Green, "Narrative and Scriptural Truth," 91.

The Internet and the Bible

The internet is home to many types of websites. Some focus on reporting world events. Others allow friends to share what's going on in their lives. Still others provide snippets of information, like recipes or weather reports. There are other sites for photos, videos, fun, travel, education, gaming, shopping, and a million other things.

As we surf the web, switching from one website to another, we automatically adjust how we read. We may not even realize it, but we process a news report differently than someone's latest update on Twitter or Facebook.

It's easy to forget that the Bible has many types of literature, just as the internet has many types of websites. The more we understand the types of literature in the Bible, the better we can grasp the Bible's message.[a]

a. See Fretheim, *About the Bible*, 59–60, on different genres in a Sunday paper.

When readers turn to the opening chapters of Genesis, they need to make a decision about the type of literature before them. Is it best understood as scientific literature? Or does it belong to a different genre? Do these chapters invite readers to see their contents as literal or symbolic? This question is absolutely crucial. If we answer it wrongly, we may end up with the sort of absurd logic Gervais proposes about "Humpty Dumpty." We may miss the very truths that God wants us to find in the Bible. (See "The Internet and the Bible.")

Symbolic and Historical Possibilities

Churchgoers frequently feel uncomfortable with the question, could parts of the Bible be more symbolic than literal? We want the Bible to be taken seriously. It's the Word of God. Saying a passage is "just symbolic" seems to be an easy way to weasel out of applying the crucial messages of the Bible to our lives. It appears that we could then give the Bible a symbolic meaning anytime we didn't like its literal meaning. Furthermore, many people are concerned that if we say one part of the Bible is figurative, it's a slippery slope that can lead to saying the resurrection of Jesus didn't literally happen. (See "Picking and Choosing?")

Yet when one studies the Bible closely, it becomes clear that the writings themselves sometimes want us to understand things literally, but other times they clearly do not. Jesus says, "And if your right hand causes you to fall into sin, chop it off and throw it away. It's better that you lose a part of your body than that your whole body go into hell" (Matt. 5:30). We read this passage and immediately know that Jesus is engaging in a bit of exaggeration to make

---

Picking and Choosing?

Richard Dawkins is a prominent atheist. He claims that Christians "pick and choose which bits of Scripture to believe, which bits to write off as symbols or allegories. Such picking and choosing is a matter of personal decision."[a]

Dawkins fails to realize that biblical texts give people important clues about whether they should be understood literally or symbolically. It's not a matter of willy-nilly choosing what one likes and doesn't like. Rather, it's an interpretive judgment using God-given reason to make sense of evidence in the text itself. Furthermore, within the grand scheme of the Christian tradition, symbols are perhaps more sacred and meaningful than historical accounts. Christians do not write off the symbols of Scripture. We live by them.

a. Dawkins, *The God Delusion*, 269.

---

a point. Thus we hear these words and invariably choose to keep our right arms. Yet Christians can still take this verse seriously without dismembering themselves: Jesus tells us that we need to be concerned not only with sin, but also with the things that lead to sin. For example, if using the internet late at night leads to viewing pornography, then our computers should stay off in the evening and nighttime hours. (See "The Bible's Alpha Rule.")

When we look at other parts of the New Testament, it's clear that Jesus's resurrection is not simply a metaphor. Rather, the resurrection is obviously something that the writers want us to understand as a historical event. Thus they correlate the life of Jesus with other historical events and historical people (Luke 3:1–2). Similarly, when they discuss the resurrection, they make references

---

The Bible's Alpha Rule

"The very first command that God gives to Adam is 'Be fruitful and multiply.' It's the Alpha Rule of the Bible.

"Now, if I were taking the Bible absolutely literally, I could be 'fruitful' by loading up on peaches at Whole Foods Market and 'multiply' by helping my niece with her algebra homework. I could scratch this commandment off my list in twenty minutes flat.

"This hammers home a simple but profound lesson: When it comes to the Bible, there is always—but always—some level of interpretation, even on the most seemingly basic rules. In this case, I'm pretty sure that the Bible was talking about fertility, not math."

A. J. Jacobs, *Living Biblically*, 19

The Word of God and History

"The idea that the Bible declares the Word of God only when it speaks historically is one which must be abandoned, especially in the Christian Church. . . . The presumed equation of the Word of God with a 'historical' record is an inadmissible postulate which does not itself originate in the Bible at all but in the unfortunate habit of Western thought which assumes that the reality of a [narrative][a] stands or falls by whether it is 'history.'"

Karl Barth, *Church Dogmatics*, vol. 3, pt. 1:82

a. Here, the word "narrative" better translates Barth's word *Geschichte* than does "history." Although *Geschichte* can mean "history," it can also mean "story" or more generally "narrative," clearly the intended sense here. Otherwise Barth would be saying it's unfortunate when people assume that a history stands or falls by whether it's history. For a later expression of sentiments similar to Barth's, see Mark S. Smith, *Memoirs of God*, 162–66, condemning the "exaltation of history as the absolute or primary measure of truth in the Bible."

to witnesses to this event (1 Cor. 15:6). The apostle Paul says that the resurrection needs to be understood literally, or else his faith is in vain (1 Cor. 15:19–20).

In the Bible, then, some passages should be understood as literal and historical, like Jesus's resurrection. But others are obviously more figurative, like Jesus's arm-cutting words. God isn't confined to speaking through history. (See "The Word of God and History.")

To understand the depths of reality, we need a variety of genres: not only historical accounts and scientific postulates, but also poetry, allegories, and symbolic stories. (See "The Limits of Science.")

To put things differently, God can speak through any type of literature. At times, highly symbolic imagery dominates the landscape of Scripture. The Psalms overflow with poetry, songs, and metaphors that speak to the depths of our hearts. For example, Psalm 18:2 is only one verse, but it uses over half a dozen metaphors to describe God:

Faithful versus Literal

"In order to be 'faithful' to the Bible, it is not necessary to read it literally."

John Rogerson,
"What Difference Did
Darwin Make?," 89

> The LORD is my solid rock,
>   my fortress, my rescuer.
> My God is my rock—
> I take refuge in him!—
>   he's my shield,
>   my salvation's strength,
>   my place of safety. (Ps. 18:2)

The Limits of Science

In the past few decades, it has become increasingly clear that subjects like science are not completely neutral, fact-finding endeavors. The impulse of *modernity*, to collect data and organize it in supposedly objective categories, has come under increased scrutiny (hence, *postmodernity*). People have realized that science prizes what can be measured and quantified, over against highly meaningful concepts like ethics and love.

Although medical science helps us understand, diagnose, and treat diseases, it's also responsible for subjecting patients to painful and humiliating procedures that only delay death—if the patients are lucky. Similarly, scientific study of the atom has led to our ability to split it, but this newfound knowledge has resulted in more death and destruction than the human mind can comprehend.

So science has deepened our knowledge of some things, specifically quantifiable and testable data. Yet science has failed to offer the moral, ethical, and critical guidance that humanity has desperately needed in the last century.

If we took this verse literally, we would be idolaters: each of us would need an actual rock, fortress, and shield to worship. However, if we take it figuratively, these images combine to show us the strength, protection, and comfort that God offers. (See "Faithful versus Literal.")

Similarly, readers of the New Testament know that Jesus loved symbolic stories. He used parables constantly. Though symbolic, these stories unfold profound theological truth. Furthermore, Jesus's parables are not open to every interpretation under the sun. Rather, the stories themselves invite a range of good interpretations.

Understanding the Bible well requires our asking, "What type of literature do we have in a particular passage? Is its truth conveyed in a more literal or a more symbolic way?"

Adam and Eve, or Humanity and Life?

There are many signs that the stories of Adam, Eve, and their children are highly symbolic.[4] Unfortunately, some of these signs have been lost in translation.

---

4. Although scholars tend to look at Gen. 2:4b–3:24 (stopping before 4:1–16), there are many parallels between Gen. 2–3 and Gen. 4 (Schlimm, *From Fratricide to Forgiveness*, 139–40). One can think of these chapters in the following terms: "If Genesis 2–3 shows humanity disobeying God in a nearly ideal environment, then Genesis 4 shows humanity sinning amid the concrete realities of the world" (ibid., 139).

This text, along with most of the Old Testament, was originally written in Hebrew. (See "A Bumpy Ride.") When one learns Hebrew and studies these chapters, different meanings emerge than if one looks only at popular English translations.[5]

Hebrew Names

Our English Bibles speak of two characters named Adam and Eve. In some ways, these

names are appropriate since they have similarities with how the names sound in Hebrew. However, the name for the first man (*adam*) is the ordinary Hebrew word for "Human." "Eve" (*havvah*) actually means "Life." Their first child's name, "Cain" (*qayin*), sounds like several Hebrew words, including "Get," "Take," "Jealousy," "Funeral Song," and especially "Spear."[6] All of these words relate to the oldest son of Genesis 4. Meanwhile, the Hebrew name for "Abel" (*hebel*) is a word used to refer to a "Fleeting Breath," like one sees on a cold morning. It's there one moment and gone the next. Obviously, the character called Abel in Genesis 4 very much resembles a fleeting breath. He illustrates in both name and character the fragility of human existence. Finally, the Hebrew term for Adam and Eve's first location, Eden (*eden*) means "Bliss," "Delight," and "Luxury." Such a title clearly matches the portrait of paradise found in these chapters.

When one studies these names in the original Hebrew, they begin to look much more like the names of characters in John Bunyan's allegorical story than the names of actual historical people. Our English Bibles could be summarized as follows:

Adam and Eve live in the Garden of Eden until they get kicked out, where Cain kills Abel.

However, given the meaning of the Hebrew, it would be more accurate to say:

Humanity and Life live in the Garden of Delight until they get kicked out, where Spear kills Fleeting Breath.

Our English Bibles suggest that *Adam* and *Eve* are our distant relatives, ancient figures we might have something in common with. However, the original

---

5. Good study Bibles and commentaries often shed light on what original languages convey. See the end of chap. 8 for recommended resources.

6. Of these Hebrew words, the one for "Spear" is the closest to Cain's name, but it only appears one other time in the Hebrew Bible (2 Sam. 21:16). Translators have debated whether it clearly means "spear," but it obviously refers to a weapon of some sort.

The Inadequacy of History

"Literary art, [Aristotle] said, is 'more philosophical' than history, because history simply shows us 'what happened,' whereas works of literary art show us 'things such as might happen' in a human life. In other words, history simply records what in fact occurred, whether or not it represents a general possibility for human lives. Literature focuses on the possible, inviting its readers to wonder about themselves."[a]

Martha Nussbaum, *Poetic Justice*, 5

a. Nussbaum is commenting on Aristotle, *Poetics* 9. See also Lesser, "Morally Difficult Passages," 301.

Hebrew text invites readers to see these characters as mirror images of ourselves, as representatives of humanity as a whole.[7] Seeing these characters as symbolic does not diminish the text's relevance. If anything, it sheds new light on how these chapters can illuminate our lives.[8] (See "The Inadequacy of History.")

Animals and Trees

Are there other clues that the opening chapters of Genesis are more symbolic than historical?[9] Obviously there is the whole matter of the talking snake. Perhaps there once really was a snake that could talk, and perhaps that snake really did speak to the first human couple. However, what makes more sense: To assume the historicity of a talking snake? Or to assume that the writers

---

7. Although some passages can be interpreted as portraying "Adam" as a literal person (Gen. 5:3–5; 1 Chron. 1:1), there are also many passages that display an understanding of this character as functioning symbolically. E.g., Ps. 144:4 appears related to Gen. 2–4. It reads, "*Humanity* [the same word as for Adam] is like a *breath* [the same word as for Abel]. Our days are like a passing shadow" (my translation; cf. NLT, "breath of air, . . . passing shadow"). The apostle Paul also seems aware of how the figure in Gen. 2–3 serves as a representation of humanity: "all die in Adam" (1 Cor. 15:22 NRSV; cf. Rom. 5:14; 1 Cor. 15:45; see Dunn, *Romans 1–8*, 289, on how Paul's theological point does not depend on seeing Adam as a literal person; cf. Kirk, "Does Paul's Christ Require a Historical Adam?"). Other early writings also display an awareness that Adam is a representative of humanity. Thus the author of *2 Baruch* 54:19 writes, "Each of us has become our own Adam" (*OTP* 1:640).

8. Some interpreters have argued that rather than representing humanity as a whole, "Adam" represents Israel in particular: Enns, *Evolution of Adam*, 65–70; Postell, *Adam as Israel*. The story of Adam and Eve certainly resonates in particular ways with Israel's story (e.g., facing expulsion from a good land as a result of disobeying God). However, the text itself has a more universal scope (e.g., Gen. 2:4b–7; 3:20).

9. This question is quite important. Many biblical characters have names with highly significant meaning. So one should not assume solely on the basis of Adam and Eve's names that the entire story is meant to be understood symbolically. The interpreter needs to see what other features are present in the text.

If God Had Literally Made a Talking Snake

The God of the Bible certainly has the power to make a talking snake.

However, what's remarkable about Genesis 3 is that it never bothers to say something like "Originally, God gave snakes the ability to talk," or "In those days, snakes could speak." At the end of this chapter, when God curses the snake to crawling on its belly, God never adds, "And furthermore, I'm taking away your voice box. Aside from hissing, you're mute from now on."

If readers were supposed to see this text as a historical account of a talking snake, the narrator could have done a better job of communicating that.

---

of Genesis wanted us to see this story as highly symbolic? (See "If God Had Literally Made a Talking Snake.")

When readers need to choose between two ways of interpreting a text, they can ask this question (sometimes called the "rule of faith" or the *regula fidei*): Which interpretation is more consistent with the rest of the Bible and our faith?[10]

On the one hand, taking the resurrection narratives as historical is consistent with a God who creates life, who loves humanity, and who loves life itself. On the other hand, there is little theological value in literally ascribing the faculty of speech to a snake.

Furthermore, if those who wrote and edited Genesis wanted us to take this text literally, then certainly there would be crystal clear agreement between what we have here and what we have in the surrounding chapters. However, such agreement isn't present. Consider a simple question, were the animals made before or after the first human? In Genesis 1:20–26, the animals come first. In Genesis 2:7, 18–19, the human comes first.[11] None of this is a problem if we're supposed to take these chapters figuratively. If they must be understood literally, however, then we have a major contradiction on our hands.[12]

10. Various parts of the Bible are quite different from one another. The same could be said of the Christian tradition. While interpreters thus shouldn't assume that one passage says something identical to another passage, one part of the OT can illuminate another part. After all, writings within the OT provide the closest linguistic, geographic, and temporal parallels we have (Talmon, "The 'Comparative Method'").

11. Genesis 1:1–2:4a was likely written at a different time than Gen. 2:4b–3:24. The editors who brought these stories together did not try to harmonize one account of creation with the other. Strawn, "Evolution(ism) and Creation(ism)," argues that because the Bible contains diverse perspectives on how creation took place (e.g., Gen. 1; Gen. 2; Prov. 8; John 1), it's mistaken to focus obsessively on just one text and the details therein.

12. Some readers of this chapter will object to my asking whether this story should be understood as *either* historical *or* symbolic, maintaining that Adam and Eve were *both* (proto) historical figures *and* symbolic representatives of humanity as a whole (cf. G. Wenham, *Genesis*

Another feature to consider: the trees described in Genesis 2–3 are unlike any trees we have ever encountered (3:22). They are called "the tree of life" and "the tree of knowledge of good and evil." These descriptions suggest that they are figurative representations, rather than particular species of vegetation. While people sometimes think of the tree of knowledge of good and evil as an apple tree, the Bible never describes it this way. In fact, the first writers and readers of this story had probably never tasted an apple. This fruit is native to the northern regions of the globe, not the Middle East, which gave birth to the Bible.

Location

Geographical clues also suggest that the opening of Genesis should not be understood as hard history. For example, when the location of the Garden of Delight (*eden*) is described, it refers more to the world as a whole than to one geographic site. In Genesis 2:10–14, we read that a river flows out of the garden and divides into four headwaters: the Pishon, Gihon, Tigris, and Euphrates.

There is no river that branches out into these four rivers. In fact, it would be impossible for there to be one.[13] These rivers flow in different directions and originate thousands of miles away from one another. While modern readers have had difficulty figuring out the exact location of the Pishon and Gihon, they likely refer to the two branches of the Nile, which flow from south to north through modern-day Sudan into Egypt before emptying into the Mediterranean Sea, which adjoins the Atlantic Ocean.[14] Meanwhile, the Tigris and Euphrates rivers begin in modern-day Turkey and flow from the northwest to the southeast into Iraq before emptying into the Persian Gulf, which connects with the Indian Ocean. (See figure 1.)

1–15, 90–91). However, the fact that Gen. 1:1–2:4a doesn't agree perfectly with Gen. 2:4b–3:24 suggests that readers are not supposed to take these two accounts too literally.

13. Some scholars suggest that ancient peoples may have believed that these rivers were joined underground (Albright, "Garden of Eden"; J. Day, *Yahweh and the Gods*, 30). Others maintain that these rivers converge at the same location, possibly in the Persian Gulf (Speiser, *Genesis*, 19–20). More convincing is the argument of Radday, "Rivers of Paradise," 31: "Eden is nowhere. . . . The passage, hence, is not one of blatant anachronism, but timelessness, nor of childlike geography, but atopism." Cassuto, *Genesis: Part I*, esp. 118, makes similar points, as does Westermann, *Genesis 1–11*, 216.

14. Aharoni and Avi-Yonah, *Macmillan Bible Atlas*, 20 (on the basis of Gen. 10:7). If the Gihon refers to a small spring in Jerusalem (which despite 2 Chron. 32:30 seems unlikely because of the end of Gen. 2:13), it would still be far removed from the other rivers. If the Pishon is the Indus River (J. Day, *Yahweh and the Gods*, 30), the points above are reinforced, particularly regarding the very different points of origination of these rivers. The Indus River begins in the Himalayan Mountains of modern-day Tibet and then flows from north to south through present-day India and Pakistan before emptying into the Arabian Sea, which is connected to the Indian Ocean.

Perhaps the authors of Genesis flunked geography or envisioned the earth as once shaped very differently. However, it seems more likely that these "directions to Eden" were intentionally unclear, inviting readers to see this garden less as a solitary geographical location and more as a symbolic locale representing a place to which humanity can never return—at least not without the earth being created anew. (See "Flaming Sword.")

A Poetic Story

Finally, the story at hand does not resemble a straightforward prose narrative like we would find in historical accounts. Instead, these chapters

Figure 1. The Rivers of Genesis 2. South of this map, the Nile's two branches flow together to form the Nile. The Pishon and Gihon likely refer to these two branches. *Wikimedia Commons*, http://commons.wikimedia.org/wiki/File:Middle_East_topo graphic_map-blank.svg.

form a poetic story—a genre that lends itself to a more figurative interpretation.[15] While English poetry displays rhyme most frequently, Hebrew poetry tends to display *parallelism, repetition, wordplay,* and *symbolic language.*[16] All of these elements are present in Genesis 2:4b–4:16.

Parallelism is seen when one line (or part of a line) is similar in form or meaning to another line (or part thereof). Already in Genesis 2:5, readers find parallel lines:

Genesis 2:5a	//	Genesis 2:5b
No plant	//	No vegetation
of the field	//	of the field
was yet on the land.	//	had yet sprouted.[a]

a. My translation.

15. Rather than seeing poetry and prose as two completely distinct categories, readers of the OT can envision a poetry-prose continuum (Petersen and Richards, *Interpreting Hebrew Poetry*, 13–14). The opening chapters of Genesis, while containing a narrative sequence, nevertheless display features of poetry such as parallelism and repetition. At the same time, they do not display all the terseness and metrical form of Hebrew poetry.

16. On this topic, see Berlin, "Hebrew Poetry," 301–15.

Flaming Sword

The end of Genesis 3 describes the Garden of Eden as cut off from humanity by heavenly beings called *cherubim*, with a whirling flaming sword (Gen. 3:24). No one has ever claimed to find a permanent geographical location where such creatures forbid entry. It would be quite a tourist attraction if that were the case! So again, it seems very unlikely that the authors of Genesis 2–3 wanted readers to take their words as hard history.

The purpose of parallelism isn't to sound redundant or to repeat things simply for the sake of repeating them. Rather, parallelism increases the beauty of the text, gives the writing a greater sense of unity, and allows a single thought to be amplified and clarified. Many verses in Genesis 2:4b–4:16 display some sort of parallel structure.

With *repetition*, entire lines may not stand parallel to each other. However, similar words appear over and over. For example, the Hebrew word for "eat" (*akal*) appears seventeen times in Genesis 3 alone (four more times in Gen. 2). Meanwhile, in 2:4b–25, the Hebrew word for "land" (*erets*) shows up seven times, while the Hebrew word for "earth" (*adamah*) shows up five times. Sometimes these words appear and reappear at key junctures. Thus the second half of 2:5 and all of 2:6 have segments that end in the Hebrew words for "land" (*erets*) and "earth" (*adamah*).

> [2:5c] For the Lord God had not sent rain on the land [*erets*],
> [2:5d] and there was no earthling [*adam*] to work the earth [*adamah*].
> [2:6a] A stream went up from the land [*erets*],
> [2:6b] and it watered the entire face of earth [*adamah*].[17]

A third important feature of Hebrew poetry is *wordplay*. In Genesis 2:4b–4:16, many words sound like one another:

- The Hebrew word for "earth" (*adamah*) frequently appears alongside the Hebrew word for "human(ity)" (*adam*). To convey this similarity, translations sometimes render *adamah* as "earth" and *adam* as "earthling." Or they translate *adamah* as "humus" and *adam* as "human."
- The Hebrew word for "stream" or "mist" is *ed* (2:6), which sounds like a shortened form of *eden*, the name of the garden (2:8, 10, 15; 3:23–24; 4:16).

17. My translation.

- "Name" (*shem*) and "there" (*sham*) appear three times each in 2:10–14.
- "Naked" (*arummim*) appears at 2:25 (see also 3:7, 10, 11). It sounds similar to "crafty" (*arum*) in 3:1.

In the appendix of this book, I have provided a translation of Genesis 2:4b–4:16 that draws attention to poetic elements in this text.[18]

Another key element of Hebrew poetry is *symbolic language*. Given the presence of the various poetic features just mentioned, readers should be on the lookout for symbolic elements in Genesis 2:4b–4:16.

The Treasures of Genesis 2:4b–4:16

To point out just some of the many symbolic meanings of this text, *Adam* (*Human*) and *Eve* (*Life*) encapsulate key features of human life. Like these characters, we have all done things God has forbidden. Rather than being thankful for what we had, we desired what wasn't ours. We doubted how trustworthy God is. We doubted God's word. We suspected that there may be a way around the negative consequences God foretold. We may not have heard a talking snake, but we heard many other voices that did not originate in God.[19] We have trusted our own sensibilities and those of others around us, while neglecting our Creator. (See "Understanding Creation in Biblical Terms.")

At the time, our actions may have seemed perfectly harmless—as harmless as taking a bite of fruit. In fact, they may have seemed advantageous: delicious, pleasurable, and leading to success.

Yet, like *Humanity* and *Life*, our actions often result in more pain and chaos than we ever imagined. Oh, to go back and do it all over again!

But there is no going back. The entry to Eden is blocked. We cannot return to paradise. We become deeply ashamed of ourselves. We find ourselves in a world that is cruel and unfair, a world where even brothers can kill one another. We walk atop cursed soil that yields its fruit only grudgingly. We make our

---

18. As noted there, other features of Hebrew poetry appear in Gen. 2:4b–4:16, including (1) alliteration (repeating consonant sounds) in Gen. 2:14 (the "h" sound); (2) assonance (repeating vowel sounds) in 2:18b (the "e" sound); and (3) an inclusio (key material at the beginning and end of a story, such as "Eden" at 2:8; 3:23–24; 4:16).

19. Ricoeur suggests that we see within the symbol of the serpent (1) "a part of ourselves which we do not recognize"; (2) the "evil *already there* . . . [as] part of the interhuman relationship, like language, tools, institutions"; and (3) "a cosmic structure of evil." "Thus the serpent symbolizes something of humanity *and* something of the world, a side of the microcosm and a side of the macrocosm, the chaos *in* me, *among* us, and *outside*" (*Symbolism of Evil*, 256–58, alt. for gender inclusivity).

Understanding Creation in Biblical Terms

"The adequacy of one's categories of thought is all-important. Belief in creation needs to be retrieved from its characteristic modern distortion in terms of 'design' and understood afresh in other, more biblical terms. These should include—at the least, in terms of Genesis 1–3—the wonder and delight of the world, creaturely contingency, creaturely responsibility, the gift of relationship between creature and Creator, and the difficulty that humans have in genuinely trusting God as a wise Creator and living accordingly."

Walter Moberly, "How Should One Read?," 17

---

way through life with sweat on our brows and thorns in our feet. We spend most of our lives working, though we may find such work downright painful. Things that bring us a level of joy, like having children, are intertwined with a great deal of pain.

Alongside *Spear*, we learn that even when we are at the altar and offering gifts to God, jealousy and anger may creep into our lives in the most insidious of ways. We hurt those closest to us, and in the end we find ourselves far away from God, wandering alone.

We retain a memory of paradise. We sense that the world should be a better place than it is. At times we are shocked to see in ourselves or our children just how fleeting life is. We are confronted with the harsh realities of death in ways we least expected it.

We are Adam. We are Eve. We are Cain, and we are Abel.

Conclusion

Storytelling is central to any close friendship. When our best friends tell their best stories, we cling to every word they say. We identify with them as they explain the twists and turns of their lives. We see ourselves in their stories. We identify with our friends, and in so doing, we grow closer to them.

As our friend in faith, the Old Testament tells incredible stories, and we can see ourselves with remarkable clarity in its characters. Rather than giving us a dry historical account about the ancestors farthest removed from us, the Old Testament tells a story about you and me. Instead of providing a technical scientific explanation of the universe's murky beginnings, the Old Testament explains the fundamentals of God, ourselves, and the world we inhabit. The

---

A Prayer

"My God, my God, . . . you are a figurative, a metaphorical God, . . . a God in whose words there is such a height of figures, such voyages . . . to fetch remote and precious metaphors, such extensions, such spreadings, such curtains of allegories . . . and such things in your words, as all secular authors seem of the seed of the serpent that creeps—you are the Dove that flies. What words but yours can express the inexpressible texture and composition of your word!"

John Donne, "Devotions" (alt. to reflect modern English)

---

significance of Genesis 2:4b–4:16 isn't diminished by seeing these chapters as a symbolic story.[20] If anything, it's increased.[21]

It's been said, "A friend is someone who knows the song in your heart and can sing it back to you when you have forgotten the words." All too often, we forget who we are. We forget our waywardness. We distrust God's trustworthiness. And like a good friend, the Old Testament helps us to remember who we are, who God is, and what our world is really like. (See "A Prayer.")

For Further Study

See the end of chapter 3, which describes resources for dealing with Genesis 1–4.

---

20. Throughout the above discussion, I have spoken plainly about the text at hand being "symbolic." While there are different types of symbolic stories (e.g., parables, allegories), I have intentionally refrained from using a more precise term, both because I wish to avoid technical terms in a book aimed at nonspecialists and because the genres we are familiar with today don't perfectly align with the genres employed by biblical writers (cf. Sparks, *God's Word*, 211).

21. Cf. Ricoeur, *Symbolism of Evil*, 236.

3

Darkness over the Face of the Deep

THE PREVIOUS CHAPTER STRESSED THE IMPORTANCE OF GENRE. It showed how the story of Adam, Eve, and their children has all the markings of a highly symbolic story. Can we say the same about the Bible's first chapter, which talks about God creating the world in seven days?[1]

The answer to this question isn't so straightforward, which is why we considered Genesis 2–4 first. On the one hand, there's evidence of highly symbolic elements within the Bible's first chapter. On the other hand, it's unclear that the original writers and authors thought of the text as *only* symbolic. This complexity brings up an important point: *Genre isn't always easy to determine. Some passages resemble more than one type of literature.*[2]

Genesis 1 as Symbolic

First, let's consider the evidence that Genesis 1 is symbolic. Kenneth Burke is one of the most influential thinkers in the discipline of rhetorical criticism, and he suggests that the days described in Genesis 1 are symbols representing categories of God's well-ordered creation. (See "Putting the World into Categories.")

---

1. In this chapter, I talk about Gen. 1 or the Bible's first chapter as shorthand for Gen. 1:1–2:4a. For a concise appraisal of different scholarly designations for this text, see Waltke, "Genesis, Chapter One."
2. On this topic, see Newsom, "Spying Out the Land." Although interpreters have suggested that Gen. 2:4b–3:24 similarly functions as both symbolic and (proto)historical literature (e.g., G. Wenham, *Genesis 1–15*, 90–91), I see an abundance of evidence that 2:4b–3:24 fits in a symbolic genre, but relatively little evidence that it functions more literally.

Putting the World into Categories

"Imagine that you wanted to say, 'The world can be divided into six major classifications.' That is, you wanted to deal with 'the principles of Order,' beginning with the natural order, and placing humanity's socio-political order with reference to it. But you wanted to treat these matters in narrative terms, which necessarily involve temporal sequence. . . .

"Stated narratively (in the style of Genesis . . .), such an idea of principles, or 'firsts,' would not be stated simply in terms of classification, as were we to say 'The first of six primary classes would be such-and-such, the second such-and-such' and so on. Rather, a completely narrative style would properly translate the idea of six classes of categories into time, as were we to assign each of the classes to a separate 'day.' Thus, instead of saying 'And that completes the first broad division, or classification, of our subject-matter,' we'd say: 'And the evening and the morning were the first day.' . . . And so on, through the six broad classes, ending, 'last but not least,' on the category of humanity and its dominion."

Kenneth Burke, *Rhetoric of Religion*,
201–2 (alt. for gender inclusivity)

There is evidence within the text to bolster this claim. As David Wilkinson puts it, "The structure of the seven days reflects a logical rather than chronological order."[3] The first three days, or categories, describe the *realms* in which life as we know it takes place. The second three days, or categories, describe the *inhabitants* of the corresponding realms:

Realms	Inhabitants
Day 1: Light (separated from darkness)	Day 4: Greater and lesser lights
Day 2: Sky (separated from waters)	Day 5: Birds and fish
Day 3: Dry land (with vegetation)	Day 6: Animals and humanity

Viewed with this interpretive lens, Genesis 1 is less about scientifically pinpointing the dawn of time and more about reflecting on the incredibly well-ordered world that God has made.[4] The text itself speaks of the goodness of this order, saying seven times that God saw what was made and deemed it "good" (1:4, 10, 12, 18, 21, 25, esp. 31).

3. D. Wilkinson, *Message of Creation*, 23–24.
4. Science is a modern endeavor, and so many people wouldn't even think to classify Gen. 1 as scientific. However, as a way of addressing the current creationism-evolutionism debate, it's necessary to make these points. On scientific knowledge standing "outside the scope of scripture," see Cosgrove, *Appealing to Scripture*, chap. 4.

The Purpose of Genesis 1

"It was never God's intention that people should think that the world was created in six days. The purpose of the narrative was not to describe origins but to deliver humanity from idolatry, from worshipping objects in the natural world or universe, by pointing humanity to the divine order that is at the heart of reality."

John Rogerson, "What Difference Did Darwin Make?,"
80 (on F. D. Maurice's thought)

"God's creation in Genesis 1 offered to Israel a vision of life and blessing, of order and holiness, in the midst of a world marred by violence and disaster, servitude and death."[a]

Mark S. Smith, *Priestly Vision*, xii

a. See also G. Wenham, *Genesis 1–15*, liii.

Others have made similar suggestions about the symbolic nature of Genesis 1. Claus Westermann, an outstanding twentieth-century biblical scholar, suggests that Genesis 1 is a parable. Accordingly, its point is not to describe with mathematic precision what happened in seven discrete twenty-four-hour blocks of time. Rather, it causes readers to imagine how God is involved in the affairs of our world. So for Westermann, this text's main point is "that time, properly ordered and directed in carefully regulated periods toward its God-given goal [that is, the Sabbath], began with creation."[5]

Others have pointed to specific features within Genesis 1 that suggest it was never intended to be understood as scientific. For example, it talks about evening and morning from the beginning, but the sun and moon are not created until the fourth day. How could one measure time without celestial bodies? As Clark Pinnock observes, "The fact that God made the sun, moon, and stars on the fourth day, not on the first, ought to tell us that this is not a scientific statement (Gen. 1:14–19). This one detail in the narrative suggests that [seeing Gen. 1 as scientific] is not going to work well and that the agenda of the writer must have been something other than one of describing actual physical processes."[6] This text appears to be more about the nature of God and the world than dating a time before history. (See "The Purpose of Genesis 1.")

5. Westermann, *Genesis 1–11*, 90.
6. Pinnock, "Climbing Out of a Swamp," 148. Other scholars have offered alternate explanations for why light was created before heavenly bodies, such as Westermann, *Genesis 1–11*, 112; and Mark S. Smith, *Priestly Vision*, 71–79, 98.

Thus one can easily argue that trying to get scientific information out of Genesis 1 is like breaking open a Fabergé egg, expecting an actual yolk and egg white to be inside. This approach misses the text's main purpose. It disregards the artful depiction of the world in Genesis 1, reducing the beautiful text to mere facts—and the wrong facts at that! The Bible's opening words seem much more concerned with instilling a sense of awe about creation and God than describing the age of the earth.

Genesis 1 as "What Happened"

The above interpretation has great merit, but it needs to be qualified. Scientific and historical questions weren't the most important issues the authors of this text addressed. At the same time, it's unclear that the writers intended this text to be understood *only* as symbolic, in no way reflecting how things actually happened.[7]

In many respects, Genesis 1 reflects an ancient understanding of the general order in which the world was created. Archaeology has unearthed creation stories from the ancient Near East, the cultures surrounding ancient Israel. We have texts from ancient Egypt and Babylonia, among other places.[8] Some of these texts appear older than Genesis 1.

In many ways Genesis 1 disagrees with these other creation stories, as we will see below. Furthermore, it's questionable whether the authors of Genesis relied directly on these other stories. However, there are significant points of agreement between Genesis and these other ancient texts. At times, then, it appears that Genesis echoes well-known ideas from surrounding cultures.[9]

For example, an Egyptian text from the ancient city of Memphis describes a creator deity named Ptah, who creates things by issuing commands. After creation, the text says that Ptah was satisfied with the "good" creation that came into being.[10] Genesis 1 similarly describes God creating the world by command and then deeming it good.

---

7. For a concise discussion of several viewpoints, see Brett, "Motives and Intentions in Genesis 1," 13–16; also Mark S. Smith, *Priestly Vision*, 63: "Genesis 1 does tell readers about how things came about. At the same time, it does not offer an explanation in any manner approaching a rational or scientific sense."

8. A brief but useful introduction to the comparative study of Gen. 1 can be found in Mark S. Smith, *Priestly Vision*, 182–85.

9. On this topic, see Walton, *Ancient Near Eastern Thought*, esp. 26–27. For an extended treatment of Gen. 1, see Walton, *Lost World of Genesis One*.

10. "The Memphite Theology," *AEL*[2] 1:54–55. Another translation, rather than saying that Ptah "was satisfied," says that Ptah "rested," which would also have connections with Genesis ("Memphite Theology," trans. James P. Allen [*COS* 1.15:23]).

Uneasiness about Old Testament Parallels

Christians often feel anxious when they hear about similarities between the Bible and ancient texts from other religions. They face questions like these:

> Is the Bible really unique?
> Is the Bible just an accident of history?

It's important to remember that the Bible portrays God's loving concern for all peoples of the world.

If God does love everyone, then surely God has given people in other religions some measure of truth, even if it isn't the fullness of truth found in the Bible.

Followers of John Wesley often talk of different types of grace. There's *justifying grace* that one receives at conversion, when sins are forgiven, as well as *sanctifying grace*, which helps believers live holy lives. Before these two types of grace, there's *prevenient grace*. It's available to all of humanity, offering some sense of right and wrong, of who God is, and of how the world works.

One can easily see extrabiblical parallels as manifestations of this prevenient grace. Ancient texts may be similar to the Bible, but that doesn't mean the Bible is an accident of history. Rather, these parallels illustrate how God's grace extends to all the people of the world.[a]

a. See Schlimm, "Wrestling with Marduk"; Strawn, "Genesis, Gilgamesh."

Or, to mention another example, a well-known Babylonian text called the *Enuma Elish* presents the universe's origins in terms of a movement from chaos to order that involves the following:

1. the creation of the firmament,
2. the creation of luminaries,
3. the creation of humanity,
4. and finally divine rest.[11]

Such an order is quite similar to what one finds in Genesis 1. (See "The Purpose of Genesis 1.")

11. "The Creation Epic," translated by E. A. Speiser, in Pritchard, ed., *The Ancient Near East*, 31–39. See esp. Tablet IV, lines 136–40 (firmament); Tablet V, lines 1–13 (luminaries); Tablet VI, lines 1–10, 33 (humanity); Tablet VI, lines 34–36 (rest/freedom from work and service). Scholars have debated whether the authors of Gen. 1 were familiar with this text. Most believe that while it's difficult to establish a line of direct dependence, there was a common pool of cultural images and assumptions that the authors of Gen. 1 drew on in formulating their work. For additional similarities between Gen. 1–3 and ancient Near Eastern mythology, see Enns, *Evolution of Adam*, 35–59; Harlow, "After Adam," 182–85.

Given the similarities between the Bible and other texts, it appears that those who first read Genesis 1 probably thought it contained fairly reliable information about the origins of the world. If nothing else, it reflected common cultural understandings of how the world came into existence.

Does this mean that Christians today need similarly to accept Genesis 1 as an accurate depiction of the order in which things came about? Not necessarily. *There are many ways a biblical text can shape our lives.*

Faithfully Finding Continuity with the Biblical Text

Our task as Christians is to work with the Holy Spirit, other Christians, and all available evidence to determine how a text can best relate to us today. Sometimes, this task calls for creativity.

In the case of Genesis 1, the authors didn't advocate an outright rejection of everything that surrounding peoples thought about the natural world.[12] They didn't assume that those outside their own faith communities were utterly bereft of God's truth. Instead, these authors presented some features of the world's origins in ways that aligned with broader cultural assumptions.[13]

Just as the writers of Genesis were open to what people in surrounding cultures thought about the world's origins, so Christians can be open to what scientists today think about the same.[14] Such an approach is much better than denying science or inventing schemes to account for the lack of alignment between science and Genesis.

To make the same point another way, becoming friends with the Old Testament does not mean we need to be enemies with everyone else. There's a biblical precedent for accepting logical and reasonable proposals about the origins of the world. Indeed, the development of modern science owes much to the biblical belief that creation reflects its Creator, operating under understandable principles.[15] If we believe that God loves all people and has given everyone abilities for understanding the world, then we can expect truth from

12. Mark S. Smith, *Memoirs of God*, chap. 3; also see 169.

13. Every text opens a field of meaning. Within such a field, many good interpretations are possible. However, there are also many poor interpretations that fall outside that field of meaning. These poor interpretations don't match the contours of the text itself, failing to align with all available evidence. Above, I speak of authorial intent, but I don't mean to suggest it's possible to reconstruct exactly who wrote each word of the Bible and what all of their intentions were. Instead, I explore what the writers of Genesis were trying to communicate as a way of talking about the field of meaning opened by the text.

14. Mark S. Smith, *Memoirs of God*, 170.

15. Goddu, "Science and the Bible," 684.

Genesis and Science

The approach here suggests that just as the writers of Genesis were open to cultural ideas, so Christians can be open to scientific ideas. As David Wilkinson explains, others relate Genesis and science differently, taking one of these approaches:

Seven-Day Creationism: The universe was literally made in seven days. Scientists claiming otherwise have it wrong.

The Gap Theory: God originally created the universe as in Genesis 1:1, which could have taken place billions of years ago. However, Satan worked ruin on the earth, so 1:2–2:4a describes how God re-created the world.

Day/Age Theory: The word "day" in Genesis 1 should be translated as "age," meaning the world could be quite old.

Seven-Day-Explanation Theory: God took seven days to explain to Adam how the world was made, but its creation took place long beforehand.

Literary Approach: Genesis 1 doesn't convey scientific truth, and we shouldn't expect it to do so. It does, however, convey important theological truth.[a]

Both Wilkinson and I have sympathies with the last position.

a. D. Wilkinson, *Message of Creation*, 271–79.

---

sources other than just the Bible. Science, including the study of evolution, can be one of these sources.

A Critical Openness

While Christians can and should be open to science, we do not need to agree with everything that has ever been claimed in the name of evolution. *Biblical authors were cautious in what they accepted from surrounding cultures.* (See "Genesis and Science.")

The writers of Genesis didn't commit themselves to everything neighboring peoples believed. While they accepted basic assumptions about the order in which the world came into being, they carefully rejected questionable theological and ethical claims. Christians can similarly exercise a critical openness to what others claim. (See "Neither Totally Identical nor Completely Opposed.")

In fact, studying how Genesis relates to its original environment can provide a useful *heuristic*, or guide, to how Christians can relate to claims made in the name of evolution. Four examples begin to illustrate this point.

Neither Totally Identical nor Completely Opposed

Biblical scholar Christopher B. Hays recommends that readers treat "biblical texts as the complex ideological and literary products that they are, rather than assuming that they should express ideas identical to those of surrounding cultures, or that they should be completely opposed to them."[a]

Christopher B. Hays, *Death in the Iron Age II*, 1

a. This point about First Isaiah applies to other parts of the Bible as well.

---

1. Human Equality

The first example pertains to human equality. Cultures of the ancient Near East didn't believe that all people were created equal. These cultures tended to hold up kings and pharaohs as distinct from others, claiming that only those with power displayed the image of God. Genesis 1 clearly rejects this claim, asserting that *all* of humanity is made in the image of God (1:26–28).[16]

At times people have taken evolution beyond the realm of science, assuming that it explains how people *should* live and how the world *ought* to work. (See "Evolution: More Than a Scientific Theory.") In the name of evolution, for example, some people have claimed that certain people are better than others. Natural selection suggests that "survival of the fittest" is a basic principle governing the world's inhabitants. Some individuals have extended this thinking to suggest that some humans are better—fitter and more evolved—than others. Thus, throughout its history, Darwinism has had connections with racism, eugenics, and even Nazism.[17]

Informed by our Scriptures, Christians can reject such notions, upholding the inherent worth of all people. Everyone bears the indelible stamp of God's image (also called the *imago Dei*). Thus we can reject selfish notions that some people are better than others, even while accepting the more substantial claims of evolution, such as how it makes sense of the available fossil record. In doing so, we resemble the authors of Genesis 1, who accepted common cultural assumptions about how the world was created while also rejecting problematic ethical claims that accompanied them.

16. See Middleton, *Liberating Image*, esp. chap. 3.

17. See the useful discussions in Cunningham, *Darwin's Pious Idea*, 186–91; S. Barton, "'Male and Female,'" 182–83. For racism itself within Darwin's writings, see Darwin, *Descent of Man*, 1:186; cf. 191, as well as his discussion of "barbarians" and "savages" throughout part 1.

There's an important difference between evolution-as-a-scientific-theory and evolution-as-an-ideological-springboard to notions like racism. On this topic, see Strawn, "Evolution(ism) and Creation(ism)"; McGrath, *Darwinism and the Divine*, 27–45.

Evolution: More Than a Scientific Theory

"The theory of evolution is not just an inert piece of theoretical science. It is, and cannot help being, also a powerful folk-tale about human origins. Any such narrative must have symbolic force. . . .

"Facts will never appear to us as brute and meaningless; they will always organize themselves into some sort of story, some drama. These dramas can indeed be dangerous."

Mary Midgley, "Evolutionary Dramas," 239, 242

"It would be hard to miss the fact that the concept of evolution lives a double life, that it references a body of technical knowledge developed through careful scientific study but also evokes a cluster of more intangible meanings at once emotive, ideological, perhaps even religious, that move in orbit around the notion of progress."

Thomas M. Lessl, *Rhetorical Darwinism*, xi

So when evidence is presented in favor of evolution, we don't need to deny such evidence or engage in mental gymnastics to explain it away. If the best scientific thinkers of our day suggest that the earth is billions of years old, the Scriptures do not implore us to challenge them.

At the same time, when individuals exalt evolution to an all-encompassing theory that denies God's existence or promotes horrendous ethical practices, we can be on the forefront of rejecting such moves. In doing so, we align ourselves with how Genesis 1 interacted with its environment.

2. Violence

A second example of the relationship between Genesis, its world, and our world pertains to violence. Many people in the ancient Near East assumed that the world was created as a result of a violent battle between competing gods. Their religious writings recount tales of these bloody conflicts, praising victorious deities for conquering others. (See "Mythic Violence at the Dawn of Time.")

Genesis 1, in sharp contrast, is refreshingly boring. There's very little drama. God simply speaks, and then things exist.[18] There's no bloodshed, no violence,

---

18. Earlier I mentioned that the Memphite Theology depicts Ptah as similarly commanding the world into being. However, unlike Gen. 1, Memphite Theology isn't free of violence. It recognizes that the quarrel between the deities Horus and Seth needs to be pacified ("Memphite Theology," AEL^2 1:52–53).

Mythic Violence at the Dawn of Time

In a Babylonian creation epic called the *Enuma Elish*, the creation of the world takes place when rival gods enter into mortal combat with one another. Marduk, the patron deity of Babylon, calls the sea goddess Tiamat into battle:

> "Stand thou up, that I and thou meet in single combat!"
> When Tiamat heard this,
> She was like one possessed; she took leave of her senses.
> In fury Tiamat cried out aloud. . . .
> They strove in single combat, locked in battle.
> The lord spread out his net to enfold her,
> The Evil Wind, which followed behind, he let loose in her face.
> When Tiamat opened her mouth to consume him,
> He drove in the Evil Wind that she close not her lips.
> As the fierce winds charged her belly,
> Her body was distended and her mouth was wide open.
> He released the arrow, it tore her belly,
> It cut through her insides, splitting the heart.
> Having thus subdued her, he extinguished her life.
> He cast down her carcass to stand upon it. . . .
> The lord trod on the legs of Tiamat,
> With his unsparing mace he crushed her skull.[a]

In what follows, Marduk slices this monster of a deity in two, making the world as we know it out of her corpse.

a. From Pritchard, *Ancient Near East*, 34–35 (Tablet IV, lines 86–89, 94–104, 129–30).

---

and no killing.[19] To be sure, as soon as humanity steps outside the garden in Genesis 4, violence does erupt. However, when it does, this violence is condemned by the Creator, both before and after it happens. Thus, instead of seeing violence as fundamental to creation, Genesis presents a world where violence is opposed to God's will. (See "Make Creation, Not War.")

19. Here I speak of violence between gods or between humans. One could argue that Gen. 1:28 condones some sort of violence, but it certainly doesn't advocate humans killing other humans. It reads, "God blessed them, and God said to them, 'Be fruitful and multiply, and fill the earth and *subdue* it; and *have dominion* over the fish of the sea and over the birds of the air and over every living thing that moves upon the earth'" (NRSV). The Hebrew word for "subdue" means treading underfoot (e.g., Mic. 7:19). It can entail violence toward humans (e.g., Esther 7:8), but here it is directed toward the earth, not other people (the Hebrew word for "earth" can also mean "land" or "ground"). The text likely envisions humans as carving out a place for themselves among the wilds of creation. The Hebrew word "have dominion" refers to the exercise of power, which can take place with or without harshness (Lev. 25:43, 46; Ps. 68:27). God's nonviolent nature elsewhere in Gen. 1 suggests that these words do not condone violence toward other humans.

Make Creation, Not War

Biblical scholar Mark Smith asks why violence is missing in Genesis 1 when it's present in other creation stories from the ancient Near East. His answer: "In this way, God can be viewed as a power beyond conflict, indeed the unchallenged and unchallengeable power beyond any powers."

Mark S. Smith, *Priestly Vision*, 69

At times evolutionary thought has been interpreted as condoning violence. Within the Darwinian world, species constantly compete with one another. The reason is simple enough: unlike the portrait of Genesis 1, the world isn't good—there's not enough to go around. And so, violence occurs naturally as species struggle with one another over limited resources in the quest for survival.[20]

In contrast to such a line of thought, Christians can reject notions that violence is fundamental to who we are and what the world is. We can reject all logics claiming we should kill others, drawing a direct line from the nonviolent Creator of Genesis 1 to Jesus's cheek-turning commands in Matthew 5.[21] While evolution can teach us much, it doesn't need to teach us that violence is justifiable. Perhaps evolution can serve a descriptive purpose, partially explaining the roots of some violence. Yet it should never serve a prescriptive function that encourages violence.

Indeed, many scientists who believe in evolution shudder when people use evolutionary theory to justify racism and violence today. They argue that civilization and culture have removed the need for humanity to practice destructive evolutionary impulses. Thus we no longer need to see ourselves as in competition with one another, violently striving to survive and reproduce.[22] Christians can subscribe to such a line of thought, seeing human communities as divine gifts that let us better reflect the God of Genesis 1, who sees all humans as having infinite worth, who sees violence as unnecessary, and who has blessed all forms of life.

20. Some of Darwin's favorite words are "competition" and "struggle," the former appearing over 40 times in *Origin of Species* and the latter over 80 times. On several occasions, including the final paragraph of *Origin of Species*, Darwin characterizes the evolutionary struggle in violent terms, calling it "the war of nature" (Darwin, *Origin of Species*, 316). On connections made between evolutionary thinking and violence, see Cunningham, *Darwin's Pious Idea*, chap. 5.

21. Or, to stay within the book of Genesis, one finds Joseph at the end of the book eventually offering forgiveness to the very brothers whom he could have further harmed, punished, or perhaps even killed (Gen. 50:15–21).

22. For Darwin's discussion of how civilization and culture curb evolutionary impulses, see Darwin, *Descent of Man*, 1:180, 185. For a more recent account of the role of cooperation within an evolutionary scheme, see Nowak with Highfield, *SuperCooperators*.

3. Pantheism, Theism, and Atheism

A third example pertains to the sacred status of the world. Religions in the ancient Near East generally saw the cosmos in divine terms. The ordinary Hebrew words for "sun" and "moon," for example, were also the names of deities.[23] Genesis firmly rejects such pantheism. It even goes so far as to call the sun the "greater light" and the moon the "lesser light"—presumably so that the names of these deities don't even enter the text (1:14–16). Genesis tells readers that there is only One who is worthy of worship, the God who spoke the world into existence.[24]

Evolutionary thought obviously does not espouse pantheism. In fact, it can be used to rule out God altogether. A number of people, taking evolution as their starting point, subscribe to atheistic materialism: they believe that matter is all that ever has existed and ever will exist. For them, the world isn't divine; there's nothing at all that's divine.[25]

Clearly, Christians don't subscribe to such a point of view. Not only do we affirm the existence of God; we also see the world and all its inhabitants as blessed by God (Gen. 1:22). We thus find a middle ground between the pantheistic idea that the world is divine and the materialistic idea that only physical matter exists. For us, creation isn't god, but it is sacred, infused with divine worth and blessing. It should be respected, protected, and seen as our partner. Just as the authors of Genesis firmly rejected pantheism, so we can reject atheism. Creation should be neither deified nor objectified. It has value from God, but it is not God. (See "Struggle versus Beauty.")

> **Struggle versus Beauty**
>
> Darwin saw the world in terms of a massive struggle for survival. In such a world, it's hard to see much value in beauty, awe, wonder, or rest. The Bible, in contrast, gives humanity permission to join God in reveling in the beauty of creation and resting amid its goodness.

4. Humanity

Finally, let's turn to the question, how did humanity get here? A number of ancient Near Eastern creation stories depict humanity as created out of the

---

23. Cf. 2 Kings 23:5, 11.

24. Genesis 1 implies there are other heavenly beings ("Let *us* make humanity in *our* image," v. 26, alt.). However, these other heavenly beings receive little attention. They are neither described nor named. The emphasis is thus on the oneness of God.

25. For a popular account of this type of view, see the description of philosophical naturalism in Dawkins, *God Delusion*, esp. 34, with the qualifications given therein.

Figure 2. Atrahasis. Both the *Enuma Elish* (see p. 37) and *Atrahasis* describe humanity as made out of the blood of a dead god. The image above shows two fragments of *Atrahasis*. Scribes made letters by pressing a reed into a clay tablet. I took this photograph at the Metropolitan Museum of Art in New York in 2005. More information is available at "Cuneiform Tablet: Atra-hasis, Babylonian Flood Myth," *The Metropolitan Museum of Art*, http://www.metmuseum.org/collections /search-the-collections/30000627?img=1.

blood of a slaughtered god.[26] In these accounts, humanity's most important function is to do the surviving gods' work for them, allowing for divine rest. (See figure 2.)

Genesis bears some continuity with these ancient Near Eastern stories. Both talk of divine rest. Both see humanity as doing some of God's work (thus Gen. 1:26, 28 talks of humanity as ruling over creation). Both see humanity as a combination of the divine and dirt: in a very ancient creation story called Atrahasis, the blood of the dead god is combined with clay; in Genesis, God's breath goes into the dust of the ground that God fashioned (2:7).

But it would be a mistake to say that Genesis is simply paraphrasing cultural ideas. It reshapes them, upholding the dignity and worth of humanity, rather

26. See "Atra-hasis," *COS* 1.130:150–244; Pritchard, *Ancient Near East*, 36–37 (Tablet VI, lines 1–38).

than suggesting that we are little more than slaves for gods. In biblical traditions, humanity ends up participating in divine rest by honoring the Sabbath (cf. Exod. 20:8–11). In Genesis, the work that humanity does for God is the honorable work of ruling over creation. In Genesis, humanity doesn't just have part of God inside it: humanity is the very image of God. (See "Human Origins.")

> ### Human Origins
>
> "In Mesopotamian tradition humanity was created from the blood of a god who represents chaos and guilt, and thus people bear within themselves elements of a life bound to failure. This negative anthropology is linked to a pessimistic idea of the aim of human life, whose purpose is to relieve gods who have become guilty of the burden of work. Work as the object of human life is seen as a punishment for the guilt of the gods. How different things are for Genesis!"
>
> Eckart Otto, *Ethik*, 62;
> via J. Barton, *Understanding*, 1, alt.

What we see, then, is that the authors of Genesis had some openness to ideas in the surrounding culture. However, these cultural ideas were critiqued, modified, and changed to affirm the great worth, responsibilities, and wonder of human beings.

Following the example of Genesis, Christians today can have a critical openness to ideas about humanity's origins. We can accept evolution's ideas of human origins, though we should never lose sight of how we are made in God's image.[27] We can stress that being distantly related to other animals doesn't mean we must act like animals.

Furthermore, we can explore ways that evolution can fruitfully inform theological thinking. Consider these questions:

- The Bible condemns pride, when people exalt themselves to a position equal to or above God. How does seeing ourselves as related to primates strengthen our understanding of ourselves as creatures, rather than the Creator? (See "Humanity and Humility.")
- Biblical scholars have emphasized biblical mandates to care for God's creation.[28] How does seeing ourselves as related to animals reinforce the idea that the earth's inhabitants should be seen as our partners, rather than as objects to manipulate?[29]
- The Bible presents lust and greed as deeply damaging sins. How can reflection on the animalistic impulse to reproduce and survive illuminate our understanding of these sins and the temptation they pose?[30]

27. Cunningham, *Darwin's Pious Idea*, 180.
28. See, e.g., Davis, *Scripture, Culture, and Agriculture*.
29. On this idea, see Santmire, "Partnership with Nature."
30. See Harlow, "After Adam," 191, as well as the literature cited there.

Rather than being fearful or hateful toward science, Christians can see scientific findings as opportunities to reflect more deeply on their faith. As Pope Benedict XVI put it, "The theory of evolution does not invalidate the faith, nor does it corroborate it. But it does challenge the faith to understand itself more profoundly."[31] Biblical writers wrestled with cultural ideas about the world's origins, and they came to a more profound understanding of their faith.

> **Humanity and Humility**
>
> "At least, evolution teaches us humility. The evolutionary perspective is a reminder that, although we are fearfully and wonderfully made, it is out of the dust of the earth. Both biology and theology insist on a dark side to human nature."
>
> Jeff Astley, "Evolution and Evil," 175

A Deeper Understanding

One way to understand a biblical passage better is to ask, what questions does this text answer? When it comes to Genesis 1, people commonly focus on just two questions:

- *When* did the world come into existence?
- In *what order* did parts of the world come into existence?

Genesis 1 takes passing glances at these questions, but as we've seen, it largely relies on common cultural knowledge of its time.

There are much more important questions that this text also answers. Sadly, the evolution-versus-creation debate has sidelined these questions that are central to the text itself. Here are the questions, as well as summaries of what the text says:

Q: Who is responsible for the world?

A: God made it and gave humanity the responsibility of caring for it.

Q: Who are we? What is our identity?

A: We are made in the image of God, blessed with infinite worth, even though we are, like animals, mere creatures.

Q: How should we relate to one another?

A: Nonviolently, given that we each bear the image of God, who made the world through speech rather than violence.

Q: What is the world? Is it divine? Is it a random array of atoms?

A: The world is not divine, but it is created by God, reflecting amazing order and goodness.

31. Quoted in Horn and Wiedenhofer, eds., *Creation and Evolution*, 16.

The Unity of Truth

The "'science and faith in conflict' narrative is deep-seated in American culture, both among Christians who find evolution a threat to the authority of scripture, and among metaphysical naturalists who view anything that cannot be tested [by] using science to be irrational. I see this narrative all the time, including in views held by my students at Colorado State, and in the local Christian schools to which my wife and I considered sending our children. It is entrenched. And that is what saddens me. Psalm 19, one of my favorite chapters in the Old Testament, paints a beautiful picture of a God who reveals himself through the majesty of his creation, and also through the inspired words of Scripture. If one believes in the unity of truth, or that 'all truth is God's truth,' this means that there is no actual conflict between what sound science discovers and what Scripture teaches, there is only apparent conflict. When such conflict appears, finite humans are getting something wrong, either in their science, or in their understanding of Scripture."

Bryan Dik, "Bill Nye vs. Ken Ham"

Q: How should we order our time?

A: In seven-day periods, allowing for a day of God-inspired rest each week.

These questions focus on what ultimately matters. They give us an identity, a worldview, and a way of life.

Conclusion

Contrary to some assumptions, scientists can and do become friends with the Old Testament. (See "The Unity of Truth.") The Old Testament is not an aloof or dishonest friend who continually denies what science discovers.

Rather, the Old Testament was open to surrounding ideas in its culture. However, it critically assessed these ideas by using the highest ethical and theological standards. As a friend in faith, the Old Testament responds to what others say with deep stories, rich poetry, and critical assessments. This friend has a way of speaking that makes us marvel in creation and worship our Creator.

For Further Study

Barton, Stephen C., and David Wilkinson, eds. *Reading Genesis after Darwin*. Oxford: Oxford University Press, 2009.

This is an excellent collection of essays written by leading scholars in the field of religion. It's a must-read book for students interested in the topic of creation and evolution.

Cunningham, Conor. *Darwin's Pious Idea: Why the Ultra-Darwinists and Creationists Both Get It Wrong*. Grand Rapids: Eerdmans, 2010.

At over five hundred pages, this work provides a careful, technical, and in-depth study of scientific proposals and biblical creation stories.

Fretheim, Terence E. *God and World in the Old Testament: A Relational Theology of Creation*. Nashville: Abingdon, 2005.

This book examines creation throughout the Old Testament. It reflects mainstream scholarship while communicating with great clarity. Written by someone sympathetic to the life of faith, it provides a host of insights into creation and its central place in the Bible.

Smith, Mark S. *The Priestly Vision of Genesis 1*. Minneapolis: Fortress, 2010.

This book summarizes a variety of scholarly arguments about Genesis 1:1–2:4a. While readers may disagree with some of Smith's conclusions, he commands an impressive knowledge of academic research.

The website www.MatthewSchlimm.com has additional resources, including group discussion questions.

4

The R-Rated Bible

T HE BIBLE ISN'T WHAT WE EXPECT. Genesis contains many stories that are neither uplifting nor inspiring. After leaving the ark, Noah gets so drunk that he passes out while naked (9:21). Abraham fools around with polygamy (chap. 16). On two other occasions, Abraham lies about his wife, giving her away to other men (12:10–20; 20:1–18). His son Isaac does essentially the same thing (26:7–11). Meanwhile, Abraham's grandnieces get their dad drunk and sleep with him (19:30–38). Abraham's grandson Jacob exploits his famished brother, Esau (25:29–34). Later, Jacob deceives his nearly dead father and again cheats Esau, who then plots to kill him (27:1–45). Jacob in turn receives his own share of harsh treatment from his uncle Laban, whom Jacob combats by running off with Laban's daughters, who steal their dad's idols (chaps. 28–31). Then Jacob's sons nearly kill their brother Joseph, choosing instead to sell him into slavery (chap. 37). As a slave, Joseph is falsely accused of trying to sleep with his master's wife, so he's sent to prison (chap. 39). Talk about dysfunction! Abraham and his descendants are a complete mess.

Beyond Genesis, readers find Israelites—fresh out of slavery—doubting and abandoning the God who rescued them. The book of Numbers describes incessant whining that brings punishment after punishment. At one point, the Bible talks about the Israelites vomiting quail out of their noses (Num. 11:20). The book of Judges abounds with stories of deception and violence. It recounts how a man killed his own daughter to fulfill a rash vow (11:29–40). Judges 19–21 tells a terrible story of rape, corpse mutilation, and killing; if it

> ### Dirty Little Secrets
>
> "Genesis is all those dirty little secrets we know about one another strung into a 'family' narrative. This family is so 'nuclear' it's fissile. Genesis is R, it's NC-17. Genesis is what spouses hide from the neighbors, hide from the children, hide from each other. . . . It's not pretty, it's not nice, it's not for polite company—and it's canonical Scripture for hundreds of millions of Jews and Christians, the background for a revelation to hundreds of millions more Muslims, and the inspiration to zillions more secular folks who just happen to enjoy reading Western literature."
>
> Burton L. Visotzky, *Genesis of Ethics*, 9–10

were a stand-alone short story and not in the Bible itself, Jews would likely denounce it as anti-Semitic, and Christians would probably try to censor it.

In the books that follow, Israel moves from judges to kings, but stories about these rulers are hardly edifying. King David embodies the corruption of power. Abusing his office, he sleeps with his friend's wife while his troops are at war. After his initial cover-up operations fail, he orders the death of his friend (2 Sam. 11–12). From there, the monarchy spirals out of control.

What do we make of these disturbing stories? Why are they part of the Holy Bible—when they seem so unholy? Why has the church kept these shocking and confusing stories in the Bible? Why do children's Bibles need to censor so much of what the Bible says? What redemptive value do these sordid stories have?[1] (See "Dirty Little Secrets.")

Searching for Saints

This chapter explores different ways interpreters have wrestled with the Bible's morally questionable stories. One approach is to search for the most saintly characters of the text, upholding them as examples to follow. Benno Jacob, a prominent biblical scholar of the early twentieth century, treats Joseph in Genesis 37–50 this way, seeing him as a moral exemplar.

To review, the story begins with Joseph making some very arrogant claims to his family. His brothers in turn sell him off into slavery (Gen. 37). Joseph goes from slave (chap. 39) to prisoner (chap. 40) to overseeing Egypt's food distribution (chap. 41). In time, Joseph's brothers go to Egypt for food (chap. 42). Joseph recognizes them, but they fail to realize who he is. Joseph eventually reveals his true identity, and the family soon dwells together in Egypt, at peace with one another (chaps. 45; 50).

---

1. I explain many of the points made here in greater depth in Schlimm, *From Fratricide to Forgiveness*, esp. chaps. 7–13.

Benno Jacob upholds Joseph as a saint that we as readers can emulate. He says that Joseph would never "invent malicious words" about his brothers. He claims that Joseph wants nothing more than goodwill for his brothers and "shows no desire for revenge." On other occasions, he asserts that Joseph "overflows with love" for his brothers, is "neither excessive, nor dangerous," and "had always been confident of regaining all of" his brothers.[2]

Benno Jacob's interpretation gives readers what they've come to expect from the Bible: stories of saints whom they can imitate in their own lives. Countless preachers and teachers make the same sort of interpretation. Unfor-

> **Exegesis versus Eisegesis**
>
> Biblical interpreters love to talk about the difference between *exegesis* and *eisegesis*. These words come from Greek terms. *Exegesis* literally means "to lead out of." Interpreters use it to describe *good interpretations* that come directly *out of* the biblical text. On the other hand, *eisegesis* means "to lead into." It describes *poor interpretations*, where people read their own thoughts *into* the biblical text instead of letting it speak clearly in its own voice. Here we could say that *pursuing paradigms* is more exegetically sound than *searching for saints*.

tunately, when you read the Bible carefully, it's clear that Joseph is far from saintly. Contrary to Benno Jacob's claims, the Bible says specifically that Joseph brings back "a bad report about" his brothers (37:2 NRSV). It says that he "spoke harshly to them" (42:7 NRSV) and accuses them falsely several times, despite their pleas to the contrary (42:9, 12, 14; cf. 42:16, 30). Joseph imprisons his brothers for crimes they did not commit (42:17) and makes them appear as thieves (44:1–15).

Although Joseph occasionally extends a nice gesture (e.g., giving food), for much of the story he appears out for vengeance.[3] Joseph once suffered at his brothers' hands. Now they suffer at his hands. He seems interested only in reuniting with his closest brother, Benjamin, not his thuggish half-brothers.

Yet, with the passing of time, Joseph has a change of heart. The brothers eventually prove that they are no longer the type of people who sell off family members to save their own necks (Gen. 44). Joseph is deeply moved. He sees that they have changed. He offers forgiveness, and the brothers make peace.[4]

---

2. Jacob, *Genesis*, 249, 253, 284, 287, 302.

3. Joseph returns the brothers' money to them, which could be another act of kindness (Gen. 42:25). However, the brothers' fearful reaction (42:28) suggests that even this "gift" of money is another way Joseph strikes terror into his brothers' hearts. They once sold Joseph for silver (37:28). Now, they are haunted by silver. See Schlimm, *From Fratricide to Forgiveness*, 173.

4. Some interpreters suggest that Joseph never actually forgives his brothers because the text doesn't say something like, "Joseph forgave his brothers, just as they requested." However, the logic of the story certainly goes in that direction. The brothers explicitly request forgiveness

Joseph finally does the right thing, but his harsh circumstances have not left him free from guilt.

As Christians, our job isn't to bleach the Bible's portrait of Joseph, attempting to clean off smudges on his moral character. The Old Testament provides no biographies of saints. When Paul says, "All have sinned and fall short of God's glory" (Rom. 3:23), he has done his biblical homework. Following Benno Jacob's lead and turning biblical characters into exemplars doesn't work when we carefully study the text itself.[5]

Pursuing Paradigms

An alternate approach to biblical stories admits that no human in Scripture provides a perfect model for us to emulate. However, readers can still look at a variety of characters, mentally putting together their best qualities to assemble a vision of who we should be and how we should act. By zeroing in on virtues, perhaps we can better understand what to pursue in our own lives.

Biblical scholar Waldemar Janzen takes this approach. He observes that most people have a mental image of a good driver and yet would have difficulty naming someone who perfectly matches that description. In a similar way, Janzen maintains, the Old Testament instills in its readers models to follow without lifting up a single individual as a perfect example.[6]

So, instead of saying that Joseph is an ideal saint, Janzen says that some of his actions can help us understand what it means to be a wise person. Thus readers can join Joseph in seeing God's hand at work in the world, particularly when life is preserved (Gen. 45:4–7; 50:20). We do not, however, need to follow in all of Joseph's footsteps.[7]

This approach of *pursuing paradigms* is better than the *searching-for-saints* approach. (See "Exegesis versus Eisegesis.") Whereas Benno Jacob's interpretations do not align with the text, there are positive qualities that biblical

---

(50:17), and Joseph's response is profoundly gracious. First, he weeps. Next, he tells his brothers not to be afraid, because he is not in the position of God to condemn. He tells them a second time not to be afraid. Then, he promises to care for their children. The pericope concludes by saying that Joseph comforted them and spoke kindly to them. It certainly seems that he is responding in a way reflective of forgiveness. While the narrator doesn't spell out every last detail, this narrator revels in being terse, speaking more through characters' words and actions than by providing unnecessary commentary.

5. Schlimm, *From Fratricide to Forgiveness*, 170, n.13.

6. Janzen, *Old Testament Ethics*, 8–9, 27–28. J. Barton (*Understanding*, 73) gets at something similar: "We may treat all of what we find in the Bible as contributing to a kind of profile of the good life by imagining possible lives or lifestyles in which its precepts are instantiated."

7. Janzen, *Old Testament Ethics*, 125.

characters do have, and readers can mentally assemble these qualities from different characters to arrive at a model toward which they can strive.

Problems remain, however. Why do biblical texts present characters with both sinful and virtuous qualities if we are supposed to focus mainly on the virtues? Biblical stories often show human nature at its worst. Why do some stories, such as the final chapters of Judges, fail to mention anything we should imitate? Can we learn something from these negative stories, as opposed to sorting out the good from the bad and focusing on

> ### God and Moral Principles
>
> "It is always easier to reduce a life with God down to 'principles.' It's our best attempt to avoid His lack of domesticity."
>
> Jonathan Martin, Twitter, August 17, 2012
>
> "He's wild, you know. Not like a *tame* lion."
>
> C. S. Lewis, *The Lion, the Witch and the Wardrobe*, 182, on Aslan, the Christlike lion
>
> "Puny indeed is the faith which constricts the richness of biblical traditions and confessions to fit into a dogmatic structure. A living faith, by contrast, opens up to embrace every authentic witness to God's presence and activity, and it is stretched in the process to ever-heightened reverence and perceptivity."
>
> Paul Hanson, *Diversity of Scripture*, 3

just the good? Janzen's project dwells on what's good. The messy stories of the Bible, however, seem determined to present good and evil as intertwined. Is there an alternate approach that better connects with biblical stories?[8]

A Matter of Principle

Some people prefer instead to search for ethical principles that undergird the Bible's stories. This tactic assumes that biblical narratives are not too far removed from Aesop's fables.[9] Aesop was a Greek slave who told stories around the time that parts of the Old Testament were written. The stories associated with him illuminate a word of wisdom that can help in life. For example, in "The Dog and His Reflection," a dog carries a piece of meat in his jaws while crossing a bridge. Glancing down at the water below, the dog sees another dog with another piece of meat. Next, the fable says, "So, without thinking twice, he opened his jaws to snatch the second piece of meat—and found himself with no meat at all. His own piece fell into the stream and disappeared. And

8. See also Schlimm, *From Fratricide to Forgiveness*, 97–98, 107–9.
9. Here, I speak of "Aesop's fables" as a way of referring to the fables commonly associated with Aesop. Historically, little is known about Aesop, and it's doubtful that he himself wrote anything (Perry, *Babrius and Phaedrus*, xxxv–xlvi, esp. xxxv–xxxvi).

Figure 3. More Meat! Wenceslas Hollar, "The Dog and His Reflection," *Wikimedia Commons*, http://commons.wikimedia.org/wiki /File:Wenceslas_Hollar_-_The_dog_and_his_reflection.jpg.

the second piece, of course, was merely a reflection of the first. *In our greed for more we may lose what we already have.*[10] (See figure 3.)

Many preachers see Old Testament stories as similar to Aesop's fables, saying that the Bible's narratives illustrate ethical principles and words of wisdom to guide along life's way. Thus some interpreters emphasize the principle of forgiveness when dealing with Joseph. One scholar says that the Joseph story suggests to readers "that they too should forgive even their long-term enemies, if they show sincere contrition."[11] There's certainly some truth here. The story illustrates that reconciliation can occur, even after horrendous ruptures in relationships.

Yet it's not as if we can disregard the story once we have arrived at an important principle. The Joseph story is much more than a way of encouraging us to forgive others. It shows, for example, just how difficult real forgiveness can be. It teaches us that the worst conflicts can arise not among enemies, but among family members. It illustrates the temptation of harming those who harmed us. It shows how lasting reconciliation does not happen overnight. It's a devastating critique of those who cheapen forgiveness, making it into something we can achieve in an instant. It shows that some wounds strike so deep that much time must pass before real forgiveness can be offered.

Our job as interpreters is *not* to boil a bunch of chapters down into a single principle. The Joseph story is much too rich and deep for that. We trivialize both the Bible and God by focusing on abstractions. (See "God and Moral Principles.") So then, how do we resist the reductionist urge to collapse larger-than-life stories into two-dimensional, self-evident moral clichés?[12]

10. Bader, *Aesop and Company*, 20.
11. G. Wenham, *Story as Torah*, 38.
12. On principles in biblical ethics, see Schlimm, *From Fratricide to Forgiveness*, 94–95, 100–107.

A Messy Moral World

Greek philosophers (and their heirs) assumed that the world was ordered in such a way that humans could easily make sense of it. Writers of Greek tragedy, however, had a very different perspective. Bernard Williams explains:

> Plato, Aristotle, Kant, Hegel are all on the same side, all believing in one way or another that the universe or history or the structure of human reason can, when properly understood, yield a pattern that makes sense of human life and human aspirations. Sophocles and Thucydides, by contrast, are alike in leaving us with no such sense. Each of them represents human beings as dealing sensibly, foolishly, sometimes catastrophically, sometimes nobly, with a world that is only partially intelligible to human agency and in itself is not necessarily well adjusted to ethical aspirations.[a]

Frequently the Bible's view of the world is closer to Sophocles and Thucydides than their philosophical counterparts. As I write elsewhere, although the Bible's "opening chapters present a carefully ordered world, the chapters that follow present a world that humans struggle to understand and master ethically. With the loss of Eden, the world's order has become partially undone, and humanity's capacity for perceiving this order has been impaired."[b]

a. Williams, *Shame and Necessity*, 163–64.
b. Schlimm, *From Fratricide to Forgiveness*, 112.

Reading Stories Well

There are important differences between what the Bible is up to and what people commonly assume is involved in ethical reflection.

We assume that moral reasoning is as simple as *focusing on the good*. As a result, we look for saints, models, or principles. However, the Bible presupposes that *the good all too often is inextricably intertwined with the bad*. We all bear the image of God, but we are all sinners. A good God created a good world, but that creation "waits with eager longing" for a brighter day (Rom. 8:19 NRSV). We're not in Eden anymore, and we shall not return any time soon. As Jesus puts it, the world is a field filled with both life-giving wheat and life-sucking weeds. Good and evil won't be sorted out until the harvest at the end of time (Matt. 13:24–30). (See "A Messy Moral World.")

Therefore, when interpreting the Bible, we dare not confine ourselves to a narrow question like, What's ideal in this text, and how can I uphold it in my life? We do much better to ask, How is this text realistic, and in what ways does it reflect the struggles of upright living?

The Art of Storytelling

"The art of storytelling is the art of exchanging *experiences*."[a]

Paul Ricoeur,
Oneself as Another, 164

"The brain, it seems, does not make much of a distinction between reading about an experience and encountering it in real life; in each case, the same neurological regions are stimulated."

Annie Murphy Paul,
"Your Brain on Fiction"

a. Ricoeur is summarizing Walter Benjamin's thought. See also Schlimm, *From Fratricide to Forgiveness*, 115–18.

In other words, we miss the big picture by searching for only what is positive. If we were already leading wonderfully good lives and just needed help continuing on that perfect trajectory, then we would need nothing but saintly examples, ethical paradigms, and good principles. As things stand, however, none of us is perfect. Our lives are frequently more complicated than we realize. We struggle to do what is right, though we deeply desire it. For these reasons, *we need stories that are just as complex and fraught with difficulty as life itself.*[13]

Stories: A Reflection of Life

Stories reflect life. Whether they are fiction or nonfiction, fantasy or history, narratives can tell us a great deal about what it means to be human.[14] In stories, people talk like they talk in real life. They act like they do in real life. They interact, feel, and think like they do in real life. When a good storyteller has our attention, we identify closely with characters in the story. We may even find ourselves moved to tears or filled with fright over events far removed from our lives. (See "The Art of Storytelling.")

When we enter into a story and identify with its characters, we gain what can be called *story experience*. Although *story experience* is not the same as *real-life experience*, it still has immense value, especially from an ethical perspective.

Most people know that you can learn only so much from rules, principles, and theories. In the final analysis, to do something well, you also need experience. (See "Prudence and Sages.")

When we read the Bible's stories, we gain some of the experience we need for moral living. The Bible's stories are like apprenticeships. They give us equipment for surviving and even thriving in a fallen world.[15]

---

13. Schlimm, *From Fratricide to Forgiveness*, 112–13. See also Goldingay, *Theological Diversity*, 87, 90–91; chap. 5.

14. Bakhtin, *Dostoevsky's Poetics*, 55; R. C. Roberts, "Narrative Ethics," 474; Hardy, "Poetics of Fiction," 5; Booth, *Company We Keep*, 345.

15. Lyotard, *Postmodern Condition*, 18–23; Burke, "Literature as Equipment," esp. 254–56, 259. See also Schlimm, *From Fratricide to Forgiveness*, 126–29.

Prudence and Sages

"Although the young may be experts in geometry and mathematics and similar branches of knowledge, we do not consider that a young person can have Prudence. The reason is that Prudence includes a knowledge of particular facts, and this is derived from experience, which a young person does not possess; for experience is the fruit of years."

Aristotle, *Nicomachean Ethics* 6.8.5 (alt. for gender inclusivity)

"Storytellers join the ranks of the teachers and sages. They have counsel—not for a few situations, as the proverb does, but for many, like the sage."

Walter Benjamin, "The Storyteller," 108 (alt. for gender inclusivity)

Remarkably, story experience may be even more important than real-life experience. Here are four reasons.[16]

Stories as Laboratories for Ethics

First, stories work like laboratories for ethics: they provide controlled environments where readers can test out experiments without too greatly fearing the consequences.[17] When faced with moral uncertainty in real life, people can make bad choices that lead to enduring, catastrophic consequences. However, when faced with moral uncertainty in stories, people can experience different things without suffering consequences in the same way. (See "Trial Runs.")

In the world of the Bible, for example, receiving blessing from another person, especially one's parent, was a sign of highest honor. In the character of Jacob, readers gain glimpses of what happens when someone stops at nothing to secure others' blessings. Jacob deceives his dying father and cheats his older brother to gain a blessing for himself. Yet he ends up exiled out of his own household because of his quest for favor and power (Gen. 27). For twenty years he's forced to work for someone even crueler than he is (Gen. 28–31). Even after two decades, his entire being is filled

Trial Runs

Stories give readers a "relatively cost-free offer of trial runs. If you try out a given mode of life in life itself, you may, like Eve in the garden, discover too late that the one who offered it to you was Old Nick himself."

Wayne Booth, *Company We Keep*, 485

---

16. I also discuss these reasons in Schlimm, *From Fratricide to Forgiveness*, 126–28.

17. Ricoeur, *Oneself as Another*, 163–66. In biblical studies, this argument of Ricoeur's has been appropriated by Parry, *Old Testament Story*, 26–29; Hettema, *Reading for Good*, 108–9.

with fear as he desperately tries to save his own life when Esau comes to meet him (Gen. 32–33).

In the end, Jacob returns to Esau the blessing he stole through deceit.[18] If only he had never snatched it in the first place! He would have been with his family when his parents died. He would have avoided his cruel uncle. He would not have been robbed of his own wages, forced to endure scorching heat by day and frigid cold at night (Gen. 31:39–40).

The story of Jacob is no biography of sainthood. Rather, it's an artfully realistic depiction of how greed even for blessings can turn to disaster. For those of us tempted to gain power, favor, and blessing wherever possible, the story of Jacob makes us pause. It teaches what can happen if one succumbs to such temptation. And fortunately readers do not need to endure all the suffering that Jacob does. We gain practical wisdom from *story experience* without having to undergo the tragic outcomes in *real-life experience*.

Gaining Experience through Reading

"We have never lived enough. Our experience is, without fiction, too confined and too parochial."

Martha Nussbaum, *Love's Knowledge*, 47

"In a month of reading, I can try out more 'lives' than I can test in a lifetime."

Wayne Booth, *Company We Keep*, 485

More Experience

Second, *story experience* is important because it lets us experience more than we ever could in our own *real-life experiences*. Sometimes we need a great deal of experience—more than we could ever accumulate in our own lives—to gain wisdom for handling life's most difficult situations. (See "Gaining Experience through Reading.")

For example, how should we respond when a family member has wronged us? Do we value justice and fairness, paying back wrong for wrong? Or do we focus on just forgiving family members who harm us—even when we open ourselves to more harm down the road? There isn't a one-size-fits-all principle that always works perfectly.

A book like Genesis gives readers many sorts of experiences to help in answering these sorts of difficult questions. We witness the conflict between Cain and Abel (4:1–16), the shepherds of Abram and Lot (13:5–18), Sarah and Hagar (chaps. 16; 21), Jacob and Esau (25:29–34; 27:1–45; chaps. 32–33),

---

18. In Gen. 33:11, Jacob commands Esau to take his "blessing" (*berakah*), the very thing he stole from Esau in Gen. 27. On how Jacob gives back the blessing he received through deception, see Schlimm, *From Fratricide to Forgiveness*, 167.

Jacob and Laban (chaps. 28–31), Jacob and Rachel (30:1–4), Leah and Rachel (30:14–16), and Joseph and his brothers (chaps. 37; 42–45; 50). Hardly any of these stories qualifies as inspirational or sentimental. Yet they give us experiences so we can better navigate hardship in our own moral lives. They expose us to a variety of bad situations so that we have something to go on when we face bad situations ourselves.

Better Experience

Third, *story experience* is important because it fills in gaps in our own *real-life experiences*. In other words, there's not only a *quantitative* but also a *qualitative* difference in the experiences that stories provide. Literature allows readers to enter situations they have not and could not have previously encountered.[19] As a result, stories can foster compassion and respect for those unlike ourselves. They can also prepare individuals for situations they may face later in life.

For example, most of us hopefully have never had someone else defame our character. We may have no idea what it's like to suffer through false accusations. The stories of the Bible help us understand what it's like. In Genesis 39, we see Joseph doing everything right, and yet he is falsely accused by Potiphar's wife and wrongfully imprisoned. Through his story, we learn something of how much destruction false accusations can bring. In the Ten Commandments, we read that false accusations are forbidden (Exod. 20:16; Deut. 5:20); in Genesis 39, we experience with Joseph the ways in which this type of lying can ruin someone's life.

> **The Vulgar Heat of Everyday Life**
>
> With stories, "we are free of certain sources of distortion that frequently impede our real-life deliberations. Since the story is not ours, we do not find ourselves caught up in the 'vulgar heat' of our personal jealousies or angers or in the sometimes blinding violence of our loves."[a]
>
> Martha Nussbaum,
> *Love's Knowledge*, 47–48
>
> a. Also see Nussbaum, *Poetic Justice*, 5–6.

Reflection

Finally, stories can focus our attention in ways that are not always possible in real life. Amid the flux of everyday life, we frequently lack the time, wherewithal, and energy to consider the ethical significance of everything we encounter. (See "The Vulgar Heat of Everyday Life.")

19. Nussbaum, *Poetic Justice*, 5, 45.

Stories, however, give us time to ponder.[20] Anger, for example, may be too strong an emotion to receive extended reflection as it is encountered in everyday experiences. However, when anger is readers' first encounter outside Eden, and when they see it leading to nothing less than Cain killing Abel, they're called to reflect on this emotion in ways that they cannot (or will not) amid their personal experiences of it.

Stories Change What We Cherish

Stories pattern desires. They summon attitudes. They instill values. They evoke views of the world. They show readers what truly matters, what is worth considering and reflecting on, what people are truly like, and what hazards and opportunities the environment has in store.

Consider, for example, the book of Numbers. It's a terrible book to read. Chapters 10–25 are a mess. The stories are disjointed. People complain. Tempers run short. God sends horrendous punishments. The people still don't learn.

In many respects, the book of Numbers is like a long car trip that won't end. The children whine. The parents don't make things any better. The air conditioner is broken. They're in the desert. And they never seem any closer to their destination.

"When will we get there?"

"In forty years."

As we read Numbers, we shouldn't expect to feel uplifted. We shouldn't look for inspiration. Instead, we should expect to feel like the Israelites did out in that desert wasteland. Ironically, you're reading Numbers *well* if you're sick of the characters and want to stop reading. You are reading well because in that moment you begin to understand in new ways what things were like for the Israelites and for God.

Through the trials of reading Numbers, we can emerge as better people. Someone might rattle off a cliché like "Count your blessings." Or we might admit, when we stop and think about it, that complaining is not a great way to go through life. However, many of us need something more to put our grumbling aside.

When we read Numbers, something interesting happens. We are exposed to constant complaining. We are forced to suffer alongside Moses and the people. We grow sick and tired of their bitterness. And hopefully, complaints in our own mouths begin to taste like ash.

20. Alter, *Biblical Narrative*, 156. See also Booth, *Company We Keep*, 223.

The Difficulty of Upright Living

If the Bible's stories do nothing else, they teach us how difficult upright living is. They show the elusiveness of righteousness. They illustrate the challenges of holiness. They describe how those with the best of intentions make the worst of mistakes.

Principles in Conflict

Moral principles can be of some value in ethical living. However, what should we do when one principle comes into conflict with another? Which principle takes priority?

The Bible's stories give us examples of how God's people have tried to navigate this difficulty. For example, in Genesis 26:12–33, the Philistines repeatedly demand that Isaac leave their land. The land was given to Isaac's father (Gen. 21:22–34), but the Philistines don't seem to care. Abraham's servants dug wells in it, but the Philistines have filled them in. Isaac has wealth and numbers at least to put up a fight (26:12–16, 28–29), but is it the right thing to do?

Peace and *justice* are clearly at conflict here. Should Isaac *avoid bloodshed*, as God has commanded earlier in Genesis (e.g., 9:5–6)? Or, should he follow in the footsteps of his father, Abraham, in Genesis 14, *protecting what belongs to his family*?

In the end, Isaac neither pretends that the Philistines are right nor resorts to violence. When they show up at his tent, he voices his complaints against them. Yet he's unwilling to go to war (26:30–31). Though this fertile land is exceedingly precious and is owned by his family, Isaac gives it up to keep peace.

In this brief story, readers see that the moral life isn't easy or fair. At times, our best moral principles come into conflict with each other. Sometimes, all our choices are bad ones. The Bible tells us we're not alone when that happens. We learn about the fundamental complexity of the moral life. (See "The Bible's Not-So-Glossy Picture.")

The Bible's Not-So-Glossy Picture

"It is not that the Bible paints a glossy picture, as many people—mostly those who have never read it—believe. No, it shows us our familiar world, with difficulties all too real, and sometimes intractable. The Bible is relentlessly realistic about the world and our situation in it. It does not pretend that things are better than they are, nor entice us to imagine that we can transcend the difficulties through some kind of spiritual superiority, innate or acquired. Nonetheless, a radical change happens as we read it deeply."

Ellen F. Davis, *Getting Involved with God*, 41

Outside Eden

"Fundamental to all of Genesis . . . is the driving metaphor WE ARE EXPELLED FROM PARADISE. No reader of Genesis has literally been expelled from the Garden of Eden. No reader has seen firsthand the cherubim and whirling, flaming sword east of the tree of life. And yet, Genesis clearly invites its readers to adopt Adam and Eve as metaphorical representations of themselves. In fact, it is a casualty of translation that the Hebrew [is] typically rendered 'Adam' and 'Eve,' when in fact their names literally are 'Humanity' and 'Life.' Few readers of the English Bible are aware of this connection, and thus they fail to realize how the text itself invites them to see these characters less as historical figures and more as metaphorical representations of the human race. Once one understands the driving metaphor WE ARE EXPELLED FROM PARADISE, however, then suddenly the remainder of Genesis and even our own lives make much more sense."

Matthew Schlimm, *From Fratricide to Forgiveness*, 125

For all of us who have experienced the difficulties of upright living, the Bible says, "You are not alone. Those who went before you struggled, too. Moral living has always been challenging, ever since humanity left Eden with its relatively straightforward choice of whether to eat from one particular tree." (See "Outside Eden.")

Lacking Access to God's Will

In a highly complicated world, even the great people of the Bible fail at leading perfect lives. In Genesis 16, Abraham and Sarah have far exceeded their life expectancy.[21] (See "Life Expectancy in Ancient Israel.") Death may come at any time. When it does, it appears that all they have will go to someone outside their family, an employee who manages the house (Gen. 15:2–3). God has promised offspring beyond number, but in the meanwhile, years pass while the elderly couple remains barren. Even Abraham and Sarah do not know how God's promises will materialize.

They decide that Abraham should try to have a child with Sarah's servant Hagar. They seem to have the best of intentions.[22] Though they are none other than Abraham and Sarah—the founders of three of the world's great religions—and though God has appeared to them in the past, they don't know

---

21. In this text, they are called "Abram" and "Sarai." However, I have chosen to go with their more familiar names "Abraham" and "Sarah," which the text uses from Gen. 17 onward.

22. Bellis, *Helpmates, Harlots, and Heroes*, 70–71; LaCocque, *Onslaught against Innocence*, 45.

how God's promises will reach fulfillment. They don't have instant access to God's will. They make the best decision they can.

And in the end, what they decide leaves everyone broken. The Bible makes clear that even Abraham couldn't make polygamy work. His family plunges into the worst of dysfunctions. By Genesis 21, Abraham needs to send away his firstborn son and one of his wives into a harsh and unforgiving desert—a place where nothing less than God's miracles will be able to save the mother and child.

For all Christians who feel like they have lacked access to God's will, Genesis shows them they are not alone. They are, instead, in the company of Abraham and Sarah. Even those whom God has chosen for the greatest of promises still fall prey to the worst of decisions.

Through Abraham and Sarah's story, readers learn that terrible decisions do not forfeit the promises God has made to us.

People sometimes complain that Christians are not authentic enough, that they hide behind veneers that thinly disguise who they really are. This complaint may be true of particular people, but it is not true of the Old Testament. The Bible doesn't try to hide who we really are. It speaks with authenticity and realism about the human condition.

> **Life Expectancy in Ancient Israel**
>
> In Genesis 16, Abraham is 86 years old, making Sarah 76. Those ages sound old to us today, but they must have sounded even older to the earliest readers of Genesis. In ancient Israel, most people died before the age of 40.[a]
>
> a. Cf. MacDonald, *What Did the Ancient Israelites Eat?*, 86.

Many pastors (myself included) have stood up on Sunday morning and acted as though they have things figured out. They have put on a mask, attempting to disguise their own sinful nature. They have pretended to know God's will, to have mastered every evil, to have conquered sin. Jesus called such people "hypocrites."

The stories of the Bible remind all of us that the moral life is downright difficult. There are no shortcuts. We are forced to make decisions in the heat of the moment. We do things that seem good at the time, but in the end lead to nothing but tears. (See "Not Simple.")

The Old Testament's R-rated stories give us God's grace by showing that even the so-called champions of our faith struggled in many ways.[23]

23. Some interpreters might argue that biblical characters never even struggle to pursue goodness. I advocate a more generous reading of the text. With Genesis, e.g., there are good intentions behind Abram and Sarai's desire to have Ishmael, Jacob's desire to receive blessing, and Joseph's desire to enact some level of justice against his brothers. The problem isn't that

---

Not Simple

"There are no simple, easy resolutions; but that's okay. Life's not simple, the Bible's not easy, so why should we expect God to be? Let's have the courage and audacity to engage the raw and uncensored God of Scripture."

Mark Roncace, *Raw Revelation*, 84

"We need to see ourselves among the plotting, whoring, murdering, blaspheming people of God and pay attention to what God makes of the mess. And hope and pray that God will make something out of our mess."

Peter John Santucci, "Telling Details"

Conclusion

The Old Testament is a friend who's unafraid to talk about R-rated material. Yet the adult nature of our friend's conversations is no reason to stop listening.[24]

We, as the church, need to hear the Old Testament's stories because we, like the characters in those stories, are sinners. Maybe if we were already saints, we would be inspired by stories of those who always knew what to do and easily conquered every evil. But as it is, we need a survival guide for making it in a fallen world. We need ways to deal with the sinful nature that resides within us. We need real stories of real people struggling in the real world. Alongside them, we gain experiences and a sense of wisdom for handling struggles within our own lives. We learn more about our world's limitations, our human imperfections, and God's grace.

For Further Study

Barton, John. *Ethics and the Old Testament*. 2nd ed. London: SCM, 2002.

———. *Understanding Old Testament Ethics: Approaches and Explorations*. Louisville: Westminster John Knox, 2003.

Booth, Wayne C. *The Company We Keep: An Ethics of Fiction*. Berkeley: University of California Press, 1988.

---

these characters are thoroughly wicked; it's that flaws in themselves and their world lead to flawed decisions that cause significant suffering.

24. In fact, one can argue that many of the Bible's disturbing stories should be shared even with children. As Bettelheim, *Uses of Enchantment*, 7, puts it, "Many parents believe that only conscious reality or pleasant and wish-fulfilling images should be presented to children—that they should be exposed only to the sunny side of things. But such one-sided fare nourishes the mind only in a one-sided way, and real life is not all sunny" (alt. for gender inclusivity).

————. *The Rhetoric of Fiction*. Chicago: University of Chicago Press, 1961.

Nussbaum, Martha C. *The Fragility of Goodness: Luck and Ethics in Greek Tragedy and Philosophy*. Rev. ed. Cambridge: Cambridge University Press, 2001.

————. *Love's Knowledge: Essays on Philosophy and Literature*. New York: Oxford University Press, 1990.

> These books by Booth and Nussbaum provide more insights into the ways of reading stories described above. Although they do not focus on the Bible, their ideas about other types of literature can be applied to Old Testament texts.

Wenham, Gordon J. *Story as Torah: Reading Old Testament Narrative Ethically*. Grand Rapids: Baker Academic, 2000.

> These books by Barton and Wenham apply insights from Booth and Nussbaum, exploring the ethical import of biblical narratives.

The website www.MatthewSchlimm.com has additional resources, including group discussion questions.

5

Killing All That Breathes

Violence in the Old Testament

THE PREVIOUS CHAPTER EXAMINED some of the Old Testament's morally questionable stories. This chapter digs deeper, turning specifically to the issue of violence.

Bloodshed dominates the Old Testament. The moment humanity sets foot outside Eden, Cain kills his own brother. The story of Noah and all the animals recounts how nearly everyone and everything drowns. Abraham comes within inches of slaughtering his own son. Moses and David commit murder. Legal codes call for the constant killing of animals, not to mention criminals. Genesis, Judges, and 2 Samuel tell stories of rape. The prophets bring a forecast of violent destruction and doom to a disobedient people. The psalmist cries out for God to kill even infants. With bloodshed, the Israelites take possession of the Holy Land, and with bloodshed, many are forced off it. The Old Testament rarely strays far from violence, mentioning it in every book except Ruth.

Frighteningly, the Old Testament connects violence with God. Exodus 15:3 puts it simply: "The LORD is a warrior." God commands the Israelites not only to defend themselves through war, but also to slaughter other tribes and seize their land. Even women and children die in this God-sponsored violence (e.g., Deut. 2:33–34). In time, God turns violence against first the northern kingdom of Israel, using the Assyrians—renowned for their atrocities—to bring about Israel's downfall in 722 BCE.[1] (See figure 4.) In 587 BCE, God appoints Nebuchadnezzar as an assassin to take out the people of Judah.

If Jesus is the Prince of Peace, what does he have to do with this sword-wielding deity of the Old Testament? Or, to stay within the Old Testament, how can this Divine Warrior also be the God whom the psalms describe as "compassionate and merciful, very patient, and full of faithful love"?[2]

Of all the issues tackled in this book, violence is the most challenging. There are no easy explanations for why the Old Testament is so violent. (See "The Troubling Bible.") While answers are elusive, we can avoid interpretive errors that only make matters worse. We can avoid ways of thinking that lead to skewed views of

Figure 4. Assyrian Siege. This relief shows Assyrians attacking a city. It comes from the palace of Tiglath-Pileser III (746–727 BCE), who exerted his power over Israel in its waning days. "Bas-relief from Palace of Tiglath-Pileser III, 746–727 BC," Minneapolis Institute of Arts. I took this photograph on March 28, 2011.

the Bible, ethics, and God. We can also arrive at a deeper understanding of how the Old Testament is our friend in faith.

We all bring assumptions to the act of reading the Bible. Some of the things we take for granted are especially problematic. This chapter tackles flawed assumptions, showing better ways of sorting through the Old Testament's violence. Here are mistaken premises that this chapter seeks to correct:

1. Christians should imitate biblical characters' actions.
2. Christians should imitate God's actions.
3. Christians should apply each individual text they read directly to their lives.
4. Christians should read individual passages in isolation from other passages.
5. Christians should have answers to every question raised by disturbing texts.

1. For a short account of Tiglath-Pileser III's involvement in ancient Israel, see V. H. Matthews, *History of Ancient Israel*, 71–73. For a description of how Assyrian rulers boasted of their brutality in war, see Crouch, *War and Ethics*, 38–48, 52–64.
2. Ps. 103:8. C. Wright, *The God I Don't Understand*, 77–80.

1. Description Is Not Prescription

Our last chapter pointed to a major mistake people can make when studying the Bible: *sometimes we erroneously assume that biblical characters are saints, people we should imitate.* This assumption is especially problematic when biblical characters commit acts of violence. If readers should imitate people in the Bible, then the Bible seems to endorse all types of killing and acts of terror.

It's essential to remember, therefore, that not all texts presenting violence are texts praising violence.[3] (See "Critiques Rather than Approvals.") From its third chapter onward, the Bible is concerned with sin and its effects. It focuses on violence precisely because violence is part of the fallen world we inhabit. The Bible does not look at reality through stained-glass windows. Readers are left face-to-face with bloodshed, cruelty, and carnage.

We expect the Bible to be inspirational. Instead, it is violent. Before we assume that's a bad thing, we should remember what literary critic Wayne Booth says: "Some of the most piously intended, openly moralistic works will reveal themselves as ethically shoddy, and some works with aggressive surface teachings of 'the wrong kind' might well prove, through the quality of the journey, ethically admirable."[4]

The Old Testament certainly has its share of "aggressive surface teachings." They are not at all what we would expect to find in Scripture.

The Troubling Bible

"I have come to regard with suspicion those who claim that the Bible never troubles them. I can only assume this means they haven't actually read it."[a]

Rachel Held Evans,
Biblical Womanhood, 51

a. See also Miller, "God the Warrior," 40–41.

But they may also provide moral guidance for precisely the horrid situations in which we need ethical direction the most. Many texts present violence in all its gore, not to *commend* it but to *condemn* it. They may not be pleasant to read. But through their disturbing content, they create in readers the desire for alternatives to violence.[5]

The Bible is filled with texts that enter the fray, that provoke questions without easy answers, that force us to wrestle with the human condition at its most brutal.

3. Lesser, "Morally Difficult Passages," 293–94.
4. Booth, *Company We Keep*, 206.
5. For an account of how Genesis creates in readers' minds a desire for an alternative to Cain and his violent ways, see Schlimm, *From Fratricide to Forgiveness*, 128–29.

Consider, for example, Genesis 34. It's one of the most disturbing stories in the Bible. Many Christians ignore it altogether. It makes people uncomfortable, but it also brings important matters to the church's attention.[6]

At the outset of this chapter, readers witness a tribal prince rape Dinah.[7] When her father—our patriarch Jacob—learns about it, he does nothing. If his response is appalling, so is that of Dinah's brothers. They slaughter not only Shechem but also every male inhabitant of his city, grossly distorting the rite of circumcision in the process.

> **Critiques Rather than Approvals**
>
> "Understanding that [the Bible's] stories are frequently told as critiques of the social situations that they portray rather than in approval of them can lead us to applaud rather than deplore their inclusion in Scripture. Contemporary readers can read with a 'hermeneutics of grace,' a method of interpretation that recognizes the basic decency and well-meaning character of the biblical authors."
>
> Tikva Frymer-Kensky,
> *Women of the Bible*, 353

If we approach the Bible while assuming we should imitate its characters, we'll give up on reading it. There's no one in Genesis 34 whom readers should try to copy. Shechem's rape, Jacob's silence, and the brothers' violence—all of these actions are horrendous. Readers expecting the Bible to contain rosy and inspiring stories are in for a sore surprise.

Similarly, readers wanting the Bible to give them a set of directions will be disappointed. Genesis 34 doesn't prescribe a course of action. It doesn't tell readers what they should do in response to the rape of a loved one. It doesn't end with a tidy solution. Instead, the story closes with an unanswered question. After Jacob condemns his sons for their genocidal vengeance, they reply, "Should our sister be treated like a whore?" (v. 31 NRSV). The text never offers a response. The story ends with a question mark.

Readers are left to wrestle with the human condition in all its limitations, confusion, and pain: What is the proper response to sexual violence? What should one do when a family member has been harmed and there are no good options for punishing the wrongdoer? How does one exact justice in the absence of possibilities commensurate with the offense? How can we create communities free from rape and violence?

We might prefer to ignore such questions because they involve unpleasant topics. But the Bible refuses to let us do so. It causes readers to recognize how

6. Cf. Fontaine, "Abusive Bible," 111.

7. The interpretation here follows Scholz, "Was It Really Rape in Genesis 34?" For alternate interpretations, see L. Bechtel, "What If Dinah Is Not Raped?"; and Wolde, *Reframing Biblical Studies*, 283–96.

damaging abuse can be and how it can spark incredibly strong reactions. Dinah's story summons readers to reflect on how abuse can be prevented and how to respond to violence when it does occur. As the text points out, answers may be hard to find—especially in the moment—but that does not lessen the need for communities of faith to reflect on abuse.

> ### Sexual Violence Statistics
>
> "Nearly 1 in 5 women (18.3%) and 1 in 71 men (1.4%) in the United States have been raped at some time in their lives, . . . and 27.2% of women and 11.7% of men have experienced unwanted sexual contact."
>
> M. C. Black et al.,
> *Sexual Violence Survey*, 1–2

Even in so-called progressive societies like the United States, many people suffer sexual violence. (See "Sexual Violence Statistics.") The trauma inflicted by such abuse can harm individuals for decades, if not lifetimes. It can and does devastate people's faith. For the church to be the church—to care for the suffering, to befriend the afflicted, to heal the downtrodden—it must tend to what this text presents.

The Bible describes a violent world because our world is violent. If we ignore the violent nature of our world, we also ignore victims of violence. And we cannot ignore those who suffer if we are God's people.[8]

2. When *Not* to Be Godly

If one mistake is assuming we should imitate people in the Bible, *another mistake is assuming that we should imitate God*. This point seems counterintuitive, but it's definitely true when it comes to God's violence.

One of the Old Testament's favorite images for God is a warrior. The common name "The LORD of hosts" appears over 250 times in the Old Testament. In many cases, the Hebrew is better translated "The LORD of armies."[9] This God of war is frequently depicted as using weapons to destroy enemies:

> The LORD thundered from heaven;
>   the Most High made his voice heard.
> God shot arrows, scattering the enemy;
>   he sent the lightning
>   and whipped them into confusion. (2 Sam. 22:14–15;
>   cf. Ps. 18:13–14)

8. I treat Gen. 34 in greater depth in Schlimm, *From Fratricide to Forgiveness*, 43–46, 160–61.

9. The CEB gets at this idea by translating it, "the LORD of heavenly forces." As noted by H.-J. Zobel, *TDOT* 12:215–32, other translations are possible. However, this translation works well with texts like 1 Sam. 15:2, where God is involved in military matters.

In Deuteronomy 32:42, God boasts of what will happen to enemies:

> I'll make my arrows drink much blood,
>> while my sword devours flesh,
>> the blood of the dead and captured,
>>> flowing from the heads of enemy generals.

These texts cannot be glossed over. They are too prevalent and too shocking.[10] Yet interpreters do well to remember that there's a universe of difference between a violent God and a violent humanity.

It's one thing to say that a just God executes judgment on a sinful humanity to keep people from destroying creation. It's an entirely different thing to say that humans have the capabilities to execute similar judgment through violent means. God alone knows everything: every motive, every past, every psychology, every limitation, every action, and every history. God alone knows how to intertwine justice with mercy, when to forgive and when to punish. Humans do not.

For decades, Christians have enjoyed reading Charles Sheldon's *In His Steps*.[11] It fixes attention on the question "What would Jesus do?" (WWJD), urging the imitation of Jesus (and God) as the guiding principle for Christian ethics.

While there's some biblical basis for such a principle (Lev. 19:2; Matt. 5:48), our ethics quickly become skewed if this principle is the sole or even the primary means of determining how to live.[12] A recurrent theme in Scripture is the fundamental difference between God and humans (Isa. 55:8–9; Hosea 11:9). The Bible portrays God as enthroned atop the ark of the covenant in the holy of holies (Lev. 16:2). A human seeking to imitate God and sit there would be nothing short of an abomination.

Similarly, humans seeking to imitate God's violence risk committing the gravest of sins. People making judgments about who should live and who should die assume God's duties—even though they are sinful and flawed. The book of Isaiah condemns the king of Babylon for precisely such a sin. Because he has acted with great violence and tried to exalt himself to a place equal with God, he shall instead descend into the depths of the grave on a bed of maggots (Isa. 14:11).

---

10. Many other texts portray God in this way, as noted by Miller, "God the Warrior," 39. These include Num. 10:35; 21:14; Judg. 5:31; 1 Sam. 18:17; 25:28; 30:26; Pss. 24:8; 74:13–14; 89:10–11; Isa. 42:13; 51:9–11; Hab. 3:8; Zeph. 3:17. See also Deut. 33:2, 26–29; Isa. 63:1–6; Amos 2:9.

11. Sheldon, *In His Steps: What Would Jesus Do?* This book was first published in 1896 by Chicago Advance, but multiple presses have published it since.

12. For a biting critique of those who see the imitation of God as central to ethics, see Rodd, *Glimpses of a Strange Land*, 65–76.

God Fights, So God's People Shouldn't

While people can use the image of a violent God to try to condone their own violent actions, the logic of many biblical texts goes in the opposite direction: God fights, so God's people shouldn't. Exodus 14:14 summarizes this thought: "The Lord will fight for you, and you have only to keep still" (NRSV).[13] The basic idea is that God fights so that God's people don't need to engage in violence. (See "Zero Human Cooperation.") Many of the Bible's stories about warfare do not glorify the nation's military prowess or recount Israel's brute force. They describe how Israel would have been homeless and dead without the miraculous workings of God. They do more to encourage trust in God amid danger than to promote the building of arsenals or trusting in weaponry.[14]

As Psalm 20:7 puts it, "Some people trust in chariots, others in horses; but we praise the LORD's name." This verse is all the more significant when we remember that chariots and horses were used for military purposes in ancient contexts.[15] Today we might say, "Some people trust in tanks, others in missiles; but we rely on the LORD." The text stands directly opposed to those who try to justify standing armies and the stockpiling of weapons.

> ### Zero Human Cooperation
>
> "The holy war [is] sheer miracle; [God's] saving act is entirely self-sufficient and does not allow any human co-operation."
>
> Gerhard von Rad,
> *Old Testament Theology*, 2:160
>
> "Biblical references to the conquest generally omit all mention of specific battles and human activity. It is God's deed; he is the sole actor; there are no human heroes."
>
> George E. Wright,
> *Old Testament and Theology*, 123

Texts about Samson should be read in a similar way. Samson's violence exceeds that of nearly anyone else in the Bible. At one point, he kills a thousand Philistines, striking them down with the jawbone of a dead donkey (Judg. 15:9–20). Just before his mass killing, the text says, "The LORD's spirit rushed over" Samson (15:14). On the one hand, it should disturb us that God is connected so closely with violence. On the other hand, we shouldn't forget that this text does nothing to encourage investing in armies and weapons. Samson

13. J. Yoder, *Politics of Jesus*, 76–88.
14. See, e.g., Deut. 4:37–38, which explicitly says that other nations were bigger and stronger than the Israelites. See also Niditch, *War in the Hebrew Bible*, esp. 143–49.
15. See, e.g., Brueggemann, *Divine Presence amid Violence*, 15–16, 33; on 55–60 he discusses texts similar to Ps. 20:7, including Pss. 33:16–17; 76:6–7a; 147:10–11; Prov. 21:30–31; Isa. 31:1, 3; 30:15–16; 43:15–17; Jer. 9:23–24; Hosea 1:7; Mic. 5:10, 15; Zech. 4:6.

rescues Israel from oppressive Philistine rulers, and he does so using only a bone from a donkey's carcass—and God's supernatural strength. The text encourages readers to trust in God for rescue from horrid situations, not to spend one's life training for combat.[16]

Other Old Testament texts similarly urge readers to rely on God rather than their own military might—even when faced with grave threats.[17] In 2 Chronicles 20, readers encounter the incredible faith of Jehoshaphat, Judah, and the Levites who turn to the Lord—not their weaponry—when the Moabites and Ammonites come to make war.[18] It tells of God's intervention and protection. Similarly, the book of Daniel provides readers with visions of hope that God will intervene against those who seek to wipe out Jews and Jewish culture. Daniel's audience can embrace nonviolence even under severe persecution because of what God will do.[19]

Maybe God Isn't on Our Side[20]

The texts just reviewed give biblical perspectives of when God is on the side of God's people. However, that's not always the case. There are times in the Old Testament when God refuses to side with the Israelites.

For example, in the book of Joshua, God generally sides with Israel against the Canaanites. Yet God favors a Canaanite prostitute named Rahab while opposing an Israelite fighter named Achan (Josh. 2:1–21; 6:17–25; 7:1–26).[21] At one point, Joshua meets an angel of the Lord. One would think that the angel would march before or even alongside Joshua. But here's what the text says:

> When Joshua was near Jericho, he looked up. He caught sight of a man standing in front of him with his sword drawn. Joshua went up and said to him, "Are you on our side or that of our enemies?"
>
> He said, "Neither! I'm the commander of the Lord's heavenly force." (Josh. 5:13–14a)

---

16. Cf. V. Matthews, *Judges and Ruth*, 153–54.

17. See Seibert, *Violence of Scripture*, 80–81, 125–28. He mentions texts such as Deut. 17:16–17; Isa. 31:1; Hosea 10:13b–14a.

18. Cf. Niditch, *War in the Hebrew Bible*, 146–49. On 144 she mentions other stories of God's miraculous deliverance in battle, including Exod. 17:8–13; Josh. 6:20; 8:18; 10:12–13; 1 Sam. 7:9–11; 2 Kings 3:20–25; 6:18; 7:5–7; 19:35–37.

19. Portier-Young, *Apocalypse against Empire*, 223–79, esp. 278.

20. There's a strong tradition of associating God and country in America, esp. during wartime; yet this tradition has grave problems, as pointed out by Hauerwas in *War and the American Difference*, *Unleashing the Scripture*, and *After Christendom?*

21. Davis, "Poetics of Generosity."

If this angel refuses to side with even Joshua, perhaps we should be cautious about assuming that God will favor whatever nation we're a part of. God may not be on our side, especially when we go to war.[22]

Outside the book of Joshua, the Bible makes clear that God will violently oppose even Israel and Judah after generations of unrepentant sinfulness. Legal codes warned of such dangers (e.g., Lev. 18:24–30). The prophets sounded alarms that such violence was coming (e.g., Jer. 4:4–8). Books like 2 Kings showed how such violent destruction fell on Israel and Judah after centuries of faithlessness (esp. 2 Kings 25).

It's wrong to imitate God's violence—or even to assume that God is on our side. We may find ourselves, like Israel or Judah, in military conflicts where God plans to punish us.

It's frightening to think of a violent God, and we will return to this issue in greater depth in chapter 11, where we deal with divine wrath. For now, we can at least see the grave error of trying to imitate God's violence.

3. The Problem with Application

A third mistake we can make when interpreting the Bible is assuming that every individual passage of Scripture should be directly applied to our daily lives. The problem with this assumption isn't the urge to apply the Bible as a whole to our lives. It's the idea that each individual passage can be directly lived out in each individual life today.[23]

Some texts describe onetime occurrences, which God doesn't intend to duplicate in the future. In fact, several biblical passages describe God's violent victory over the Egyptians and Canaanites in precisely these terms (Exod. 34:10–16; Deut. 4:32–38). We shouldn't jump from the violence of Joshua to violence in our day. As George Ernest Wright

> **Never Meant to Become a Model**
>
> "So the conquest of Canaan, as a unique and limited historical event, was never meant to become a model for how all future generations were to behave toward their enemies (whether future generations of Israelites or, still less, of Christians)."[a]
>
> Christopher Wright,
> *The God I Don't Understand*, 90–91
>
> a. For frightening accounts of how people have used biblical images to justify violence today, see Jenkins, *Laying Down the Sword*, e.g., 19–20, 155–57.

22. See also 1 Sam. 4–6, where the Israelites mistakenly assume that God will be on their side if they take the ark of the covenant with them into battle.

23. On the urge to apply individual passages to lives, see C. Smith, *Bible Made Impossible*, 5, 69–72; Frykholm, *Rapture Culture*, 111–15.

said decades ago, "Israel's wars of conquest become no mandate for wars by God's people today."[24] (See "Never Meant to Become a Model.")

Some texts are in the Bible less for our own benefit and more for the benefit of people very different from ourselves. Rather than trying to apply each text to our individual lives, we sometimes need to ask if a text addresses someone other than ourselves.

Who Should Pray Psalm 137:9?

Psalm 137:9 is perhaps the most disturbing text of the Old Testament:

> Happy is the one who seizes your [Babylon's] infants
> and dashes them against the rocks. (NIV)

At first glance, it's almost inconceivable that such a verse ever made it into the Bible. How is *this* Holy Scripture? Applying this verse to our lives in a straightforward manner may well constitute an act of sin. Jesus, after all, said that simply calling someone a "fool" could jeopardize one's entire salvation (Matt. 5:22). How could we wish that babies die?![25]

In thinking about this text, it's important to remember: the Bible is a book for the ages. We are *not* its only audience. It speaks to people in many cultures, times, and places.[26] Sometimes it speaks more to others than to us.

It may be wrong for most of us to pray the words of Psalm 137. Yet I wonder about those who have suffered the unspeakable in war, who have seen their own children dashed against rocks, who know atrocities others cannot imagine. For these people, praying with rage—even hateful rage—isn't a sin, but a refusal to give up on God. For those who have seen their loved ones tortured and killed, prayer of any type, no matter how violent or how wrathful, may constitute a more profound act of faith than any I will ever know. (See "Violent Psalms.")

Claus Westermann, one of the most respected biblical interpreters of the last century, describes how his view of the Bible changed during World War II, as he faced persecution in Germany and later wound up in a Russian prisoner-of-war camp:

> The Bible was no longer merely an uplifting book, as it had been in my childhood and my parental home. Life had gotten too hard for that. The only thing in the

24. G. E. Wright, *Old Testament and Theology*, 130. See also Walzer, *Exodus and Revolution*, 144.
25. Possibly Babylon is here conceived as a mother, with the "infants" of this verse referring to the city's inhabitants (cf. Isa. 49:21–23; 60:4; 66:7–13). However, other texts suggest that Ps. 137:9 should be understood literally (Nah. 3:10). In either event, the desired violence is highly problematic.
26. Cf. Ḥakham and Berman, *Psalms with the Jerusalem Commentary*, 1:xvii.

Bible with enduring value was that which spoke directly to my present existence. First and foremost, that was the psalms. . . . Under the influence of my wartime experiences, I realized that the people who had written and prayed the psalms understood prayer differently than we do. Prayer was closer to life, closer to the reality in which they lived, than is true with us. For us, prayer is something a person does or is admonished to do—a human act. But in the Psalter, crying to God grows out of life itself; it is a reaction to the experiences of life, a cry from the heart.[27]

As Westermann suggests, our Scriptures speak with authenticity to war-torn people, the traumatized, the wounded. The Bible reminds the inhabitants of a broken world that we remain children of God's promise. (See "Veterans and the Bible.")

Turning Psalm 137:9 Around

Thus far, I've stressed that individual texts of the Bible may not apply *directly* to our lives. God can still speak to us through texts like Psalm 137:9, but it might be in a roundabout way. Old Testament scholar Ellen Davis describes how many psalms of the Bible express anger (a topic we'll return to in chap. 10). She wonders whether these psalms can prove useful when we are free from anger. Davis writes, "If you have the courage (and it will take some), try turning the psalm a full 180 degrees, until it is directed at yourself, and ask: Is there anyone in the community of God's people who might want to say this to God about me—or maybe, about us?"[28] When I do that with Psalm 137:9, I am reminded of military action my country has taken that has left countless children dead. I think not only of the horrors of Hiroshima and Nagasaki, but also of more recent wars in Iraq and Afghanistan that have made it

---

Violent Psalms

"Violent psalms reflect the emotions of those at their weakest state, who, given the threat of their enemies, are in no position to fight back through their own power. [They] are the prayers of the powerless, whose only source of strength is the hope that God will act powerfully for their salvation. . . .

"The sensitive community is aware both that violent prayers have value and also that they can be abused, for example, when nonvictims pray for God's violent judgment."[a]

Joel LeMon,
"Saying Amen to Violent Psalms," 108–9

a. Wolterstorff ("Reading Joshua," 256) makes a similar point. LeMon's essay offers a fine overview of how other scholars have treated violent psalms (99–102).

---

27. Westermann, "Bible and the Life of Faith," 340.
28. Davis, *Involved with God*, 28.

Veterans and the Bible

"For soldiers who had experienced and even committed atrocities in war, there is tremendous value in learning that Scripture knows their horror and shame and knows the dehumanizing effect of war. Finding these horrors contained within sacred Scripture might suggest to combat veterans that they are not cast outside the orbit of God's power to redeem. . . . There is no horror we dare not speak before God, no crime we dare not confess, because there is no horror that God does not see and know. In these Scriptures God's Spirit has chosen not to hide the worst of our humanity from us—even these horrors of killing, wounding, and shaming in God's own name—and instead brings us to these texts to wrestle and struggle with our sinfulness and our limitations even as we seek so desperately to approach and talk about God and uncover God's ways."[a]

Anathea Portier-Young, "Drinking the Cup of Horror," 407,
summarizing the work of Mel Baars

a. See also Kelle, "Trauma of Defeat"; Smith-Christopher, *Theology of Exile*.

---

so mothers and fathers will never again see life in their own infants, toddlers, and children. I am made deeply concerned and ashamed about my country resorting to military action under any circumstances. Strikingly, a text that initially seems morally repulsive actually causes me to face the horrors of war and oppose violence under any conditions.

The Old Testament is a friend who has seen the horrors of war and lived to talk about it. The Old Testament doesn't come to us with quaint memories of a rosy childhood and a two-parent family. It's more like a war veteran with symptoms of posttraumatic stress. This friend can thus offer deep resources to the war-torn, refugees, and those exposed to violence. This friend reminds us all of the brutality of war.

4. The Right Word for the Right Situation

A fourth interpretive mistake is to assume we should read individual passages in isolation from other passages. On most vexing topics like violence, the Bible gives more than one perspective.[29] Psalm 137 is hardly the only text to deal with violence, and we shouldn't assume that the perspective offered by it

---

29. Sometimes different perspectives are embedded within the same text. Some scholars suggest that even within a book like Joshua, there is uneasiness about the conquest: Stone, "Ethical and Apologetic Tendencies"; Seibert, *Violence of Scripture*, 98–100; Hawk, "God of the Conquest," 144–46.

is the best viewpoint for us to adopt with whatever we face in our particular context. Rather, we should work cooperatively with other Christians and the Holy Spirit to discern which texts provide the best resources for what we face. To put it differently, we cannot randomly apply one text to our lives without bringing it into conversation with other related texts.

Christians should wrestle not only with this question:

- How should we live out a particular text in our individual lives?

We must also struggle with other questions:

- How do different biblical texts provide a conversation with one another?
- Which texts speak most directly to us in our context?
- Where do we most closely align with the biblical text? Where do we diverge? Why?[30]

> **Part and Whole**
>
> "As in any literary work, individual verses and passages matter less for themselves than for the role they play in the composition of the whole work. . . .
>
> "In fact, the more we explore the darkest Bible passages, the more they would benefit from being brought back into the wider story through public or liturgical readings. They should not be presented in isolation as frightening injunctions, but placed alongside the other passages that frame and expound their meaning, especially from the prophets."
>
> Philip Jenkins,
> *Laying Down the Sword*, 235, 241

Interpreting the Bible is less a science and more an artistic expression. A great artist finds the perfect color to place alongside other shades and hues. A great interpreter finds texts aptly spoken in particular situations.[31] Proverbs 25:11 uses a vivid metaphor to get at this idea: "A word fitly spoken is like apples of gold in a setting of silver" (NRSV).

Readers of Psalm 137 aren't left alone with it, as though it were the only text in the Bible dealing with violence. Instead, we have a great range of texts that need to be studied and brought into conversation with one another.[32] (See "Part and Whole.")

A text highly relevant for the church today is Amos 1:3–2:3. It constitutes one of the earliest denunciations of atrocities in

---

30. Cf. Cosgrove, *Appealing to Scripture*, chap. 2, esp. 66; Goldingay, *Theological Diversity*, chaps. 2–3.

31. See Davis and R. Hays, *Art of Reading Scripture*, xv–xvi.

32. R. Hays, *Moral Vision*, 187–205, is helpful for engaging in this process. While his concern is NT texts, many of his insights can easily be transferred to the OT.

war from the ancient world. In a sense, Amos was a champion of human rights centuries before his time. The prophet denounces torture, imprisonment, slavery, indiscriminate killings, violence against women, and the desecration of the dead.

This text may be far more relevant for mainline American churches than a text like Psalm 137. The atrocities that Amos denounces are increasingly prevalent in armed conflicts today. As Nobel Peace Prize nominee Lloyd Axworthy has pointed out, "In the First World War, approximately 10% of casualties of conflict were civilian. Now, 90% of these casualties are civilian."[33] One only needs to think of war crimes committed in Vietnam, Sierra Leone, Rwanda, Tibet, Darfur, Iraq, Afghanistan, or Syria to begin to imagine how this text connects with contemporary realities. Everything that Amos condemns in this passage is similarly condemned by the Geneva Conventions. A text such as this one, denouncing those who disregard human life in times of war, may be far more relevant to many of us than texts that bless those who kill enemies. Amos reminds the church that God opposes those who senselessly kill and harm others, even in times of war.[34]

Amos and the Geneva Conventions

Amos (NRSV)	Geneva Conventions (GC)
"Thus says the LORD: For three transgressions of Damascus, and for four, I will not revoke the punishment; because *they have threshed Gilead with threshing sledges of iron*" (1:3).	"[Mutilation is] and shall remain prohibited at any time and in any place whatsoever, whether committed by civilian or by military agents" (Protocol I.75; cf. GC I.3, 12; III.17; IV.32; Prot. II.4, §2A).
"Thus says the LORD: For three transgressions of Gaza, and for four, I will not revoke the punishment; because *they carried into exile entire communities*, to hand them over to Edom" (1:6; cf. 1:9).	"Individual or mass forcible transfers, as well as deportations of protected persons from occupied territory to the territory of the Occupying Power or to that of any other country, occupied or not, are prohibited, regardless of their motive" (GC IV.49; III.52).
"Thus says the LORD: For three transgressions of Edom, and for four, I will not revoke the punishment; because *he pursued his brother with the sword and cast off all pity; he maintained his anger perpetually, and kept his wrath forever*" (1:11).	"In the conduct of military operations, constant care shall be taken to spare the civilian population, civilians and civilian objects" (cf. Prot. I.57; cf. Prot. I.85, §3).
"Thus says the LORD: For three transgressions of the Ammonites, and for four, I will not revoke the punishment; because *they have ripped open pregnant women in Gilead* in order to enlarge their territory" (1:13).	"Expectant mothers shall be the object of particular protection and respect" (GC IV.16; cf. IV.27, 38, 50, 89, 132; Prot. I.69, 76; II.6, §4).

33. Axworthy, "Opening Remarks, . . . Singapore, July 27, 1999."
34. Schlimm, "Teaching the Hebrew Bible"; cf. "Geneva Conventions."

Amos (NRSV)	Geneva Conventions (GC)
"Thus says the LORD: For three transgressions of Moab, and for four, I will not revoke the punishment; because *he burned to lime the bones of the king of Edom*" (2:1).	"The parties to the conflict . . . shall . . . ensure that the dead are honourably interred, if possible according to the rites of the religion to which they belonged, [and] that their graves are respected" (GC 1.17).

In addition to Amos 1:3–2:3, many texts within the Old Testament urge not violence toward foreigners, but love, care, and protection. Immigrants are particularly deserving of respect. Leviticus puts it this way: "The foreigner residing among you must be treated as your native-born. Love them as yourself, for you were foreigners in Egypt. I am the LORD your God" (Lev. 19:34 NIV).[35]

For many Christians, violent texts are a stumbling block. But surrounding these stumbling blocks are fields of goodness that we must not ignore.[36]

5. We Don't Have All the Answers

A woman in my church named Janelle recently received a call from a friend. This friend had been going through a difficult time. Like many Christians, she turned to the Bible for help. However, she was quickly confused by what she found. Her confusion in turn led to feelings of guilt and stupidity: "Why can't I get it? Why can't I make sense of it?" She stopped reading the Bible.

After hearing her friend's story, Janelle replied, "If you don't understand the Bible, that doesn't mean you're reading it wrong. It means you're actually paying attention! Everyone has trouble understanding it at times."

Janelle's reply made me smile. *One of the biggest mistakes we can make when reading the Bible is to assume we should always be able to make sense of it.* A much better response involves humility and asking God questions. (See "Living with Questions.")

---

35. C. Wright, *The God I Don't Understand*, 103–4, identifies many texts that uphold the "well-being and protection" of foreigners: Exod. 12:45–49; 20:9–11; 22:21; 23:9, 12; Lev. 16:29; 19:9–10, 33–34; Deut. 5:12–15; 10:17–19; 14:28–29; 16:1–22; 24:17–22; 26:12–13; 29:10–13; 31:12.

36. Many of these texts can be found in the NT (e.g., Matt. 5:43–48). While Christians should take notice of these texts, there are problems with those who claim, "Old Testament portrayals that correspond to the God [whom] Jesus reveals should be regarded as trustworthy and reliable reflections of God's character, while those that do not measure up should be regarded as distortions of the same" (Seibert, *Disturbing Divine Behavior*, 185). Such arguments go in the direction of Marcion, can jeopardize Christian-Jewish friendships, and give insufficient attention to violent texts within the NT (e.g., Matt. 10:34).

> **Living with Questions**
>
> "Concrete answers to key questions about the Bible are not always available. But even without definitive answers, asking questions sometimes provides the most helpful avenue to insight. Living with questions about the Bible over time is important because they keep us thinking about matters that are central to the faith. Living with questions will mean we can better recognize answers if and when they come our way. Even more, we are called to live the questions with other people who ask them; in other words, we are called to *a ministry of questions*. Being called to such a ministry means caring about the questions people have, understanding that questions have no little potential to draw you and others more deeply into the mystery."
>
> Terence E. Fretheim, *About the Bible*, vii

Humility

Not all of the Bible's violence can be explained away. *The necessary starting point for interpreting any passage of Scripture is a spirit of humility.* Biblical scholar Richard Briggs has written a book on the types of virtues that the Old Testament encourages in its readers. He holds up *humility* as one of the most important virtues readers can bring to the text.[37]

Briggs makes an excellent point. We are mortals trying to understand the Infinite through texts that are thousands of years old. Not all of it will make sense to us. Even with all our centuries of reflection, painstaking research, archaeological findings, and critical scholarship, we remain ignorant and flawed. When God speaks to us in powerful ways through Scripture, it's often amid our weaknesses, not because we are perfect interpreters. We will never solve all the Bible's problems.[38]

Prayerful Questions

One approach then is to prayerfully question violent texts. Terence Fretheim observes that many biblical characters question God's actions. Similarly, we can question God's Word.[39] (See "Those Very Responses.")

Consider Abraham in Genesis 18:16–33. God appears poised to destroy Sodom and Gomorrah. Abraham is deeply concerned: his nephew Lot lives

---

37. Briggs, *Virtuous Reader*, chap. 2.

38. For a good example of humbly trying to deal with violent texts of the OT, see C. Wright, *The God I Don't Understand*, 86–87.

39. Fretheim and Froehlich, *Word of God in a Postmodern Age*, 102–3. Similar remarks appear elsewhere, as in Seibert, *Violence of Scripture*, 62–72, esp. 64–65.

Those Very Responses

"The Old Testament portrays the world as it is, no holds barred. In its pages you will find passionate stories of love and hate, blood-chilling stories of rape and dismemberment, matter-of-fact accounts of trafficking in slaves, honest tales of the high honor and cruel treachery of war. Nothing is neat and orderly. Spoiled brats like Solomon and Samson get supernatural gifts; a truly good man like Job gets catastrophe. As you encounter these disturbances, you may recoil against them or turn away from a God who had any part in them. The wonderful quality of the Old Testament is that it contains those very responses as well! God anticipates our objections and includes them in his sacred writing."

Philip Yancey, *The Bible Jesus Read*, 11–12

---

in Sodom. Will Lot and his family die in the destruction? Driven by this concern, Abraham begins to barter with his Creator. Here's how he begins:

> Abraham approached and said, "Will you really sweep away the innocent with the guilty? What if there are fifty innocent people in the city? Will you really sweep it away and not save the place for the sake of the fifty innocent people in it? It's not like you to do this, killing the innocent with the guilty as if there were no difference. It's not like you! Will the judge of all the earth not act justly?" (Gen. 18:23–25)

In what follows, Abraham talks God down to sparing the city if ten innocent people are there. While many things could be said about this text, the important thing for our purposes is that Abraham is perfectly content with confronting God with difficult questions. He never says, "God, your plan makes no sense to me, but I'll hold my tongue and blindly trust." Instead, Abraham confronts God with tough questions about God's violence. Strikingly, God yields to Abraham. This example suggests that we have the freedom to ask God questions, too—especially questions about violence in the Bible. (See "Telling God What We Think.")

The writers of the psalms join Abraham in questioning God. At the outset of Psalm 10, the person praying launches accusing questions at God:

> "Why, O Lord, do you stand far off?
>   Why do you hide yourself in times of trouble?" (Ps. 10:1 NRSV)

Psalms like this one will receive more attention in chapter 10. For now, it's important to note that the writers of this Psalm felt they had permission to question God when life made little sense to them.

In a similar way, readers of the Bible have the freedom to question biblical texts that make little sense to them. When God commands the Israelites to go to war or to wipe out everything that breathes, people of faith can join the assembly of voices in the Bible that questions what God is doing. (See "David's Anger at God's Violence.")

Christians' moral responsibility isn't to explain away violent texts or to be less than honest about their disturbing contents. We can, however, humbly and prayerfully ask why these texts are in our Bible. In fact, if the church established a tradition of prayerfully questioning these texts, individuals might be less likely to use them to try to justify present-day violence.[40]

We don't need to pretend that we have all the answers. And we certainly don't need to feel guilty or embarrassed by our lack of solutions.

A Final Example: The *herem* Texts

As a way of drawing this chapter to a close, let's look at one of the most challenging sets of texts in the Old Testament: the *herem* texts.

When the Israelites are told to take the land of Canaan, God commands the people to kill every inhabitant of the land, offering these people to God as a sacrifice (see Deut. 7:2; 20:17; Josh. 6:17–21). These texts are highly disturbing. On the surface of things, they appear to praise genocide—just the opposite of what Amos did.[41] In Joshua 10:40, to name one of many possible examples, the warrior Joshua is commended for "utterly destroy[ing] all that breathed, as the LORD God of Israel commanded" (NRSV).[42]

These texts appear to operate with the following logic.[43] First, the practice of slaughtering the Canaanites means that idolatry is uprooted from the land (cf. Exod. 22:20; Deut. 7:1–4; 20:17–18).

---

40. See the points made by Seibert, *Violence of Scripture*, 74–75, 91–92, about the importance of "Naming the Violence" of biblical texts.

41. However, C. Wright, *The God I Don't Understand*, 92, points out: "As used in the modern world, 'genocide' goes along with vicious self-interest usually based on myths of racial superiority, and therefore it is sometimes also called 'ethnic cleansing'. . . . But the conquest of Canaan is *never* justified on ethnic grounds in the Bible, and any notions of ethnic superiority—moral or numerical—are resoundingly squashed in Deuteronomy." He then points to Deut. 9:4–6, which dismantles the notion that the Israelites are righteous while the Canaanites are wicked (94). Seibert, *Violence of Scripture*, 96–97, challenges C. Wright.

42. There are many studies of these *herem* texts; Niditch's *War in the Hebrew Bible*, esp. chaps. 1–2 (albeit dated), provides a useful survey of both scholarship and other attitudes toward war in the Hebrew Bible.

43. See the useful discussions in Chapman, "Ban, The" and "Holy War"; cf. Schlimm, "Prisoners of War"; G. E. Wright, *Old Testament and Theology*, 128–29; Niditch, *War in the Hebrew Bible*, 50; Jenkins, *Laying Down the Sword*, 43.

Second, this practice of *herem* ensures that people don't go to war for personal gain. In the ancient Near East, warfare was the easiest way to get rich quick. After battles, military victors often seized all that remained, grabbing goods and making prisoners of war their slaves. Rather than promote such a violence-for-finance scheme, the text makes clear that the Israelites did not seize Canaan to become rich through slavery.

> **David's Anger at God's Violence**
>
> The violence of the Bible doesn't make sense to many of us. It didn't make sense to David either. In 2 Samuel 6:2–9, God kills a man named Uzzah for touching the ark of the covenant. This made David angry and frightened. Rather than remain silent, he raised questions about what God had done. The text implies that God's ways won't always make sense to us. Sometimes we must honestly ask God our haunting questions.

Third, this practice recognizes God as the military victor of Israel's battles. Because God miraculously intervened on Israel's behalf—because Israel had neither the weaponry nor the soldiers to put up a fight—all spoils of war, including both goods and prisoners of war, belong to God. Thus they are sacrificed to God (Deut. 7:1–6).

While we can begin to see some of the logic for these commands, these passages nevertheless should always leave us uncomfortable. They may have relatively little relevance for most churches today. Some interpreters think they were just metaphors, telling the Israelites that they should have nothing to do with Canaanite religious practices.[44] Yet even if they are only metaphors, they remain disturbing.[45] Perhaps the best Christians can do is prayerfully ask why God would ever allow such a command to enter into the Bible.

> **Telling God What We Think**
>
> "We should be bold enough to tell God what we think. Like a good teacher would welcome a student's challenge, God too is open to our assessments of his character, as he was with Abraham. Instead of offering God our praises, we should offer our appraisals."
>
> Mark Roncace, *Raw Revelation*, 81–82

It's also useful to remember that some texts of the Bible describe one-time events—not anything that should be repeated in later generations. Exodus 34:10–11, for example, talks about violently defeating the Canaanites. In this text, God stresses that what will happen is unlike what has "been performed

---

44. MacDonald, "Deuteronomy," esp. 275 OT; cf. Jenkins, *Laying Down the Sword*, 235–38; Wolterstorff, "Reading Joshua," 248–56; Rowlett, *Rhetoric of Violence*, 12–13, 183.

45. Collins, *Does the Bible Justify Violence?*, 3; Seibert, *Violence of Scripture*, 97–98.

in all the earth or in any nation" (NRSV). Verses like this one suggest that the *herem* texts should not be applied outside of ancient Israel.

Even within ancient Israel, there came a time early in Israel's history when God abandoned this plan of killing all the Canaanites (Judg. 2:20–23; cf. Zech. 14:11). As God says in Judges 2:21, "I will no longer drive out before them any of the nations Joshua left when he died" (NIV). If God gave up on this practice, we should too. It's nothing to be exercised today. Biblical scholar Brent Strawn correctly observes, "In the very way the Old Testament speaks of these things, it suggests that the conquest of Canaan is a limited, time-bound phenomenon never to be repeated."[46]

Finally, it's important to bring *herem* texts into conversation with other biblical texts. When we do so, we find that our Scriptures uphold images of holistic peace, *shalom*, as the goal for which creation yearns. Some interpreters have even suggested that *shalom* is central to all of the Old Testament.[47] Isaiah and Micah join in one chorus, speaking of a time free from weapons, violence, and warfare (Isa. 2:1–4; Mic. 4:1–4).

As the book of Isaiah draws to a close, it looks back at a planet soaked in blood (cf. Isa. 34:3). Using startling imagery, God promises a new heaven and earth, one where wolf, lamb, lion, and ox dwell beside one another, free from premature death (Isa. 65:17–25). It inspires the image of the new Jerusalem found at the close of the Bible (Rev. 21:1–4), and it continues to inspire all of us who live in the violent land of Cain, homesick for Eden.

The diverse texts of the Old Testament present the realities of violence alongside the ideals of shalom. It never denies the harsh brutalities that life can entail. But it never relinquishes hope that a brighter day shall come. It unflinchingly looks at the human condition at its very worst while simultaneously yearning for its very best.

Conclusion

Sometimes people have urged the church to remove violent texts from the Bible.[48] Such an approach will not work with Christians firmly committed to

46. Strawn, "Teaching the Old Testament," 8; cf. Lesser, "Morally Difficult Passages," 298.

47. Although it's dated and has some problems, Hanson, "War and Peace in the Hebrew Bible," contains some interesting proposals. See also C. Wright, *The God I Don't Understand*, 98–106. Ratheiser, *Mitzvoth Ethics and the Jewish Bible*, esp. §2.3, argues (in a technical way, presupposing knowledge of Hebrew) that when God's commandments are kept, God's people enjoy shalom as a society guided by holiness and justice. However, this work goes on to explore Joshua as exemplary (chap. 3).

48. This plea is made explicitly in Avalos, "The Letter Killeth." Other sources lean in this direction or at least discuss it: Collins, *Does the Bible Justify Violence?*; Cowles et al.,

the sacred status of the Bible. What Christians need instead is a model that allows them to question and perhaps even disagree with violent texts while still revering the Bible as sacred. The metaphor THE OLD TESTAMENT IS OUR FRIEND IN FAITH provides a way forward, giving Christians permission to question the Bible even as they take its words seriously, respecting it as they would a friend.

In any friendship, there will be disagreements. Some of us will disagree with Old Testament texts about violence. Yet one of the beauties of friendship is that people remain committed to one another even when there are differences. Although we may clash with parts of Scripture, we don't need to give up on it altogether. The Old Testament can remain our friend in faith, even if we don't see the usefulness of every one of its texts in our own lives. (See "Honest Doubt.")

> **Honest Doubt**
>
> "Your absolute certitude does not help the skeptic, . . . but your honest doubt might."
>
> Brian Zahnd,
> Twitter, August 23, 2012

If the truth be told, friendship with the Old Testament isn't for the faint of heart. This side of Christ's return, answers to many of the Old Testament's perplexing questions will remain elusive. But in my experience, faith is rarely found in watertight answers or absolute certitude. Real, honest faith emerges in the midst of unsettled ambiguities, unanswered questions, and unresolved problems. Amid the messiness, suffering, and tragedies of a violent world, God shows up.

For Further Study

Davies, Eryl W. *The Immoral Bible: Approaches to Biblical Ethics*. London: T&T Clark, 2010.
    This book describes the strengths and weaknesses of five ways of dealing with morally problematic texts of the Old Testament, particularly Joshua 6–11: (1) dismissing violent texts as primitive and inferior to later teachings like the Sermon on the Mount, (2) stressing that the cultural distance between biblical times and today forbids an application of violent texts in the contemporary world, (3) preferring some biblical texts over others or at least reading particular texts in light of the overall drift of the Bible, (4) seeking to apply the Bible's underlying principles rather than specific commands, and (5) entering into conversation with the biblical text and critiquing it if necessary (which the author advocates). Although this is an academic book, Davies's writing style is accessible.

Seibert, Eric A. *Disturbing Divine Behavior: Troubling Old Testament Images of God*. Minneapolis: Fortress, 2009.

Show Them No Mercy, 13–60, esp. 36, 47; Jenkins, *Laying Down the Sword*, 198–208. See also Avalos, *Fighting Words*, 371, which invites readers "to eliminate religion from human life altogether."

———. *The Violence of Scripture: Overcoming the Old Testament's Troubling Legacy*. Minneapolis: Fortress, 2012.

> These works stress the problems of violence in Scripture, advocating ways Christians can approach the Old Testament nonviolently. Written in a more academic style, these books interact with a great deal of scholarly writings. Some readers will find these books too critical of the Old Testament. Seibert's 2009 book suggests that readers evaluate Old Testament texts by how well they match with the God whom Jesus reveals.

Wright, Christopher J. H. *The God I Don't Understand: Reflections on Tough Questions of Faith*. Grand Rapids: Zondervan, 2008.

> Only one of this book's four sections focuses on "the Canaanites." However, the account there does an excellent job of dealing with the problem of violence in the Old Testament, humbly being realistic about the problems while also pointing to helpful reading strategies. This account is informed by scholarly writings but accessible to a general audience. Some readers will find that it doesn't go far enough to wrestle critically with the Bible.

The website www.MatthewSchlimm.com has additional resources, including group discussion questions.

6

Male and Female God Created Them

Gender and the Old Testament

IMMORALITY AND VIOLENCE ARE NOT THE ONLY THINGS that trouble readers of the Bible. An equally widespread problem is how the Old Testament treats women. Readers face at least three difficulties: (1) the Old Testament focuses on men more than women, (2) the Old Testament contains texts that are biased against women, and (3) the Old Testament contains texts that can be used to condone violence against women.

Men can open to almost any passage of the Old Testament and find a character with whom they can identify. On the other hand, female examples are downright scarce. Consider these numbers: Abraham's name shows up 236 times in the Old Testament, compared with 55 times for Sarah.[1] The Old Testament mentions Moses by name 766 times and his brother Aaron 347 times, but the name of Moses's sister Miriam shows up only 14 times, and his wife, Zipporah, is mentioned just three times.[2]

These numbers illustrate why women sometimes find it difficult to feel "at home" within the Bible. Texts that focus on men more than women are *androcentric*, male-centered. Women usually need to relate themselves not only

1. This number includes "Abram" and "Sarai" as well. Even if one included "Hagar" and "Keturah" in the counts, Abraham's wives are mentioned by name only 71 times, less than one-third as frequently as Abraham.

2. These numbers are the times these character's names appear, not the times they are mentioned, e.g., with pronouns.

Male-Centered Portrayals of God

Old Testament texts are male-centered not only in how they focus on men more than women, but also in how they portray God.

On some occasions, the Old Testament portrays God with female imagery. For example, in Isaiah 49:15, God says, "Can a woman forget her nursing child, fail to pity the child of her womb? Even these may forget, but I won't forget you."

While a number of examples like this one can be found, masculine imagery is far more common. God is often called a king, but never a queen. Furthermore, the pronouns used to describe God are masculine.

Although the Old Testament never envisions God below the waist, its tendency to ascribe masculine qualities to God unfortunately implies that men are somehow more like God.

---

to a different culture and time, but also to characters of a different gender. When biblical texts focus on men and sideline women, they come across as suggesting that women don't matter as much as men. (See "Male-Centered Portrayals of God.")

On top of simply focusing on men more than women, some texts are *patriarchal*: they favor men having an unequal share of power and privilege. To give a straightforward example, Leviticus says that when a woman gives birth to a daughter, she is ceremonially unclean for twice as long as when she gives birth to a son (12:1–5). Religious purity will be dealt with in chapter 7, but already we can see that there are two standards, one for males and another for females.

Another example of the Bible's problems: many prophets portray Israel as a faithless wife who deserves punishment, while God is the righteous husband. These prophets often condemn Israel for social evils, and yet it's easy to see how their images could themselves be oppressive, suggesting to self-righteous men that they can punish their wives for disagreeing with them. The Bible never tells readers to understand this metaphor as condoning spousal abuse. However, metaphors influence people's thinking in powerful ways. Why didn't the Bible use a different image?[3]

What can Christians make of these troubling features of the Old Testament? For many Christians, the question boils down to asking, Is it possible to

1. affirm gender equality,
2. regard the Bible as God's Word, and
3. still be honest about what is in the Bible?

3. Cf. Weems, *Battered Love*, passim, e.g., 72.

Can a Man Be a Feminist?

As biblical scholar Esther Fuchs explains, some feminists would answer this question negatively, claiming that "feminism is a negotiation between women." However, Fuchs disagrees, arguing that men can "take a stand against patriarchy and sexism."[a]

With this implicit invitation in mind, I write this chapter, hoping that women and men unite in opposing those who use the Bible to oppress women.

a. Fuchs, "Men in Biblical Feminist Scholarship," 113.

This chapter focuses on this question.

In many respects, I'm woefully underqualified to write this chapter. I'm a man, and I have no firsthand experience of what it's like to read the Bible as a woman. Throughout my life, I've received male privileges that I've taken for granted. I've never felt the bite of overt or covert sexism.

Yet, failing to write this chapter would be a great mistake. Gender issues are too important for anyone—males included—to remain silent. Furthermore, any book on the problems of the Old Testament would be incomplete without a treatment of gender. I also refuse to remain silent about this topic because my silence only helps those who use the Bible to oppress women. While I naturally open myself to critique by adding my male voice to this discussion of how the Bible regards women, there's a moral responsibility to resist those who use the Bible for oppressive ends.[4] (See "Can a Man Be a Feminist?")

Approaches to Gender in the Old Testament

People have approached gender in the Old Testament in many ways. For the sake of convenience, here are three of the most basic approaches to this topic:[5]

1. Some people say that the Bible exalts men over women. Because they see the Bible as God's Word, they therefore reject gender equality, claiming that it's God's will that women serve in positions subservient to men.

4. As the sidebar "Can a Man Be a Feminist" suggests, Esther Fuchs is in favor of men taking feminist stances. I should note, however, that Fuchs would be critical of the approach I advocate here, characterizing it as insufficiently radical and complex, too "reformist and gradualist," too "informed by neoliberal idealizations of 'strong' and 'assertive' women" (Fuchs, "Reclaiming the Hebrew Bible for Women," esp. 48, 54). I certainly am guilty of criticizing some strands of feminist thought (e.g., those rejecting the Bible as God's Word), which has certain problems, given that feminism "was created specifically so as to evade male judgment, authority, and hegemony" (Fuchs, "Men in Biblical Feminist Scholarship," 110). However, feminism is so diverse and filled with so many competing approaches that it's impossible for anyone (males included) to make any contribution to this field without aligning more with some feminists than with others. In my case, I try to follow respected female interpreters like Jacqueline Lapsley and Ellen Davis.

5. For similar categories, see Lapsley, *Whispering the Word*, 3; Rodd, *Glimpses of a Strange Land*, 250–51.

2. Others agree that the Bible exalts men over women, but they go in the opposite direction, deciding to *reject the Bible as God's Word* because of its gender bias.

3. Alternatively, some people look for middle ground, insisting that *both women and the Bible are sacred*. They admit that there are problems when it comes to gender and the Bible. Yet they are unwilling to follow the first group and reject gender inequality, or the second group and reject the Bible. This mediating approach claims that the Bible contains many voices. Some biblical voices reflect a male-dominated society. However, such voices aren't so pervasive that the Bible should be rejected. Other voices in the Bible are sympathetic to the plight of women. Thus, those taking this approach often (a) *reject biased interpretations* that favor men over women, (b) *imaginatively counteract male-centeredness* in texts, (c) *question troublesome texts*, and (d) *recover neglected texts that work against male domination.*[6]

As we will see, I favor the last approach. I am unwilling to give up on either the sacred status of women or the Bible. Moreover, the Bible contains too many voices to adopt one hard-line approach.

In the Beginning

Let's begin by examining the Bible's first statement about gender. In Genesis 1:27, we read:

> God created humanity in God's own image,
>   in the divine image God created them,
>   male and female God created them.

This text describes both genders as made in the image of God.

As mentioned in chapter 3 of this book, the phrase "image of God" was used by Israel's neighbors. However, when people around Israel used it, they described kings and rulers with this term: a group of men with power. (See "The Image of God for Genesis 1 and Israel's Neighbors.") In a truly remarkable move, Israel's Scriptures apply this designation to everyone, women and men alike.[7]

So, in the Bible's first and foremost statement about men and women, the text affirms the sacred value of both genders, making a countercultural statement that blatantly opposes those who think only men with authority reflect God's image.

6. Cf. Scholz, *Women's Hebrew Bible*, 25.
7. Middleton, *Liberating Image*, 204–7.

The Image of God for Genesis 1 and Israel's Neighbors

"But whereas power in the Babylonian and Assyrian Empires was concentrated in the hands of a few, power in Genesis 1 is diffused or shared. No longer is the image of God or its associated royal language ('rule' or 'subdue') applied to only some privileged elite. Rather, all human beings, male and female, are created as royal stewards in the world, entrusted with the privileged task of ruling on God's behalf."

J. Richard Middleton, *Liberating Image*, 206

In the Bible "it is not a prince who is the image, representative, deputy and reflection of God; it is the human being—men and women in like degree, all human beings and every human being."

Jürgen Moltmann, *God in Creation*, 219

Rejecting Equality

Already we can begin to see the problems with *rejecting gender equality*. People who use the Bible to demean women apparently don't know the first thing the Bible says about gender. They certainly don't take the Bible's first statement on gender seriously enough. (See "Equal Worth but Different Roles?")

Men who favor men having more power than women also seem to ignore the fact that the God of the Bible consistently opposes people who lord authority and power over others.[8] Both Testaments repeat that God humbles people who exalt themselves and exalts people who humble themselves.[9] When men use the Bible to give themselves power over women, therefore, they risk divine judgment.

Unfortunately, one doesn't need to look very far to find those who reject gender equality on biblical grounds. Russell D. Moore, a prominent figure in the Southern Baptist Convention, declares, "Patriarchy is good for women, good for children, and good for families."[10] He tries to defend such claims on biblical grounds:

Patriarchy . . . is essential—from the begetting of Seth in the image and likeness of Adam to the deliverance of [God's] son Israel from the clutches of Pharaoh to the promise of a Davidic son to whom God would be a Father (2 Sam. 7:14; Ps. 89:26) to the "Abba" cry of the new covenant assembly (Rom. 8:15).[11]

8. See, e.g., Ps. 94:2; Prov. 3:34; Isa. 2:10–12; Mark 10:42–45; James 4:6.
9. As in 1 Sam. 2:3, 7–8; Matt. 23:12; 1 Pet. 5:5.
10. Moore, "After Patriarchy, What?," 576.
11. Ibid., 575. Moore is undoubtedly aware of Gen. 1:27. My point is that this article functions rhetorically to sideline texts such as Gen. 1:27.

Equal Worth but Different Roles?

Some Christians claim that men and women have equal worth—but then they say that men and women should have different roles in the home and society. For example, an official document from the Southern Baptist Convention declares:

> The husband and wife are of equal worth before God, since both are created in God's image.

Yet it goes on to say:

> [The husband] has the God-given responsibility to provide for, to protect, and to lead his family. A wife is to submit herself graciously to the servant leadership of her husband.[a]

The idea that men and women have separate social roles but equal worth sounds doomed to failure, much like the "separate but equal" plan of segregated schools. It's morally reprehensible to affirm equality in principle while denying it in practice.[b]

a. Southern Baptist Convention, *Baptist Faith and Message*, §18, "The Family."
b. On the complexities of gender in conservative Christian circles, see Frykholm, *Rapture Culture*, 100.

Such arguments should make us suspicious. They are advanced by a man, value patriarchy, and ignore texts such as Genesis 1:27.

There are three rules of interpretation that expose the problem with rejecting gender equality. First, Christians need to *avoid selfish readings of biblical texts* when there are more viable readings that advance the good of all members of the community. Chapter 2 talked about the *rule of faith*, the idea that we should favor interpretations more consistent with the rest of the Bible and our faith. The Old and New Testaments speak repeatedly about the importance of sacrifice, of giving to others, and of avoiding selfishness. We should therefore be suspicious of men saying the Bible gives them power over women. Such claims go against the generous tenor of Scripture.[12] (See "Reading for Good.")

Second, Christians need to *give special weight to foundational texts*. Most pieces of literature say something very important at the outset. The Bible's first statement on a topic like gender should not be overlooked. It takes a term used to describe kings in the ancient world and applies it to women and men alike. So much for the idea that women must be subservient to men!

12. Perhaps Moore would claim that his reading isn't selfish; he does write, "Male headship is not about male privilege" (ibid., 576). However, power of any type brings with it certain privileges.

> ### Reading for Good
>
> "There *are* many legitimate readings of a single text, but for Christians I suggest the use of Jesus' measuring stick: 'by their fruits you shall know them.' Does a way of reading produce shame, terror, helplessness and self-hatred? or does it empower survivors to action, peace, love and self-acceptance?"
>
> Carole Fontaine, "Abusive Bible," 110–11

Rather than sidelining Genesis 1:27, Christians should amplify it. For much of its history, the church has ignored this Genesis text and denied women the equality they deserve. The church today needs to repent of its sin of sexism and let life-giving verses speak loud and clear. Genesis 1:27 should now take center stage.

Third, Christians shouldn't *take the most problematic cultural dynamics of biblical times and transfer them uncritically to the twenty-first century.* The Bible was written in a patriarchal culture, and it often reflects the norms of its time.[13] This isn't surprising. What *is* surprising is how the Bible also makes daring, countercultural statements like Genesis 1:27 that affirm the worth of both genders. Such a text is well suited for application today.[14] (See "Should Christians Own Donkeys?")

> ### Should Christians Own Donkeys?
>
> Genesis 22:3 says that Abraham used a donkey to transport supplies. Legal codes assume that people will own donkeys (e.g., Exod. 23:12). Yet I don't know any Christians today who feel obliged to use donkeys rather than their cars to move things and themselves. If Christians have the freedom to move beyond primitive modes of transportation, then we certainly have the freedom to move beyond ancient conceptions of gender—especially when the Bible itself has texts that break free of old, constricting ideas.

Rejecting the Bible

The Bible's first statement about gender shows not only the problems with *rejecting gender equality*, but also the follies of *rejecting the Bible altogether.* Biblical scholar Esther Fuchs says that the Bible "not only presents women as marginal, it also advocates their marginality. It is not merely a text authored by men—it also fosters a politics of male domination." She adds that the Old Testament "promotes a male supremacist social and cognitive system."[15]

13. Meyers, *Discovering Eve*, argues that while women may have enjoyed more equality before the institution of the monarchy, the kingship structured society in patriarchal ways.

14. On according greater weight to countercultural witnesses within the Bible, see Cosgrove, *Appealing to Scripture*, 90–115.

15. Fuchs, *Sexual Politics in the Biblical Narrative*, 11–12. Milne, "Patriarchal Stamp of Scripture," makes similar arguments.

These sorts of blanket statements fail to do justice to the complexities of the Old Testament. Genesis 1:27 alone gives people reason to see that the Bible, for all its difficulties, nevertheless can be a positive force in our lives today, even on gender issues.[16]

It's easy to fault the Bible—and all other literature written before the 1960s—for failing to measure up to current standards of gender equality.[17] What's more challenging is to admit how difficult it is to get gender equality right, even in our own society.[18] For Christians committed to the Bible as God's Word, it won't work to reject the Bible, throwing out the champagne with the cork, so to speak.[19] We need a multipronged approach to the Bible that allows us to use it in ways that counteract inequalities in our day. (See "What about Rejecting Parts of the Bible?")

Rejecting Biased Interpretations

The church has a long and sad history of using the Bible for wrong, especially when it comes to gender. Here are some of the disturbing things that church leaders have said over the centuries:

You [women] are the devil's gateway.[20]

I cannot work out what help a wife could have been made to provide the man with, if you take away the purpose of childbearing.[21]

The domination of men and the subjection of women continue. You must endure them.[22]

16. For additional reasons to refuse jettisoning the Bible simply "because we see it with all its pits and valleys," see Fontaine, "Abusive Bible," 112.

17. While I agree with contemporary standards of gender equality, I do recognize that my culture occupies a relatively small place in comparison with all the cultures that have been and will be. I am sure that generations from now, when people look back at my culture, they will find many shortcomings and failings that seem almost unbelievable by their standards.

18. Even though, e.g., the US has laws in place to prevent employers from discriminating on the basis of gender, women still earn about 80 percent of what men make (see "Equal Pay").

19. The suggestion that some parts of the Bible should be rejected can be made in various ways. Fontaine ("Abusive Bible," 112–13) refuses to give up on the Bible (since it contains liberating texts), but then also says that the "content, form and function" of biblical texts "must be either *resisted* or *reaffirmed*."

20. Tertullian, *Apparel of Women* 1.1 (*ANF* 4:14).

21. Augustine, *Gen. litt.* 9.5.9 (Augustine, *On Genesis* [trans. E. Hill], 380).

22. Luther, *Luther's Works*, 28:279.

What about Rejecting Parts of the Bible?

Some people see certain parts of the Bible as truly inspired, but outright reject other parts.

Obviously, this idea won't work with those who affirm that the entire Bible is God's Word. Most Christians don't feel they have the authority to decide what should and shouldn't be included in the Bible.

Furthermore, there are texts that may strike us as very problematic in the present moment. Yet when we return to these texts at different times, we may see things differently. Chapter 4 discussed the rape of Dinah (Gen. 34), and chapter 5 dealt with the psalm that prays for the death of infants (Ps. 137). Many people may want, on first reading, to exclude these passages from the Bible. Yet, as I have discussed, both can function positively among Christians in particular situations.

As we will see, there are ways of dealing with troublesome texts besides rejecting them outright.

Christians today need to repent of the church's grave sins.[23] One way to do that is by counteracting biased interpretations.

Consider Eve in Genesis 2–3. Earlier, I suggested that previous translations and interpretations could have done more to recognize that her name literally means *Life*. It turns out that interpreters have gotten many other things about her wrong as well.

First, some interpreters have claimed that women are inferior to men because Eve was made after Adam (2:22). However, Genesis consistently values what comes later, rather than what comes first. It expresses a preference for Abel over Cain, Isaac over Ishmael, Jacob over Esau, Rachel over Leah, and Joseph over his older siblings. Eve isn't an afterthought. She's the crown of creation.[24] Notably, the first time the Bible records human speech, readers find a poem praising how wonderful Eve is (2:23).[25]

Second, it's asserted that women are inferior to men because Eve was created to be a "helper" for Adam (2:18). The assumption is that a "helper" is

---

23. While the church today needs to repent of the sins of previous generations, Thompson (*Writing the Wrongs*) shows that precritical commentators were often more sympathetic to female characters in Scripture than one might expect. On the complexities of Augustine's thought, see Harmless, *Augustine in His Own Words*, 302–5, 366–67.

24. Here and elsewhere, the pioneering work of Phyllis Trible has influenced my thinking. In this case, her "Depatriarchalizing in Biblical Interpretation" (esp. 36) makes the same argument with similar language. Admittedly, this interpretation stands at odds with 1 Tim. 2:11–14. On tensions between biblical texts, see chap. 9 below.

25. Binz, *Women of the Torah*, 18.

like an "assistant" or even a "servant" today: a subservient and second-class person who obeys superiors.[26] However, the Hebrew word for "helper" (*ezer*) generally isn't used to describe slaves, assistants, or even humans in the Old Testament. Typically, it describes God. So much for it being a sign of inferiority! Eve's being a helper means she's more like God, not less.[27]

Third, it's assumed that because Eve ate the forbidden fruit first, she's the most evil. For example, Debi Pearl, in a popular book that urges women to be submissive to their husbands, writes, "Satan was able to deceive [Eve] when she left Adam's side and confronted the Devil's logic alone."[28] However, the Bible itself never says that Eve left Adam to eat the forbidden fruit. Instead, we read that Eve "took some of its fruit and ate it, and also gave some to her husband, *who was with her*, and he ate it" (Gen. 3:6, italics added).[29] The point of the story has more to do with the communal nature of sin than blaming one gender. Given that *Adam* means *Humanity* and *Eve* means *Life*, readers should see themselves in both characters, regardless of their genders. Eve certainly didn't cram the fruit down Adam's throat or secretly sneak some into his favorite fruit salad.

Finally, it's claimed that women are always supposed to serve men because God tells Eve in Genesis 3:16:

> You will desire your husband,
>   but he will rule over you.

However, as with violent texts, it's important to ask whether the Bible is being more *descriptive*—talking about negative features of our fallen world—or *prescriptive*—telling people how things are supposed to be.[30]

The surrounding verses describe pain in childbirth, the difficulties of physical labor, and the certainty of death (Gen. 3:15–19). None of these things are

---

26. Spong, *Sins of Scripture*, 78.

27. Trible, *Rhetoric of Sexuality*, 90. See, e.g., Pss. 54:4; 70:5; 115:9–11.

28. Pearl, *Created to Be His Help Meet*, 108.

29. In addition to verses like Gen. 3:6, readers should pay close attention to texts like Gen. 31:35. There Laban enters his daughter Rachel's tent, looking for household idols that she secretly stole. She has hidden them beneath where she sits. She tells her father, "Let not my lord be angry that I cannot rise before you, for I have the way of women" (31:35, trans. by Lapsley, *Whispering the Word*, 22). At first glance, it appears that Rachel is keeping herself from getting into trouble, suggesting that she can't stand because she's menstruating. However, biblical scholar Jacqueline Lapsley shows that Rachel's words function on a deeper level to protest how she has been oppressed and is unable to rise up before her father, who has severely mistreated her. As Lapsley puts it, Rachel's words "constitute a discourse of resistance, a subtle protest against the patriarchal discourse and social structures that attempt to silence her" (ibid., 34).

30. Trible, *Rhetoric of Sexuality*, 128; Trible, *Texts of Terror*, passim; Olson, "Untying the Knot?," 76; cf. M. Jacobs, *Gender, Power, and Persuasion*, 241.

Symmetry in Song of Songs

"There is one place in the Song that makes it unmistakably clear that the long sad history of asymmetry between man and woman is a thing of the past, and a new paradigm is being established. In Eden, it seemed that the woman's own sexual desire condemned her to subordination: 'toward your husband will be your desire [*t'shuqah*], but it is he who will rule over you!' (Gen. 3:16). But here, after a lengthy exchange of poetic compliments (5:10–7:10), the woman exults: 'I am for my lover, and toward me is *his* desire [*t'shuqah*]!' (7:11). Because that word *t'shuqah* is a rare one, occurring only here in the Song and in Genesis (3:16 and 4:7), the line the poet is drawing stands out clearly. This is an intentional echo and a reversal of the sad ending of the idyll in Eden. No longer, the poem declares, are desire and power unequally distributed between woman and man. The woman proclaims a true partnership of unrestrained self-giving and mutual advocacy: 'I am for my darling and he is for me' (6:3, compare 2:16)."

Ellen F. Davis, *Getting Involved with God*, 71–72

---

good. Not surprisingly, Christians and non-Christians alike try to counteract all of them. Mothers lessen the pains of childbirth through things like Lamaze and medicine. Laborers use tools to make physical labor easier, such as farm implements. Most people see doctors to prevent premature death. In a similar way, Christians can work to counteract ways that men rule over women.[31] In fact, there are places elsewhere in the Bible that do just that, envisioning greater gender equality.[32] (See "Symmetry in Song of Songs.")

John Shelby Spong writes, "Women were indeed evil to their core. That was the message of the Christian church and it was built quite specifically on the story of Eve."[33] As it turns out, the story of Eve is a poor foundation for such a message. When people use Eve to demean women, it says more about them as interpreters than about the Bible itself.

Genesis 2–3 is hardly the only text that interpreters have misused to exert male superiority.[34] Christians have a moral responsibility to study the Bible carefully and work against interpretations used to exert power over others.

---

31. Lamb, *God Behaving Badly*, 59–60.
32. Cf. Trible, *Rhetoric of Sexuality*, 161.
33. Spong, *Sins of Scripture*, 91.
34. To name one of many possible examples, Debi Pearl blames Bathsheba, not David, for what happens in 2 Sam. 11: "Her lack of discretion cost her husband his life, his comrades-in-arms their lives, her baby son his life, and the integrity of one whom God upheld as a man after his own heart." This interpretation, remarkably far from the biblical narrative (see 2 Sam. 12),

---

A Spur to Imagination

"The women who appear in biblical stories are often striking characters, distinct personalities who have gone beyond the confines of the tales in which they appear to become important figures in our cultural memory. At the same time, these women are not fleshed-out individuals. Many of them appear in only one story, and that story tells us only those facts that serve the writer's agenda. The Bible tells us nothing of their backgrounds, nothing of their future, nothing of their thoughts; solely their actions in a particular context. The striking incompleteness of these portraits has sometimes proved frustrating and infuriating. Many contemporary women feel that this fragmentary presentation exploits and abuses the characters; they want the narrators to care about the lives and thoughts of the women about whom they write. But these partial images have also been a spur to literary and poetic imagination. Readers of the Bible, millennia past and present, have brought these characters out of the confines of the narrative, adding personality traits and personal history in an ongoing process of midrash and story."

Tikva Frymer-Kensky, *Women of the Bible*, 333

Imaginatively Counteracting Male-Centeredness

Sometimes, however, the problem has less to do with faulty interpretation and more to do with the text giving women little attention. What can we do when stories don't tell us women's names, perspectives, thoughts, or feelings?

One approach is to interact imaginatively with the biblical texts. Every story has gaps: things it doesn't tell readers. When we envision stories of the Bible, we use our imaginations to fill in these gaps. Preachers, for example, typically retell biblical stories in ways that add colorful details to what happened. Christians aren't alone in this sort of practice. The Jewish tradition contains the *midrashim*: a collection of musings by rabbis and other writers who added vivid details to things only hinted at in Scripture.[35] Or consider art depicting biblical scenes. The artist imagines what things looked like, even though the text doesn't spell out every detail.

As we interpret the Bible and add imaginative details, we should do so in ways that respect and honor female characters of the Bible. By doing so, we recognize the full humanity of women, as Genesis 1:27 teaches. An excellent example of this activity is provided by literary scholar Mieke Bal. In Judges 19, readers never learn the name of the Levite's concubine. Yet Mieke Bal has

---

appears in a book currently in its eleventh printing (*Created to Be His Help Meet*, 207). For a much better interpretation, see J. Barton, *Ethics and the Old Testament*, 19–36.

35. There are many other types of midrashim, as usefully explained in Porton, "Midrash."

suggested that we imaginatively supply a name for her as a way of recognizing her humanity. Bal suggests that we find a name matching features of the
text itself. She proposes that we call this woman "Beth," which is the Hebrew
word for "house," a key word that appears seventeen times in this chapter. This
sort of imaginative approach adds details to female characters in scripture,
working against the text's androcentrism, while still respecting the text itself.[36]
(See "A Spur to Imagination.")

Another example is in the book of Esther, as Queen Vashti is deposed for
failing to come when summoned by the king. Esther takes Vashti's place. Carol
Lakey Hess imagines what it would have been like if, at a later time, Esther
came to Vashti for advice. Her point isn't "to recover past meaning but to
imagine and to celebrate present relevance."[37] To that end, Hess's imaginary
account invites readers deeper into the biblical text, causing them to appreciate Vashti and Esther as real characters and wonder about them as people.
Like any interpretation, these imaginative renderings do not have the same
authority as the biblical text itself. Yet they can help the text come to life in
ways that recognize the full personhood of female characters.[38]

Questioning Biased Texts

Sometimes the problem isn't that women receive less attention than men. It's
that the text appears intrinsically biased against women. The more we study
such texts, the more they trouble us. Neither rejecting problematic interpretations nor adding imaginative details lessens the problems.

However, many of the same options used to deal with violent texts are
helpful with gender-biased texts. As mentioned above, we can ask if a text is
describing its patriarchal world or *prescribing* patriarchy for all time. We can
bring biased texts into conversation with more liberating texts, resisting the
urge to apply each individual text to each circumstance of our lives. We can
also humbly and honestly admit in prayer that we don't know what to make
of such texts.

Consider Leviticus 27:1–8. It deals with making vows to God. In the ancient
world, people sometimes wanted to make promises to God like this: "God,
if you do such-and-such for me, then I'll sacrifice such-and-such to you." At

36. Bal, "Dealing/With/Women," 319–20.

37. Hess, *Caretakers of Our Common House*, 26–29, esp. 26.

38. Note also chap. 9 below, which poses a conversation between Ruth and Ezra. I could have
posed a similar conversation between Boaz and Ezra, but it's important to give voice to female
characters in Scripture.

times, people even promised human beings to God. Leviticus 27 addresses these promises. It says that people can substitute money in the place of sacrificing an actual human.

Leviticus 27 explains what to pay instead of people. To modern eyes, it's a tragically sexist and ageist text. Here's what it says people are worth:

Age	Male	Female
1 month–5 years old	5 shekels	3 shekels
5–20 years old	20 shekels	10 shekels
20–60 years old	50 shekels	30 shekels
Over 60 years old	15 shekels	10 shekels

In every case, females are worth less than males.

Why is this passage in the Bible?!

I have no simple solutions. Obviously, it's good to have an alternative to human sacrifice, but do we have to assign humans monetary value? Do we have to assign men and women different amounts? Do we have to assign people different worth depending on their age? What do we do with this text?

As I mentioned earlier, it's often helpful to ask whether texts of the Bible apply to someone other than ourselves. It's also helpful to remember that we shouldn't expect ancient texts to match modern standards. At the same time, I shudder at the thought that any group of people would agree that women are worth less than men. What else can help?

The metaphor THE OLD TESTAMENT IS OUR FRIEND IN FAITH points to some answers. In the closest of friendships, there are moments of difference and disagreement, times when one person can say to the other, "I don't understand what you're saying. Can you explain?" Sometimes close friends even dare to tell each other, "What you're saying sounds wrong to me."[39]

> **Loving the Bible**
>
> "To love [the Bible] is not to claim that it is without faults, imperfections, violence, and evil. To the contrary, to love this book is to understand that a single text may yield life in one setting and death in another. And to love this book is to understand that it places upon us, readers and listeners alike, the responsibility to choose rightly."
>
> Phyllis Trible, "Take Back the Bible," 431
>
> "It is precisely because we affirm scripture's authority that we sometimes must struggle with it, rather than ignore or dismiss texts that trouble us."
>
> Joel B. Green, "Authority of Scripture," 528

39. Cf. Lancaster, *Women and the Authority of Scripture*, 174.

I know there have been times in my life when my friends told me that, and it was exactly what I needed to hear. It wasn't an easy thing for them to say, and they certainly wouldn't say such words to a stranger—someone they couldn't care less about. However, my friends said it to me because they loved me and respected me.

What if, as a sign of our love and respect for the Bible, we honestly voiced our reaction to verses like Leviticus 27:1–8? What if we said to the Old Testament, "When you spoke about men and women both being created in the image of God—I was with you. I clung to every word you said. But now, you seem like a different person."

What if, like the psalmists, we asked God piercing questions: "Lord, what are these verses doing in the Bible? They sound so opposed to the wonderful things you say elsewhere."[40]

Some people might dismiss this sort of reaction as failing to revere the Bible. For me, however, it's an honest cry of the heart—a sign of taking the Bible honestly and seriously. (See "Loving the Bible.") Piercing questions require trust; they are more common among close friends than total strangers. It's easy to ignore problematic texts. However, my commitments not only to gender equality but also to the Bible require an honest response.

To make the same point in a different way: I don't see the need to respond to every idiotic thing that people say on television or the internet. But I do see the need to respond to the words of people I love. Replying to troubling texts with honest questions reflects a far deeper commitment to the entirety of Scripture than the cold response of ignoring whatever we don't like. (See "Take Back the Text.")

> ### Take Back the Text
>
> "Do not abandon the Bible to the bashers and thumpers. Take back the text. Do not let go until it blesses you. Indeed, make it work for blessing, not for curse, so that you and your descendants, indeed so that all the families of the earth, may live."
>
> Phyllis Trible, "Take Back the Bible," 431

Recovering Neglected Texts

As mentioned above, the Old Testament comes out of a male-dominated society. Not surprisingly, it typically reflects that society. Yet interspersed among

---

40. Such a response seems especially appropriate when reflecting on the implications of metaphors that portray God as the righteous husband who will punish the disobedient spouse. On this topic, see Weems, *Battered Love*.

patriarchal voices are daring statements that affirm the great dignity and worth of women. Many people have overlooked, neglected, or minimized these daring statements. As a way of working against these errors, Christians have a responsibility to recover these texts and bring them back to the center of people's attention. We furthermore can work against interpretations of these texts that minimize their helpfulness on gender issues.[41]

The book of Genesis, for example, gives access to women's points of view, causing many to wonder if women played a role in the creation of its stories.[42] Readers not only learn about characters like Hagar, Sarah, Rebekah, Rachel, and Leah; they even see God siding with Sarah over Abraham (21:10–12).[43] On another occasion, Hagar (a woman) names God—and she's the only person in Scripture to do so (16:13). In a different story, Tamar (also a woman) faces capital punishment, but then, because of a series of events, the man leading the charges against her ends up declaring, "She's more righteous than I am" (Gen. 38:26).

In its opening chapter, the book of Exodus slows down to tell readers about two Hebrew midwives who, to save the Israelite people, boldly defied the orders of Pharaoh (1:15–21). The text praises them for their actions. It tells readers their names (Shiphrah and Puah)—but then refuses to let readers know the name of Pharaoh. It's a subtle way the text suggests that these two Hebrew women are more important and more worthy of memory than the king of all of Egypt, with all his might.[44]

In the book of Judges, we learn of Deborah, a woman who ruled Israel early in its history (chaps. 4–5). For all of the United States' commitments to equality, it hasn't had a female president at the time I write this book, even after more than two centuries of leaders. Yet an ancient group of tribes on the other side of the world was ruled by a woman: "Now Deborah, a prophet, the wife of Lappidoth, was a leader of Israel at that time" (Judg. 4:4).

41. As Darr notes throughout her book (*Far More Precious Than Jewels*), many interpretations are possible of women in the Bible like Ruth, Esther, Sarah, and Hagar. Given the authority these texts have in communities of faith, it's important to read the Bible in life-giving ways that reflect the Bible's foundational statement on gender, Gen. 1:27.

42. See the useful overview in Meyers, "Hebrew Bible," esp. 9–10; cf. Goitein, "Women as Creators of Biblical Genres"; Bloom, *The Book of J*. In addition to texts in Genesis, it's also quite likely that a woman wrote Ps. 131, as is helpfully explored by Miller, *They Cried to the Lord*, 239–43. Also, Prov. 31:1–9 recounts the teaching of King Lemuel's mother.

43. Gen. 21:10–12 is a complicated text. While God sides with Sarah over Abraham, God also seems to be siding against Hagar. Yet God does not abandon Hagar, but rather intervenes miraculously. On the complexities of this story, see Schlimm, *From Fratricide to Forgiveness*, 154–58.

44. Cf. Exum, "'Let Every Daughter Live,'" 46.

The book of Esther also displays great concern for gender issues. As mentioned earlier, the Persian king Ahasuerus becomes enraged because his wife, Vashti, refuses to come when he calls for her. The king and his officials become fearful that news of Vashti's refusal will spread, and soon women everywhere will disregard what their husbands say. So Vashti is essentially fired from her role as queen.

> **Irony in the Bible**
>
> *Irony* describes reversals. When we expect something to mean one thing and then it means something completely different, we have irony.
>
> The book of Esther revels in irony. The chauvinistic king Ahasuerus ends up doing Esther's bidding. The evil Haman is hung on the very gallows he intended to use to kill his enemies, the Jews.
>
> Irony is seen elsewhere in the Bible. The opening of the book of Ruth describes a famine in Bethlehem. The name Bethlehem literally means "House of Bread." So it's ironic that a famine there forces Naomi and her family to leave.

Esther takes over in Vashti's place. Meanwhile the evil official Haman hatches a plan to commit genocide against the Jewish people. In an act of supreme courage, Esther goes and appears before the king, defying royal decrees that said she could die for doing so.

Yet in a reversal of what happened with Vashti, the king not only lets Esther remain as queen (and live) but also agrees to whatever she says. In a wonderful dramatic twist, it's almost as though Esther is ruling over the king, who simply carries out her orders. (See "Irony in the Bible.") The Jews are spared extermination, and their savior—who risked death—is a woman.[45]

Meanwhile the book of Ruth sympathetically portrays two women, Naomi and Ruth, who face hunger and poverty. It shows these women working cooperatively to overcome the harshest of conditions with bravery and shrewdness. In the end, Ruth is praised as being more valuable than seven sons (4:15)—not exactly what one would expect from a patriarchal text!

As mentioned above, the Bible even dares to use female images to describe who God is. In Hosea 11, God is portrayed as a mother who lovingly feeds

45. Grossman, *Esther*, 240–41. According to Sharp (*Irony and Meaning*, 65–83, esp. 72–73, 80), it is Vashti, more than Esther, who is the model of resistance in the story: "Vashti's example makes clear at the beginning of . . . the Book of Esther one crucial point: it is possible to maintain one's integrity, defy the king openly, and avoid execution while not taking part in the florid overreacting that surges all about one. It is possible to resist royal coercion without engaging in hyperbolic countermeasures" (72–73). For Sakenfeld (*Just Wives?*, 64–66), Esther and Vashti share common goals even if they take different approaches to achieving them. For McBride ("Esther Passes," esp. 213), "Esther does not merely [sit upon] Vashti's throne; she transforms that previously passive office into a vehicle for legislative action by issuing edicts."

and cares for her toddler Israel.[46] Jeremiah 31:20 describes how God, like Rachel, has "motherly-compassion" for her "darling child" (to use Phyllis Trible's language)[47] Isaiah 42:14 goes so far as to describe God as a mother painfully giving birth:

> Like a woman in labor I will moan;
>   I will pant, I will gasp.[48]

At the end of the book of Isaiah, the text again describes God in maternal terms:

> As a mother comforts her child,
>   so I will comfort you. (66:13)[49]

Countering male domination, the Bible uses female images to describe the very nature of God.

Christians today face a moral choice: will we draw attention to texts that point to the worth of women? Or will we remain silent while people use the Bible to oppress women?[50] (See "Moral Choices.")

Conclusion

In every friendship, we sooner or later realize that the other person has limitations. They do things that make no sense to us. They let us down.

In response, we can choose to stop being friends. Or we can go to the other extreme, naively denying that our friends ever do things differently than we would. There's also a third option: we can remain committed to our friends, being honest about their limitations while also remembering their best characteristics.

46. This mother image is more implicit than explicit. However, breast-feeding typically continued through the toddler years in biblical Israel (Westermann, *Genesis 12–36*, 338), meaning that Hosea's image of a parent who feeds the child is that of a mother (so Fretheim, *Suffering of God*, 120).

47. Trible, *Rhetoric of Sexuality*, 45. Although Trible's treatment of the Hebrew word *rehem* ("womb") may fall prey to some of the criticisms made by Barr, *Semantics of Biblical Language*, 100–160, her work on the whole brings to light many overlooked female images for God in the Bible. For a more theological discussion of God as mother, see McFague, *Models of God*, chap. 4.

48. Cf. Job 38:29.

49. See Trible, *Rhetoric of Sexuality*, chaps. 2–3.

50. West, review of R. S. Sugirtharajah, ed., *Voices from the Margin*; Lapsley, *Whispering the Word*, 10.

Moral Choices

The God of the Bible loves putting moral choices before humans. God puts *Humanity* and *Life* (Adam and Eve) in a garden where they must struggle with whether to eat the forbidden fruit (Gen. 2–3). God tests Abraham and Job to see how they will respond (Gen. 22; Job 1). In Moses's final sermon, he tells the people that they have the choice of life or death, prosperity or adversity, blessings or curses (Deut. 30:15–20). The book of Proverbs describes God as setting two paths before humanity: the wise way of righteousness and the foolish way of wickedness (e.g., 15:9).

The Bible itself presents another moral choice. Will we use it for life, love, and all that is good? Or will we use it for patriarchy, inequality, and evil?

For people today, the Old Testament has limitations in the sense that it originally addressed people in ancient times. It makes many Christians uncomfortable to talk about the Bible having any limitations, but think about it: the Old Testament doesn't tell us the best recipe for making apple pie or what type of motor oil to put in our cars. There are limits to what it can tell us. It originally addressed people who had never heard of automobiles, the internet, nuclear power, space flight, or phones. The Bible uses ancient languages, and its people use primitive technologies. Many of its texts also reflect ancient ideas of gender.

When we encounter these texts, we can ignore them, reject them, or try somehow to hold on to Iron-Age conceptions of gender. A much better choice is to be honest about scars that patriarchy has left on the text, even as we remain open to how God can use the Old Testament as a whole to bring about goodness on matters of gender today. We do so by counteracting biased interpretations, by searching for life-giving ways to read the Bible, by questioning troublesome texts, and by recovering neglected texts that work against male domination.

If we are patient, we'll often be rewarded for our efforts. For although the Old Testament comes from a male-dominated society, it has moments when it breaks free of the prejudices of its time to envision a better world. It begins by saying that women are made in God's image. Along the way, it ventures to say that Tamar is more righteous than Judah, that Deborah ruled over Israel, that Ruth is more valuable than seven sons, and that Esther gave commands to a king who tried to make women more submissive to their husbands.

I rejoice in these texts, even as I'm unsure of what to make of other texts. I don't have all the answers. But maybe that's okay. God created us for love and holiness, not for solving every problem.

For Further Study

Lapsley, Jacqueline. *Whispering the Word: Hearing Women's Stories in the Old Testament*. Louisville: Westminster John Knox, 2005.

> Exploring Genesis 31; Judges 19–21; Exodus 1–4; and Ruth, this book provides an excellent and nuanced account of how biblical texts function. It approaches the Bible as God's Word while also embracing a critical feminist perspective.

Meyers, Carol, ed. *Women in Scripture*. Grand Rapids: Eerdmans, 2000.

> This resource provides a brief scholarly introduction to every named and unnamed woman in the Bible. It's an excellent starting place for further research.

Newsom, Carol A., Sharon H. Ringe, and Jacqueline E. Lapsley, eds. *Women's Bible Commentary: Twentieth-Anniversary Edition*. Rev. and updated ed. Louisville: Westminster John Knox, 2012.

> Another excellent starting place for research, this commentary is written by many of the leading feminist biblical scholars of the last generation. It discusses each book of the Bible, focusing on texts of particular significance to women.

Scholz, Susanne. *Introducing the Women's Hebrew Bible*. New York: T&T Clark, 2007.

> This work provides a solid introduction to the paths that feminist biblical scholarship has taken. It's useful for students new to the topic.

Trible, Phyllis. *God and the Rhetoric of Sexuality*. Overtures to Biblical Theology. Philadelphia: Fortress, 1978.

> This book is a classic when it comes to gender in the Old Testament. Trible works against biased interpretations and recovers neglected texts that portray women sympathetically.

The website www.MatthewSchlimm.com has additional resources, including group discussion questions.

7

God Commands Us to Do *What*?!

The Strange Laws of the Bible

For a number of reasons, Christians have a hard time with Old Testament law. First, there are *many* rules, regulations, commandments, and laws in the first five books of the Bible, often called the *Torah* (meaning "teaching"). By some counts, there are 613 commandments.[1] People often have trouble remembering the Ten Commandments, so keeping all 613 straight seems overwhelming. Second, the New Testament isn't always positive about Old Testament law. The apostle Paul, for example, associates it with death and sin (1 Cor. 15:56). Third, the church has sometimes set the law in opposition to grace. Who would want to engage with legal teachings when we have good news to think about? Finally, many laws are very strange, as we'll see in a moment.

What can Christians make of this portion of Scripture? Why has the church dared to claim that such writings are God's authoritative word? How could they possibly guide our lives today?

Strange Laws

Not every commandment in the Old Testament is unusual. Some regulations seem perfectly reasonable to us today. We should strive for holiness (Lev.

---

1. See *b. Makkot* 23b–24a; in Neusner, *Babylonian Talmud*, 17:120.

11:44–45; 19:2; 20:7–8, 26; 21:8). Bowing down before idols doesn't make God happy. Don't have sex with animals (Lev. 18:23; 20:15–16). Kidnapping is wrong (Exod. 21:16; Deut. 24:7). When your child is discerning a vocation, try to discourage a life of whoredom (Lev. 19:29).

While such expectations are reasonable, other Old Testament laws seem quite strange to us today. They show up alongside the normal-sounding stipulations. As one author puts it, "It's not like the Bible has a section called 'And Now for Some Crazy Laws.' They're all jumbled up like a chopped salad."[2] The following seem, at least initially, to qualify as extremely strange to us today:

1. *Dietary restrictions*: various regulations about which *animals* were "clean" and "unclean." The second type could not be eaten. For example:
   You shall not eat these: the camel, the hare, . . . the rock badger, . . . and the pig. . . . You shall not eat their meat, and you shall not touch their carcasses. (Deut. 14:7–8 NRSV)

2. *Purity laws*: various regulations about when *people* were "clean" and "unclean." One's cleanliness determined whether one could enter the place of worship. For example:
   If a man has an emission of semen, he shall bathe his whole body in water, and be unclean until the evening. (Lev. 15:16 NRSV)

3. *Sacrificial instruction*: regulations about sacrificing animals. For example:
   The bull shall be slaughtered before the LORD; and Aaron's sons the priests shall offer the blood, dashing the blood against all sides of the altar that is at the entrance of the tent of meeting. (Lev. 1:5 NRSV)

4. *Ritual instruction*: regulations about how to observe ceremonies each year. For example:
   For seven days you must live in huts. Every citizen of Israel must live in huts. (Lev. 23:42)

5. *Tabernacle-building instructions*: guidelines explaining how Israel's traveling sanctuary (also called the "tent of meeting") should be constructed. For example:
   Moreover you shall make the tabernacle with ten curtains of fine twisted linen, and blue, purple, and crimson yarns; you shall make them with cherubim skillfully worked into them. (Exod. 26:1 NRSV)

6. *Laws with severe punishments*: For example:
   Anyone who curses their father or mother should be put to death. (Exod. 21:17)

2. A. J. Jacobs, *Living Biblically*, 43.

A False Dichotomy

"Many people, many Christian people, look at the Old Testament as unchristian. . . .

"They have misread or misunderstood what Paul says about law vs. grace and works vs. faith. They come away with the idea that the Old Testament teaches you're saved if you keep the law, if you go by the book, if you keep all the rules, but in Jesus there is grace and mercy.

"That's a false dichotomy. I would challenge anybody who suggests that the Old Testament teaches that you are saved by works or you are saved by keeping the law. It's possible that in some of the intertestamental Judaism that concept may have emerged, but if Jesus is challenging it in the Sermon on the Mount, he's not challenging Moses, he's challenging the misinterpretation of Moses."

Victor Hamilton, "One on One," 8

Jesus "rejects the superficial interpretation of the law given by the scribes; he himself supplies the true interpretation. His purpose is not to change the law, still less to annul it, but 'to reveal the full depth of meaning that it was intended to hold.'"

John R. W. Stott, *Sermon on the Mount*, 72

"It is not correct to say that [Jesus] replaces the law with his own commands, for in no case does he relax a provision of the law. Rather, he shows that, rightly understood, the law goes much further than his hearers had reckoned."

Leon Morris, *Matthew*, 114

"Jesus manifests his perfect union with the will of God as revealed in the Old Testament law and prophets. He has in fact nothing to add to the commandments of God, except this, that he keeps them."

Dietrich Bonhoeffer, *Cost of Discipleship*, 122

---

7. *Laws that prescribe odd things*, such as driving an awl through your slave's ear if, after you set the slave free, the slave opts to stay in slavery (Exod. 21:6; Deut. 15:17).

8. *Laws concerning bizarre occurrences*, such as Deut. 25:11–12:

> If men get into a fight with one another, and the wife of one intervenes to rescue her husband from the grip of his opponent by reaching out and seizing his genitals, you shall cut off her hand; show no pity. (NRSV)

One has to wonder, did this seizing-your-husband's-opponent's-genitals crime happen frequently in ancient Israel? Why on earth did it become a law—much less make it into the Bible?

Three Options

Christians tend to take one of three approaches to Old Testament law.

Splitting Grace and Law

One approach is to say that *Old Testament commandments are outdated and obsolete.* Some people claim that Old Testament laws are a feature of legalistic religion, where you try to earn God's favor through obedience. Accordingly, Christians should reject this legalism and set Old Testament law aside. After all, many laws are so strange that it's unclear how we could ever carry them out.

This view of the law has many problems. It ignores key parts of Scripture. When you study the Old Testament carefully, it's clear that these texts are not about legalistically earning God's favor. In the Old Testament, just like the New, grace comes before obedience. Thus God *first* rescues the Israelites from slavery and *then* gives them the law. Many New Testament passages carry a similar idea: "We love because God first loved us" (1 John 4:19). (See "A False Dichotomy.") The law is less about getting God to like you and more about a larger covenant relationship between God and Israel that focuses on loyalty, love, and faithfulness.

In many respects, the law itself is a form of God's grace. The law's purpose is abundant life (Deut. 5:33). Obeying God's requirements means living in harmony with creation and the Creator.[3] God's commandments stand in contrast to the oppressive demands of Pharaoh. Thus the Ten Commandments require things like taking a day of rest—lest people revert back to Pharaoh's workaholic demands (Deut. 5:12–15). The great risk of disobeying God's commandments is that Israel becomes a house of oppression. (See "Law and Life.")

Those who set aside Old Testament laws seem to miss that New Testament texts often quote and build on these very laws. In the Sermon on the Mount

> **Law and Life**
>
> "God gives the law in the service of life. Scholars have written about the law as a gracious gift of God for the sake of the life, health, and well-being of individuals in the community. Unfortunately, grace is often equated with gospel. But law is as much a gracious gift of God as the gospel. . . . God gives the law not only for the life of those who receive it, but also for the life of the neighbor, indeed all of creation, whom the people of God are called to serve."
>
> Terence E. Fretheim, *About the Bible*, 87

---

3. Fretheim, *God and World*, 133–56.

(Matt. 5–7), Jesus calls for deep obedience to many parts of the law.[4] Paul equates obeying the Ten Commandments with loving others (Rom. 13:8–10). We cannot do away with the entirety of Old Testament law without also doing away with key parts of the New Testament.

Dividing the Law into Categories

Another approach is to see *some* types of Old Testament laws as binding, but *other* commandments as things we can safely set aside. For example, many Christians have claimed that there are three types of commandments in the Old Testament—*moral, ceremonial,* and *judicial*—and that only the *moral* commandments are still binding on the church.[5]

According to this logic, commandments to refrain from stealing fall into the moral category and should be practiced by Christians. However, commandments to make sacrifices or to kill those who curse their parents would fall into the ceremonial and judicial categories, respectively. Using this framework, we might quickly relegate many of the strangest laws to ceremonial and judicial categories. As such, it would seem that we can easily dismiss their relevance and focus on other biblical texts.

Certainly some laws will require that we prayerfully question why they are in the Bible, as we discussed in our last two chapters.[6] Yet we should not be too quick to give up on strange laws. Even commandments that cannot be carried out today may nevertheless inspire the church into deep theological reflection. By rejecting parts of scripture, we make ourselves deaf to what God wants to say through such texts.

Deep friendship develops when people are patient with each other and willing to stay together, even if they do not fully understand each other. Abandon patience, and the Old Testament quickly becomes a mere acquaintance.

---

4. In Matt. 5:17–20, Jesus explains he is not doing away with the law. In what follows, his message has many points of continuity with the OT. His warning about anger in Matt. 5:22 is similar to Prov. 12:16; 14:29; 16:32; 19:11; 29:11, 22. His words against making vows in Matt. 5:37 are similar to Eccles. 8:2–5. His prohibition of lust in Matt. 5:28 aligns with the Ten Commandments' prohibition of coveting a neighbor's wife (Exod. 20:17). When Jesus tells people to avoid vengeance and to love their enemies in Matt. 5:39–44, he echoes OT texts like Exod. 23:4–5; Lev. 19:18; Prov. 25:21. Jesus tells people to pray for those who persecute them (Matt. 5:44), and as we will see in chap. 10 below, the psalms are filled with prayers for one's enemies. Thus Jesus's Sermon on the Mount extends OT law naturally, rather than replacing it with something new. Jesus's words are not aimed at abolishing OT law, but rather at bringing out its fullest sense (Matt. 5:17–18).

5. Dividing the law into these three categories is seen in the writings of Thomas Aquinas, *Summa theologica* 2.99; and Calvin, *Institutes* 4.20.14 (ed. McNeill). Sometimes two divisions are made: e.g., John Wesley, preaching on the "Sermon on the Mount: Discourse the Fifth," in *Sermons,* 1:551 (I.2), talks about the moral and ceremonial law.

6. E.g., see Lev. 25:44–46.

Roll Up Your Sleeves

Leviticus 11:22 permits people to eat certain kinds of locusts. Why?! A. J. Jacobs struggles with the same question, choosing to stick with the Bible and consult commentaries. He eventually finds a great insight:

> In biblical times, swarming locusts would often devour the crops and cause famines. The only way for the poor to survive was by eating the locusts themselves. So if the Bible didn't approve of locust eating, the poorest Israelites would have died of starvation. This I like. More and more, I feel it's important to look at the Bible with an open heart. If you roll up your sleeves, even the oddest passages—and the one about edible bugs qualifies—can be seen as a sign of God's mercy and compassion.

A. J. Jacobs, *Living Biblically*, 176

Sticking with It

This brings us to a third approach to Old Testament law: *sticking with it*. As mentioned in the introductory chapter, rabbinic writings say that with the Torah, readers should "turn it this way, turn it that way, everything is in it; keep your eye on it, grow old and aged over it, and from it do not stir—for you have no better portion than it."[7] In other words, some passages seem at first to have little to offer. Yet we should stick with them, turning them to different angles, considering them in different lights, reading and rereading them slowly. (See "Roll Up Your Sleeves.")

Reading carefully does not come naturally in our age of information overload, where we like to process words as quickly as possible. However, things we quickly process rarely affect us in the long run. It's the questions and mysteries we return to time and again that have a much deeper impact on our lives. Reading slowly leads to personal transformation.

Consider, for example, the very odd law from Deut. 25:11–12 pertaining to seizing the genitals of your husband's opponent. What good could come of it? What does it have to offer us? I have never heard someone say that their "life verse"—that is, a verse of the Bible they return to again and again—deals with genital-grabbing. I have never seen a Christian T-shirt with those verses on the back, or gone to a church retreat where we just sit and reflect on these verses.

Yet what would happen if we carefully considered these verses, returning to them, asking others about them, and consulting commentaries?

7. Goldin, *Living Talmud*, 223, alt.

Recently I had a conversation with a close friend of mine about this passage. After a few moments of awkward laughter and disbelief that these verses were even in the Bible, my friend shared a great insight:

> Matt, I just thought of this. Having children was one of the greatest values in ancient Israel. When you read Genesis, it's constantly concerned with having kids. The Bible's first chapter commands humans to be fruitful and multiply, and then Genesis lists genealogies and describes God's miraculous intervention with a series of barren couples. Maybe this law made it into the Bible because of the sanctity attached to fertility, reproduction, and children.

Immediately I knew he was right. The Bible is profoundly concerned with starting families. The psalms speak repeatedly about how important children are, describing them as one of God's greatest blessings.[8]

Injuring a man's genitals might be an easy way to make him stop attacking your husband, but it also damages that man's future. It destroys opportunities for his wife and him to experience God's grace. In a sense, this commandment tells us that we need to consider the well-being of our enemies—even when they are attacking those we love and depend on for survival. It's a startling commandment that actually has elements in common with Jesus's commandment to love our enemies (Matt. 5:43–48).

These verses bring us to areas where the church needs to engage in ethical reflection. Nowadays, when we find ourselves at war, what is the church doing to protect *even our enemies* from atrocities and crimes against humanity? What steps are we taking to ensure that armed conflicts avoid creating relentless cycles of violence that haunt future generations?

Or, to turn to the issue of fertility, how should the church respond to the array of technologies aimed at preventing pregnancies in some cases and causing them in others? Deuteronomy 25:11–12 reminds us that such topics are not secular affairs. There frequently are ethical, moral, and theological issues at stake, and Christians do well to reflect on them together. Even when we cannot follow Old Testament law literally, it frequently shows us areas where the church needs to devote serious theological and ethical reflection.

Skepticism or Sympathy

In a world quite different from Iron-Age Israel, we cannot expect to obey the *letter* of the law. However, we can work with other Christians to discern how

---

8. Pss. 113:9; 115:14; 127:3–5; 128:3, 6.

to be faithful to the *spirit* of the law. Old Testament scholar John Rogerson makes precisely this point. He says that while we may not rigidly order our lives after each individual *precept* of Old Testament law, we can be inspired by legal *examples* of how God's people chose to be faithful amid changing times.[9]

In fact, many scholars have suggested that even within ancient Israel, biblical law functioned more to illustrate underlying principles and values than to prescribe rigidly what had to happen in every legal case. If this argument is correct, then using Old Testament laws as inspiring examples rather than as hard-and-fast precepts has much in common with how they were used in ancient times.[10]

It's easy to read Old Testament laws with skepticism and suspicion, rejecting texts left and right because they seem odd. But if we instead read Old Testament law with sympathy and openness, sticking with it, we will find ourselves renewed and transformed.

Viewing Another Culture's Customs

One way of opening ourselves to Old Testament law is keeping in mind that almost all cultures seem strange when viewed from the outside looking in—at least at first. Earlier I mentioned the odd practice of driving an awl through a slave's earlobe. It seems very strange, if not cruel—though many people today are quite comfortable with ear piercings in themselves and their children.[11]

To give another example, people outside the United States are sometimes disgusted by how, after going to the bathroom, Americans are comfortable cleaning their bottoms with only dry paper—no soap or even water (at least in the short term). To Americans, however, bidets seem strange.

In a popular article written in *American Anthropologist* in 1956, Horace Miner describes the exceedingly odd behaviors of a tribe of people called the Nacirema. He says these people believe

> that the human body is ugly and that its natural tendency is to debility and disease. Incarcerated in such a body, a person's only hope is to avert these

9. Rogerson, *Old Testament Ethics*, 27–28, 35–36, 133; Rogerson, *According to the Scriptures?*, 80–86; cf. Cosgrove, *Appealing to Scripture*, chap. 1.

10. Patrick, *Old Testament Law*, 189–222; Kazen, *Emotions in Biblical Law*, 53–56; cf. Sparks, *Ancient Texts*, 417–34.

11. It's also possible that the slave's ear was specifically chosen, not only because of its visibility, but also because in Hebrew words for "obeying" and "hearing" are closely related. Cf. MacDonald, "Deuteronomy," esp. 290 OT (see n. on Deut. 15:17).

characteristics through the use of the powerful influences of ritual and ceremony. Every household has one or more shrines devoted to this purpose. . . .

The focal point of the shrine is a box or chest which is built into the wall. In this chest are kept the many charms and magical potions without which none of the natives believe they could live. These preparations are secured from a variety of specialized practitioners. The most powerful of these are the medicine men, whose assistance must be rewarded with substantial gifts. However, the medicine men do not provide the curative potions for their clients, but decide what the ingredients should be and then write them down in an ancient and secret language. This writing is understood only by the medicine men and by the herbalists who, for another gift, provide the required charm.

The charm is not disposed of after it has served its purpose, but is placed in the charm-box of the household shrine. . . .

Beneath the charm-box is a small font. Each day every member of the family, in succession, enters the shrine room, bows his or her head before the charm-box, mingles different sorts of holy water in the font, and proceeds with a brief rite of ablution. The holy waters are secured from the Water Temple of the community, where the priests conduct elaborate ceremonies to make the liquid ritually pure.[12]

As you may have suspected, Miner is talking about American culture (*Nacirema* spelled backward), our bathrooms, and our personal hygiene habits. Miner's point is that our culture seems quite strange when viewed from the outside too. People in the developed world have their own obsessions with the body, its borders, and purity. Our rules and rituals seem perfectly normal to us. We take them for granted. Yet they seem very strange to those not raised in our culture.

Relating Particulars to the Whole

Many parts of Old Testament law seem exceptionally odd. Yet if we stick with Old Testament law, turning it one way, then another, some interesting features begin to emerge. Biblical scholars frequently describe these features, and trustworthy commentaries on books like Leviticus share a variety of insights. Study Bibles are also useful. (See the end of the next chapter for recommendations.) Although biblical scholars once thought of Old Testament customs as irrational and arbitrary, many interpreters now see them as part of a broader coherent system.[13]

12. Miner, "Body Ritual," 503–4, alt.
13. See the discussion in Douglas, *Purity and Danger*, 43–46. For a more arbitrary interpretation, see J. Z. Smith, *To Take Place*, 108–9.

Clearly one of the centerpieces of Old Testament law is *holiness*. The books of Exodus, Leviticus, Numbers, and Deuteronomy make over three hundred references to this concept. Being holy means being set apart, distinct, dedicated, and belonging to God. It relates closely to purity, completeness, integrity, unity, and perfection.[14] What is *holy* is dedicated to God.[15]

Because commandments to "be holy" regularly show up alongside concerns for diet and cleanliness, it appears that the Old Testament envisions the ceremonial purity of the people as reflecting the holiness of God. The people remove dirt from their lives because, as cleansed individuals, they reflect the purity and holiness of God. In other words, daily hygiene was a

> **Constant Reminders**
>
> Dietary regulations "would have been like signs which at every turn inspired meditation on the oneness, purity and completeness of God. By rules of avoidance holiness was given a physical expression in every encounter with the animal kingdom and at every meal. Observance of the dietary rules would thus have been a meaningful part of the great liturgical act of recognition and worship which culminated in the sacrifice in the Temple."
>
> Mary Douglas, *Purity and Danger*, 57

sacrament. By cleaning themselves before encountering God in the sanctuary, they reminded themselves that God is "holy, holy, holy"—utterly pure and opposed to evil.[16] They came before the Creator of the universe with respect. (See "Constant Reminders.") More will be said about holiness in the next chapter.

Interpreters have found other themes running throughout purity regulations. A number of interpreters believe that Old Testament customs are ultimately concerned with *death* and removing deathlike things from the sanctuary. God, after all, never dies. So skin diseases, which look like decomposing flesh, are not permitted within the "holy place."[17]

Others have suggested that *compassion* and nonviolence are at the core of many Old Testament commandments. Bloodlust in society is held in check by limiting who kills animals (i.e., only priests) and which ones can be killed

---

14. See, e.g., Lev. 10:10; 11:43–45; Ezek. 22:26; Douglas, *Purity and Danger*, 55–57.

15. See *TDOT* 12:521–45; Douglas, *Purity and Danger*, 49–57. On the importance of holiness, esp. as it relates to Lev. 17–26, see Balentine, *Torah's Vision of Worship*, 167–72.

16. Douglas, *Purity and Danger*, 49–57.

17. Ibid., 51. Cf. Milgrom, *Leviticus*, 11–13; Milgrom, "Seeing the Ethical," 6, 13; Milgrom, "Biblical Impurity"; Harrington, "Clean and Unclean," 688. While there's some truth here, many of these interpreters overemphasize the avoidance of death. Animals were constantly being killed at the temple; the blood of the slain was even brought into the holy of holies (Lev. 16:15). Furthermore, childbirth—the opposite of death—causes one of the longest-lasting periods of impurity mentioned in the Bible (Lev. 12). Purity is related to death, but it's not ultimately concerned with only favoring life over death.

(i.e., only clean animals).[18] We are told not to harm vulnerable animals because they symbolize the vulnerable among us.[19] Thus it's okay to eat fish with scales, but not more vulnerable sea creatures that lack scales or fins for protection (Lev. 11:9–12).

That's Disgusting

A number of biblical scholars have recognized that many biblical laws are related to the emotion of *disgust*.[20] Our families and societies teach us at a very young age what is gross and disgusting, things we should either avoid altogether or else cleanse ourselves from after contact is made. We often feel disgust in response to animallike behavior and death.[21] Modern research about our own society points to the following things as common causes of disgust:

1. Certain types of *food*, such as rotten meat.
2. Certain types of *animals*, such as cockroaches and rats.
3. Certain things associated with *disease*, such as germs on public handrails.
4. Certain types of *body-envelope violations*, such as open wounds.
5. Certain types of *bodily secretions*, such as nasal mucus.
6. Certain things related to *death*, such as a decomposing corpse.
7. Certain types of *morally problematic behavior*, such as torture.
8. Certain types of *sex*, such as incest.
9. Certain types of *people*, such as corrupt rulers. As a well-respected discussion of disgust puts it, "People of diverse cultures and languages apparently *feel* some similarity in their emotional reactions to feces and to sleazy politicians."[22]

The above examples all come from modern society. Interestingly, when we read books like Leviticus, Numbers, and Deuteronomy, we see similar concerns for what's disgusting. (See "Natural Reactions.") The particular examples

18. Milgrom, "Food and Faith," 5, 10.
19. Douglas, "Holy Joy," 12–13; Douglas, "Forbidden Animals in Leviticus," 21–23; Douglas, *Leviticus as Literature*, 168–69. See Milgrom, "Biblical Impurity," 107, for a list of other possible reasons for impurity.
20. Kazen, *Emotions in Biblical Law*, 33–36, 71–94; Feder, "Between Contagion and Cognition," 155–56, 165–66.
21. Curtis, Aunger, and Rabie, "Disgust Evolved to Protect"; Haidt, McCauley, and Rozin, "Sensitivity to Disgust."
22. Rozin, Haidt, and McCauley, "Disgust," 763. See also Haidt, McCauley, and Rozin, "Sensitivity to Disgust."

don't always line up with modern society, but all of our nine areas of concern are also areas of concern in Old Testament law.

Food and Animals

Regarding *food* and *animals*, Leviticus 11 and Deuteronomy 14 outline which animals are "unclean" and which are "clean." Clean animals, such as cows, can be eaten. Unclean ones, such as eels, should not be eaten. (See "The Bible and Flexitarianism.")

If you touch the carcass of an unclean animal, you become unclean yourself. This is not a sin, as long as you clean your clothes and wait until evening before going somewhere like the sanctuary (e.g., Lev. 11:24–25). This type of uncleanness was fairly common. It was also harmless when outside the sanctuary.[23]

Disease

Regarding *disease*, Leviticus 13–14 gives rules regarding skin disorders, ex-plaining different types, when quarantin-ing is necessary, and how an infected individual can come back into full par-ticipation in society. While some of us today may be judgmental toward the ancient practice of quarantining individuals, modern public health officials agree that in some cases, isolation and quarantining are appropriate.[24] In Le-viticus, we also see a concern for *bodily envelope violations*, such as scarring from boils and burns (13:23, 28).

> **Natural Reactions**
>
> "Many people wince at having to pick up a dead animal; most people (except two-year-olds) try to avoid touching defecation; corpses inspire a natural feeling of awe, and we hesitate to touch them; washing off semen and blood is almost natural, and certainly not hard to remember. Even gnat-impurity, which sounds picky, is not hard to understand. Who wants a fly in one's soup?"
>
> E. P. Sanders, *Jewish Law*, 145

Bodily Discharges

Certain *bodily discharges* can also make someone unclean for a period of time. Thus Leviticus 15 explains that menstruation and semen make a person temporarily unclean. (Childbirth similarly requires cleansing, as Lev. 12 explains.) Like touching an unclean animal, this impurity was not in itself considered a sin.[25] Rather, it meant that you were unfit to enter the sanctuary

---

23. Milgrom, *Leviticus*, 9; Milgrom, "Jews Are Not Hunters," 27–30.
24. T. Day et al., "When Is Quarantining a Useful Control Strategy?"
25. Klawans, "Concepts of Purity," esp. 2043; Klawans, *Impurity and Sin*, 24.

The Bible and Flexitarianism

Most of us are familiar with *veganism*, which involves abstaining from all animal products, and *vegetarianism*, a refusal to eat meat.

Many of us also know people who prefer to eat vegetarian, but then are willing to eat meat on special occasions like holidays or when other protein sources are unavailable.

At times the Old Testament's diet code is similar to this *loose vegetarianism*, often called *flexitarianism*. It places no constraints on the fruits and vegetables people can eat, but severely limits which and when animals could be consumed. In essence, the people could eat only certain domesticated plant-eating animals: sheep, goats, and cattle (as well as a few wild counterparts). Moreover, the average person did not eat these meats every day. They were consumed only at the temple, where priests slaughtered the animals humanely. Like flexitarianism today, eating meat was not an everyday occurrence.

---

and excluded from certain ritual activities. This type of uncleanness naturally happened in the course of life's events.[26] Nowadays most of us wash ourselves before going to church—particularly if we have a bodily fluid on us or have touched something dead. Showers were not available in ancient Israel. So people had to undergo a different type of cleansing activity, such as taking a bath, washing clothes, making sacrifices, and waiting things out before they were ready to enter a holy place.

Today we clean ourselves and dress up for special dinners. In ancient Israel, worshipers similarly prepared themselves before going to the temple to have a feast with their Creator.

Death

Death can trigger disgust not only in our culture but also in the biblical world. Coming into contact with a human corpse made an Israelite ceremonially unclean, as described in Leviticus 21 and Numbers 19. To be made clean again, the person who touched the corpse needed to wait a week. During that time, water mixed with the ashes of a burned, sacrificed cow was used to clean the person. Such a practice sounds bizarre to modern readers. What many people overlook, however, is that soap today can be made with lard from a cow (called tallow), and soap has historically had many connections with ashes.[27] We aren't too different from the Israelites.

26. Even priests could contract impurity through ritual (see Lev. 16:28; Num. 19:8).
27. Davidsohn, "Soap and Detergent." Peoples in the ancient Near East, such as the Sumerians, have historical connections with the invention of soap (Salzberg, *From Caveman to Chemist*, 6–7).

Morally Problematic Behavior

Biblical scholar Jonathan Klawans argues that there are two types of impurity in the Bible: ritual impurity and moral impurity.[28] The impurities discussed above (involving food, animals, bodily discharges, bodily envelope violations, and death) have to do with *ritual impurity*. However, Klawans notes that there's another type of impurity that has several differences from ritual impurities: *moral impurity*.

Here's how he characterizes each one:[29]

Ritual Impurity	Moral Impurity
usually isn't sinful.	results from very serious sin.
is wrong to bring into the temple, but is also a natural part of the land.	damages the land and may lead to expulsion from it.
can make others defiled.	cannot defile others (so there is no need to cleanse yourself after contact with an idol-worshiper).
is temporary.	is long lasting or permanent.
is cleansed by rites of purification (bathing, waiting, or sacrifice).	is cleansed by punishment, atonement, or exile.
is excluded from the sanctuary.	(surprisingly) does not exclude people from the sanctuary.
is called "impure" but not an "abomination" or "pollution."	is called not only "impure" but also an "abomination" that "pollutes."

So, whereas coming into contact with a corpse would make you ritually impure, such contact wouldn't make you morally impure. The key exception would be if you were somehow responsible for the death of another. When describing (a) violence (Num. 35:33–34) or (b) sacrificing one's child to the ancient god Molek (Lev. 20:1–5; Deut. 12:13; 18:10), the Bible uses different language to suggest that such impurities are of a different class than the everyday uncleanness associated with things like bodily discharges. These impurities are seen as polluting the perpetrators and even the land, inciting God's punishment. (See "The Land as God's Agent of Justice.")

28. Klawans, "Concepts of Purity"; Klawans, *Impurity and Sin*, 21–42; cf. Thomas Aquinas, *Summa theologica* 2.102.5; 2.103.2.
29. This chart is a close paraphrase of lists Klawans gives in both "Concepts of Purity," 2045, and *Impurity and Sin*, 27. Although some scholars have found fault with some of the particulars of Klawans's classifications (e.g., Kazen, *Emotions in Biblical Law*, 26–31), his categories provide useful starting points for thinking about differences between everyday sorts of impurity and much more serious types of impurity.

> ### The Land as God's Agent of Justice
>
> Severe moral impurities contaminated both the sinner and the land itself. Leviticus 18 says that the land itself is sickened by such pollutions:
>
> > Do not defile yourselves in any of these ways, for by all these practices the nations I am casting out before you have defiled themselves. Thus the land became defiled; and I punished it for its iniquity, and the land *vomited* out its inhabitants. But you shall keep my statutes and my ordinances and commit none of these abominations, . . . otherwise the land will *vomit* you out for defiling it, as it vomited out the nation that was before you. (18:24–26, 28 NRSV, italics added)
>
> In the Bible, the land is not a passive object that humans can simply manipulate. It is one of God's agents in the world.[a]
>
> a. On this topic, see Fretheim, *God and World*, chap. 6.

Sex

Certain things related to *sex* are also linked to ideas of disgust in the Bible. Childbirth, menstruation, and male ejaculation make one temporarily unclean and are *not* morally problematic. On the other hand, sex with animals *is morally problematic*. Like child sacrifice, this type of behavior is called an "abomination."[30] Punishment, atonement, and exile were the primary ways to be cleansed of this type of impurity.

People

The Old Testament suggests that *people* who commit extremely heinous acts become repulsive themselves. It thus has harsh words against intermarriage

---

30. Lev. 18 names several other sexual behaviors that it strongly condemns. One of them is homosexual practice among males (18:22). I have intentionally chosen *not* to discuss homosexuality in this book because churches have already spent too much time debating this extremely divisive topic. The church today should try to figure out how to embody purity in all facets of its life, rather than focusing so narrowly on purity in conjunction with this one topic. Only after the church has adopted purity as a way of life will it be able to determine whether the OT's homosexual prohibitions are more like its prohibitions of incest (i.e., something the church adheres to today) or more like its commandments about circumcision (i.e., something the church doesn't adhere to today).

For those wanting to think more deeply about homosexuality, Nussbaum (*Hiding from Humanity*) draws attention to the link between disgust and perceptions of homosexuality, albeit focusing on secular law. Brueggemann links homosexuality with issues of purity in his *Theology of the Old Testament*, 194–96. R. Hays, *Moral Vision*, 379–406, is also aware of connections between homosexuality and purity, though he reaches a very different conclusion than Brueggemann.

between the Israelites and other peoples who do not worship the LORD (Deut. 7:3–4). The fear is that these other groups of people would tear Israelites away from worshiping the LORD alone. The Old Testament is well aware that some people may be so morally corrupt that spending considerable time with them will result in the contamination of one's own moral nature (cf. Prov. 13:20).[31] Such a conviction is not unheard of in our own culture. For example, many people prefer not to associate with criminals, feel disgust toward Nazis, and treat those who have committed serious wrongs as outcasts.[32]

Conclusion

Initially, Old Testament laws may look primitive and savage. However, such appearances belie the multiple points of continuity between modern society and ancient Israel. Like the Bible, we ourselves are shaped by the emotion of disgust and ideas about purity.

The chief difference between the Bible and ourselves is not that the Bible is concerned with purity, disgust, cleanliness, and bodily borders—while we are not. Rather, the key contrast is that the Bible thinks of impurity as a religious topic, whereas we usually assume it's a secular concern. In the Bible, God is above all else pure and holy, undefiled and perfect, worthy of adoration, awe, and worship. We humans are not. At times we are disgusting creatures, unlike our Creator.

Thus the Bible teaches us that in the course of life's events, we regularly encounter impurities that remind us of our distance from God. Some impurities, like bodily discharges, are natural occurrences reminding us that we are creatures and not gods, finite and not infinite, mortal and not eternal. We can resemble animals more than the divine. Other impurities are more moral in nature, reminding us of the distance our sin creates between God and ourselves.

In either case, our impurities mean that we cannot take coming into the presence of a holy God lightly. It's necessary to purify ourselves, preparing to encounter One who is far greater than any figment of our imagination. The purity rules of ancient Israel seem quite specific to the culture of that time.

---

31. The OT and NT alike testify to the importance of loving one's enemies and welcoming sinners back into the fold. At the same time, we should not assume that we have the moral fortitude of saints. Sometimes spending time with unrepentant sinners has negative effects on our own moral lives. Jesus excluded merchants from the temple (e.g., Mark 11:15–17), Paul excluded people from table fellowship (1 Cor. 5:9–11), and the OT similarly excludes certain people for detestable practices (e.g., Deut. 7:3–4).

32. Rozin, Haidt, and McCauley, "Disgust," 763.

Yet our theology will be richer and our worship will be more meaningful if we don't lose sight of God's holiness and purity.[33]

The Old Testament is like a friend from another country. Its ways don't always make sense to us. We could easily ignore this stranger in our midst and continue in our same ways. However, by spending time with the Old Testament, we find a common humanity beneath our differences. From our friendship with the Old Testament, we learn about the significance of coming into God's presence. We learn that everyday rituals can be structured to focus our attention on God's holiness. In the end, we discover new ways of experiencing God.

For Further Study

See the end of chapter 8, which describes resources for interpreting Old Testament law.

33. Daniels and Archibald ("Levitical Cycle of Health") describe one way that parts of Leviticus have been appropriated in a church setting. While I disagree with some of their interpretations and appropriations (e.g., focusing on psychological health), I applaud the effort to apply Leviticus today.

Some interpreters suggest that the NT does away with purity and holiness concerns, given texts like Mark 7 and Acts 10; 15 (cf. Brueggemann, *Theology of the Old Testament*, 194–96). While the NT obviously displays an evolving awareness of what purity and holiness look like in its time, it doesn't dismiss these concerns. Thus even when Jesus says that food doesn't make people unclean, he retains the language of cleanliness, using it to talk of what people do with their bodies (Mark 7:15). When the Jerusalem Council removed the circumcision requirement for entrance into the church, it still expressed concern for what people ate and how they acted sexually (Acts 15:28–29).

8

Is the Law Engraved in Stone?

The Dynamic Nature of God's Law

I N AN ENTERTAINING AND FUNNY MEMOIR called *The Year of Living Biblically*, A. J. Jacobs undertakes an experiment: for one year, he follows as literally as possible every commandment in the Bible while living in New York City. His adventure leads to some rather humorous undertakings. He meets a man on a park bench who admits to having an extramarital affair. Compelled to stone the man (see Lev. 20:10), he throws a pebble at the man's chest. During this year, Jacobs also tries to avoid sitting where a menstruating woman has sat, in accordance with Leviticus 15:20. However, in a bout of anger, Jacobs's wife sits in every chair in the house. As a thirty-eight-year-old man, he is forced to sit on the only chair she missed—his toddler's six-inch-high bench.[1]

While Jacobs's memoir is a delight to read, both for its humor and its religious insight, it illustrates the difficulty of trying to replicate biblical purity laws today. And it raises important questions: Do Christians have the freedom to adapt God's law to changing times? Can we revere the Old Testament as God's Word, even while choosing *not* to follow everything it prescribes?

1. A. J. Jacobs, *Living Biblically*, 51–52, 92–93.

The Dynamic Nature of God's Law

People sometimes assume that God's law is static, fixed, and unchanging. After all, God—who is eternal—is the One giving the orders. It seems that God's commandments at one place and time would extend to everyone in all places and times.

There's some truth in such a claim. The Ten Commandments, for example, were literally written in stone (e.g., Exod. 34:1). They have an abiding truth that extends across generations and cultures.[2] Certainly some other laws have enduring significance, such as the overarching commandments to be holy (Lev. 19:2), to love God (Deut. 6:5), and to love neighbor (Lev. 19:18). But what about laws that are more specific? What about some of the strange laws mentioned in the previous chapter that we couldn't and shouldn't follow today (like killing those who curse their parents, Exod. 21:17)?

One of the most important features of biblical law is that while the essentials remain fairly constant, other parts are reshaped in different times and seasons. The Old Testament doesn't contain just one legal code binding for all people in all times. Rather, the Old Testament contains a series of law codes for different times in Israel's history:

- The Ten Commandments (Exod. 20:1–17; Deut. 5:6–21)
- The Book of the Covenant (Exod. 20:22–23:33)
- The Holiness Code (Lev. 17–26)
- The Priestly Code (other laws in Exodus, Leviticus, and Numbers)
- Deuteronomic Code (Deut. 12–26)

These law codes relate to different times and places.[3] For example, the Book of the Covenant has connections with early periods of Israelite history (such as the early monarchy in the tenth century). Meanwhile, Deuteronomic Law connects in many ways with later times, particularly the reforms of Josiah in 622 BCE (recounted in 2 Kings 22–23).

Interestingly, the different legal codes of the Bible have different emphases, sometimes even different expectations. When readers compare them, it's apparent that God and God's people responded creatively to new situations as

2. The Babylonian Talmud similarly testifies that some commandments, such as avoiding adultery and bloodshed, are binding on all peoples, unlike much of the rest of the law (*Sanhedrin* 56). On a different but related matter, although the Ten Commandments transcend cultures, they are addressed to a narrow audience in ancient Israel: individual men with property, wives, living parents, and the like (Smith-Christopher, *Jonah, Jesus, and Other Good Coyotes*, 12).

3. Texts can be not only time-specific and place-specific, but also people-specific. E.g., Num. 6 concerns the Nazirites: a group of people who made a specific type of vow.

Evolving Speed Limits

The Old Testament isn't the only place where one sees laws changing over time. Consider speed-limit laws.

In 1901, Connecticut enacted the first speed limit for motorized vehicles in the US, specifying that they could not move faster than 12 mph in town and 15 mph in the country.[a]

Similarly, *The Onion* jokingly contains the following Q & A in its fictional portrayal of a 1928 newspaper:

> Q: What would happen if an automobile were to ever reach a speed of sixty miles per hour?
>
> A: The driver of that vehicle would die.[b]

Obviously, perceptions of vehicles and laws governing speed limits have changed with time. To a certain extent, biblical law has evolved as well.[c]

a. "May 21, 1901."
b. Dikkers, *Our Dumb Century*, 37.
c. Cf. Fretheim, *About the Bible*, 87.

---

they arose.[4] For example, Deuteronomy's laws can be seen as a revision of older material. These newer laws revolve around a central temple rather than multiple sites of worship.

To give another example of how biblical law changed with time, the Ten Commandments forbid killing and give no additional explanation (Exod. 20:13; Deut. 5:17). Yet, elsewhere in the Torah, laws recognize that unintentional deaths do occur, so people need to distinguish between willful attacks and accidental deaths (Exod. 21:12–14; see also Num. 35:12; Deut. 4:41–43; 19:1–13; Josh. 20).

Other variations are also visible:

- Exodus 22:31 forbids people from eating animals killed by other animals, whereas Leviticus 17:15 permits it under certain circumstances.
- Exodus 27:1–2 specifies that the sacrificial altar should be made of acacia wood, but Exodus 20:24–26 says that it can be built of uncut stones.[5]
- Leviticus 3:1–17 and 17:1–7 stipulate that beef and mutton need to be eaten at the tabernacle, but Exodus 20:24 and Deuteronomy 12:15–25 permit it elsewhere.

4. On this topic, see Rogerson, *Old Testament Ethics*, esp. 1–39; Rogerson, *According to the Scriptures?*, 81–82; Fretheim, *God and World*, 148–56; Milgrom, *Leviticus*, 1–6; Gossai, "The Old Testament," 156; cf. Douglas, *Purity and Danger*, 4–5.

5. Sparks, *Ancient Texts*, 431. He also mentions the tension between Exod. 12:8–9 and Deut. 16:7, which is more obvious in the Hebrew than most English translations.

- Leviticus 7:19 prohibits those who are unclean from eating meat, whereas Deuteronomy 12:15 and 12:22 allow unclean people to eat it.
- Exodus 23:13 is open to various interpretations, but it appears to forbid people from mentioning the names of other gods, while Leviticus 18:21 and 20:2–5 call the deity "Molek" by name.
- Slavery is seen differently in Deuteronomy 15:12, where female slaves are set free every seventh year, and Exodus 21:2–7, where they aren't.[6]
- Readers find different ways to *tithe* (i.e., donate one-tenth of their income) in Leviticus 27:30 (the gift is given to God), Numbers 18:21 (it's given to the Levites), and Deuteronomy 14:23 (it's given back to the giver).[7]

Do these differences suggest that the Bible contradicts itself?

No. They suggest that God and God's people responded creatively to changing times.[8] (See "Ethics and Context.") The notion that God's law is absolutely static and unchanging fails to do justice to the Bible, God, and our world. Some things remain constant, like the need to love God and neighbor. In this sense, God is the same yesterday, today, and forever. However, other things change with times and seasons. In this sense, God is living and interactive, enmeshed in close relationships with creatures whose circumstances change. (See "Evolving Speed Limits.")

Jewish interpreters of the Bible don't believe that animals should be sacrificed today. There's no standing temple in Jerusalem where such sacrifices could take place. Instead of sacrifice, other parts of the law have taken on added significance, such as observing the Sabbath (a weekly day of rest).

Christianity began as a sect of Judaism. However, as more and more *gentiles* (that is, those not of Jewish descent) wanted to convert to Christianity, the church had a

---

Ethics and Context

"God is cast as the *principal instigator of change within law*. . . . God's will for Israel is understood as a living will. God moves with this people on their life's journey, and God's will for them changes because they change. For God's will to be linked to life in such a central way makes the law an even more gracious gift than if understood as unchangeable."

Terence E. Fretheim,
About the Bible, 91

"Scripture 'authorizes' its own reinterpretation."

Luke Timothy Johnson, "Bible's Authority," 69 (italics removed)

---

6. Enns, *Inspiration and Incarnation*, 85–97, esp. 90–91; cf. Greenstein, "Biblical Law," 97–98.

7. Milgrom, *Leviticus*, 1–2. Note also the differences between Deut. 23:1 and Isa. 56:4–5 (as well as the discussion in Middleton and Walsh, *Truth Is Stranger*, 179–80).

8. See Fretheim, *God and World*, 153; Carroll R., introduction to Rogerson's *Old Testament Ethics*, 10; Hanson, "Theological Significance," 129–30.

question to answer: should these converts adhere to Jewish expectations about diet and circumcision? The church met together, debated, and worked with one another and the Holy Spirit.

In Acts 15, the church reached a somewhat daring decision. They concluded that gentiles should not be under the same regulations governing diet and circumcision.

At the same time, the church did *not* adopt an "anything goes" mentality. They retained a concern for what gentiles did, displaying continuity with Old Testament law even while departing from some parts of it. A council in Jerusalem wrote a letter to gentile churches containing these words (Acts 15:28–29 NRSV):

> For it has seemed good to the Holy Spirit and to us to impose on you no further burden than these essentials: that you abstain from what has been sacrificed to idols and from blood and from what is strangled and from fornication. If you keep yourselves from these, you will do well. Farewell.

Several things are significant about these verses.

First, the church's decision to adapt to changing times and seasons has much in common with the evolution of legal codes in the Old Testament. The earliest Christians followed the precedent in the Old Testament of recognizing that God's requirements evolve in new circumstances. Even as the church moved in new directions, they mirrored the Old Testament tradition of adapting to new times and seasons. (See "The Law Is Like a Nanny.")

Second, the church's decision wasn't made by one person. Instead, Christians came together and worked with the Holy Spirit and one another to discern what God wanted. Such a practice is an important check against individualistic decisions, which are particularly susceptible to sin. We best discern God's will when we gather around the Bible with other Christians. (See "God's People.")

Third, the church did not abandon a concern for food or sexual organs, even in a time and culture that was centuries removed from ancient Israel. New Testament Christians forbade people from eating food sacrificed to idols, from ingesting blood, and from fornication. In so doing, they focused on what was most "essential," as the text puts it.

God's People

"The biblical documents were written by God's people for God's people, so that it is with and among God's people that we are best positioned to read the scriptures faithfully."[a]

Joel B. Green,
"Authority of Scripture," 527

a. On the community's role in moral discernment, see Verhey, *Remembering Jesus*, 71–76.

The Law Is Like a Nanny

In Paul's day, many households had servants who functioned like nannies do today. They protected children from harm, tended to their moral character, traveled with them, and helped them to become better people.

In Galatians 3:23–25, Paul says that the law functioned much like one of these nannies. It had custody of God's people, serving like a nanny until Christ came. Now that Christ is here, it's as though we have reached a certain age of maturity and no longer need the same supervision we once did.

While this image is very positive, some translations do not recognize it as such. The NRSV, for example, could have better translated these verses as follows (changes are in brackets):

> Now before faith came, we were [protected] and guarded under the law until faith would be revealed. Therefore the law was our [nanny] until Christ came, so that we might be justified by faith. But now that faith has come, we are no longer subject to a [nanny].[a]

Christians are no longer under the same guidance of their nanny (the law), but that does *not* mean that we now do the opposite of what God's law taught us (Gal. 3:21). Rather, it means that we now have the freedom to work with one another and the Holy Spirit to judge how to apply the essentials of God's instruction.

a. Although I have not encountered the translation of "nanny" for the Greek word *paidagōgos* elsewhere, it seems much more appropriate than "disciplinarian" or "taskmaster" (since the term is not derogatory: *TDNT* 5:596–625, esp. 620). It's also better than "tutor," "educator," or "pedagogue" (since this term did not refer to teachers in Paul's day: *BDAG* 748). For secondary literature on this image, a good starting point is M. J. Smith, "Role of the Pedagogue in Galatians." On the broader topic of the law in Paul's thinking, see N. T. Wright, *Climax of the Covenant*; Dunn, *New Perspective on Paul*. For other texts where Paul deals with the Moses, the law, and Israel, see Rom. 9–11; 2 Cor. 3.

Finally, the pattern used by the early church is a useful guide for the church today.[9] We can focus on essentials, working with one another and the Holy Spirit to discern how we can best be faithful in a rapidly changing world. (See "The Law: Then and Now.") We need to exercise humility, never assuming that having located some essentials, we can do away with the particularities of the Old Testament texts.[10] Rather, we should return again and again to the Old and New Testaments, expecting to discover anew their life-giving resources.[11]

9. As Kuhn (*Having Words with God*, 89) puts it, "Scripture itself provides no indication that the dynamic nature of God's instruction is suddenly to cease." For more on discerning how the diversity of the Bible relates to us today, see McKnight, *Blue Parakeet*.

10. Cf. Bauckham, "Reading Scripture as a Coherent Story," esp. 44.

11. Cf. Goldingay, *Old Testament Interpretation*, 51–55.

The Law: Then and Now

"Different eras and social, political, and economic settings require ethical insights and solutions specifically intended for their particular problems. That is why Christians today cannot duplicate the details of the legal system or the practices of the Old Testament. Today's needs are not the same as ancient Israel's, and the ethical challenges of modern societies cannot be met by reproducing what was done among and for that people so long ago."

M. Daniel Carroll R., introduction to Rogerson's *Old Testament Ethics,* 10

"To freeze any portion of scripture into an immutable theological or ethical system would run counter to the dynamic unfolding within scripture itself. Rather, it is a dynamic which must be viewed as continuing to unfold within our own experience as well and in a steady movement toward the eschatological Kingdom which is a part of God's plan for creation."

Paul D. Hanson, "Theological Significance," 129–30

Essentials

How can the church today continue to focus on what's essential in Old Testament law, even as it recognizes the need to adapt to new times and places? Fortunately, the Bible itself gives readers many clues about what is most essential. There are three primary ways it does so: (1) repetition, (2) location, and (3) special designations.

Consider, for a moment, the Ten Commandments, which are sometimes called the *Decalogue.*[12] The Old Testament goes to great lengths to emphasize the Ten Commandments' significance. First, the Torah engages in *repetition,* listing the Decalogue in part or in full several times (Exod. 20:1–17; 31:12–17; Deut. 5:6–21; cf. Lev. 19). On other occasions, it speaks of the Ten Commandments without quoting them (e.g., various times in Exod. 32; 34; Deut. 9–10).

Second, when the Decalogue appears, it's at highly significant *locations.* The Ten Commandments are one of the first things we hear from God on Mount Sinai, and they begin Moses's longest address in Deuteronomy.

Third, *special designations* also draw our attention to the Ten Commandments' significance. Two times they are portrayed as being written "with the finger of God" (Exod. 31:18 NRSV; Deut. 9:10). The two tablets of stone are so precious they are placed within the ark of the covenant (Deut. 10:1–5).

---

12. Although our culture is more familiar with the term "the Ten Commandments," the original Hebrew instead speaks literally of "ten words," which is what the word *Decalogue* means (Exod. 34:28; Deut. 4:13; 10:4).

The Torah also says that God spoke the Ten Commandments directly to the people, whereas other commandments were mediated through Moses (Deut. 4:12–13; 5:22–33).[13]

Given these special features, it's not surprising that the New Testament also sees the Decalogue as foundational.[14]

Many other essentials are present in Old Testament law. The following table points to some of these essentials, explaining why they are important, using the three criteria described above:

Some Essential Themes in Old Testament Law

Essential	Repetition	Location	Special Designations
Holiness	Words like *holy* appear in the Bible more frequently than words like *love*.[a]	Example: the "central turning point" of Leviticus is chapter 19,[b] which begins with the command, "You must be holy, because I, the LORD your God, am holy" (Lev. 19:2).	Holiness is central to the identity of both God and the Israelites (e.g., Lev. 20:26).
Disgust	Example: purity regulations concerning food appear in both Leviticus 11 and Deuteronomy 14.	Purity concerns are found throughout much of the Torah. (See the discussion of disgust in chap. 7 above.)	Strong rhetoric: Failure to abide by certain purity regulations means the land will vomit the Israelites out of it (Lev. 18:24–30).
Caring for the poor	Repeatedly, laws require no interest on loans, the freeing of slaves, the cancelation of debt, allowances for gleaning, and care for immigrants.[c]	Leviticus 19, the central chapter to the book, contains many commandments to care for the poor (e.g., Lev. 19:9–10, 13–15, 33–34; cf. 19:3, 11, 30, 32).	Exceedingly harsh punishments await those who treat the poor badly (e.g., Exod. 22:22–24).
Tabernacle	The end of Exodus describes the design of the tabernacle not once but twice. In Exodus 25–31, God gives the instructions; in Exodus 35–40, those instructions are carried out.	The final third of Exodus focuses on the construction of the tabernacle. Much of Leviticus and Numbers are concerned with what happens at the tabernacle.	Many texts strongly associate the tabernacle with holiness and the dwelling place of God.

13. Another marker of the Ten Commandments' importance is that they appear to undergird a variety of different texts. As Milgrom (*Leviticus*, 2) puts it, "The book of Leviticus and many of its sometimes contradictory laws can be understood as the various manifestations of the principles of the Ten Commandments." See also the discussion in Goldingay, *Theological Diversity*, chap. 2, about certain trajectories of OT thought reaching a high point (e.g., 47).

14. See Matt. 15:19 and parallels; Matt. 19:17–19 and parallels; Rom. 13:8–10.

Essential	Repetition	Location	Special Designations
Sacrifice	Leviticus 1:1–6:7 describes several sacrifices. Leviticus 6:8–7:38 then revisits the same sacrifices, focusing on the priests' portion.	The opening chapters of Leviticus are dominated with a concern for sacrifices.	Some of the instructions related to sacrifices are described as "a lasting ordinance for the generations to come" (e.g., Lev. 3:17 NIV).

a. Hebrew (*qdsh*) and Greek (*hagios*) words relating to holiness appear more frequently in the Hebrew Bible and Greek NT (1,147 times) than Hebrew (*'hb* and *hsd*) and Greek (*agapē* and *phileō*) words relating to love (940 times). For more on the importance of holiness, particularly in Leviticus, see Milgrom, *Leviticus*, 8; Balentine, *Torah's Vision of Worship*, 167–72.

b. Milgrom, *Leviticus*, 7.

c. Taking interest on loans is prohibited in Exod. 22:25–27; Lev. 25:35–37; Deut. 23:19–20. Slaves are freed in Exod. 21:1–11; Deut. 15:12–18. Debt is cancelled in Lev. 25:8–55; Deut. 15:1–11. Gleaning is commanded in Lev. 19:9–10; Deut. 24:19–22. Care for immigrants is required in Exod. 22:21; 23:9; Lev. 19:33–34; Deut. 24:17–22. For more on biblical perspectives on immigration, see Carroll R., *Christians at the Border*; Milgrom, "The Alien in Your Midst," 18, 48.

The Relevance of Legal Essentials

While holiness, purity, poverty, the tabernacle, and sacrifices are essential to the law, many Christians struggle with how at least some of these concerns relate to them today.[15] Before concluding this chapter, it's worth reflecting on the relevance of these topics to the contemporary church.

Holiness

As mentioned in the last chapter, the word *holy* describes who God is, what belongs to God, and who God's people should be. It relates closely to purity, completeness, integrity, unity, and perfection. What is holy is set apart from the world.

In our present age, the church has much to learn about the importance of being distinct from the rest of society, set apart for God's purposes, no matter how unpopular it may be.[16] We have entered a secular age, a time when people embrace a practical atheism. They are perfectly happy going through most of their lives as though God doesn't exist. The church, however, embodies an alternate set of practices. We stand against the rampant forces of greed, lust, violence, gluttony, and individualism in our culture. We offer sanctuary to those whom society rejects. We prefer a narrow and difficult

15. As mentioned above, the Ten Commandments are also essential to the Torah. For useful resources connecting the Ten Commandments with our own day, see Hauerwas and Willimon, *Truth about God*; Harrelson, *Ten Commandments for Today*; Miller, *Ten Commandments*; Brueggemann, *Covenanted Self*.

16. On this topic, see Hauerwas and Willimon, *Resident Aliens*.

passageway that leads to life, rather than a broad and wide path that leads only to destruction.

Retraining Disgust

As shown above, at the heart of many Old Testament regulations is a concern for the emotion of disgust. How can the church retain a focus on this emotion even as it recognizes changing times and seasons?

Today our society has a tendency to avoid particular emotions whenever possible. In particular, it's reluctant to express emotions involving some type of negative judgment about the world around us, such as *anger* (negative judgment: an injustice has occurred), *sadness* (negative judgment: a loss has occurred), or *fear* (negative judgment: we are threatened).

However, Old Testament scholar Christine Roy Yoder points out that, for the most part, the Bible doesn't instruct people to avoid particular emotions. Instead, it sees experiences like anger, sadness, and fear as natural feelings that happen in the course of life's events. The Bible's concern is that our emotions are *directed at the right things*. Thus hatred can be immensely problematic in many cases. Yet it's good to hate things like evil, deceit, and unjust gain (Ps. 97:10; Prov. 14:17; 15:27; 28:16; Rom. 12:9).[17]

Yoder's point makes especially good sense of the basic emotion of disgust. The Bible is quite concerned that this emotion is directed toward the right things. Thus the Israelites leave the wilderness and enter a land whose inhabitants do not see idolatry or child sacrifice as repulsive. Deuteronomy describes such practices as "an abomination," instructing its audience to be disgusted by them:

> Do not bring an abhorrent thing [an idol] into your house. . . . You must utterly detest and abhor it. (7:26 NRSV)[18]

In the New Testament, both Jesus and Paul work to reshape assumptions of their day about what is disgusting. Thus, for Jesus, prostitutes aren't revolting (Matt. 21:31–32), but rather hypocritical religious leaders. He describes such leaders with nauseating terms, saying they are "like whitewashed tombs, which on the outside look beautiful, but inside . . . are full of the bones of the dead and of all kinds of filth" (Matt. 23:27 NRSV).[19]

17. C. Yoder, "Shape and Shaping of Emotion"; C. Yoder, "Objects of Our Affections."
18. See also Deut. 7:25; 12:31; 13:14–15; 17:4; 18:9, 12; 20:18; 27:15; 32:16.
19. For more on how Jesus interacted with purity concerns of his day, see Kazen, *Jesus and Purity.*

Meanwhile, Paul spends a great deal of time teaching that uncircumcised gentiles should not be seen as disgusting. He targets that emotion on the Christians who demand circumcision, whom he calls "dogs" and "mutilators of the flesh" (Phil. 3:2 NIV).[20]

The church today can follow the biblical precedent of recrafting our conceptions of disgust. Such an endeavor isn't easy. It's only through repeated, community-based activities (like worship) that emotions start to shift. Furthermore, disgust is a difficult emotion to get right. On the one hand, we need to reject forms of disgust that lead to social exclusion like racism.[21] On the other hand, our moral life may be easier if we direct disgust toward things opposed to God. For example, we should feel disgusted by pornography. Similarly, a recovering drug addict may need to develop a healthy level of disgust toward drug culture and those who flaunt their drug use. We can also follow biblical precedents of feeling disgust toward some types of food, directing this emotion toward groceries that are harmful to our bodies and God's creation.[22]

Poverty

Today, people sometimes view the poor with extreme negativity, assuming that they are lazy individuals who feel entitled to financial assistance (like food stamps) that they never earned. The Torah has a very different perspective on poverty. It urges readers to have compassion on the poor and care for them. Some biblical interpreters speak about "God's preferential option for the poor," which essentially means that God levels the playing field, favoring the poor, the oppressed, and the powerless because of their great need and disadvantages.[23] Legal codes suggest that just as the Egyptians suffered for oppressing the impoverished Israelites, so the Israelites will suffer if they act like the Egyptians (Exod. 22:21–24).[24]

In continuity with the Old Testament, Jesus links salvation to how one treats the poor. When a young man asks Jesus what he needs to do to receive eternal life, Jesus tells him to sell all he has and give it to the poor (Matt. 19:16–30; Mark 10:17–31; Luke 18:18–30). When Jesus describes judgment at the end

---

20. See also the verses that follow, where he describes reasons for being confident in the flesh as *skybalon* (3:8). The NRSV translates this word as "rubbish," but it can refer to "human excrement" (*BDAG* 932).

21. On the problems of disgust, see Beck, *Unclean*.

22. See Berry, "Pleasures of Eating"; also in *What Are People For?*, 123–25. For a longer treatment, see *Bringing It to the Table*.

23. Magallanes, "Preferential Option for the Poor."

24. Another vulnerable group in the OT is immigrants, and texts like Exod. 22:21 protect them. See also Carroll R., *Christians at the Border*; Milgrom, "The Alien in Your Midst," 18, 48.

of time, the single most important issue is how people treat those in need: the hungry, the thirsty, the stranger, the naked, the sick, the prisoner—"the least of these" (Matt. 25:31–46, esp. 40).[25]

Sometimes Christians try to excuse a lack of concern for the poor by Jesus's remark that "the poor you will always have with you" (Matt. 26:11 NIV; Mark 14:7; John 12:8). However, Jesus is here paraphrasing Old Testament law that encourages generosity. In Deuteronomy 15:11, God says: "Since *there will never cease to be some in need on the earth*, I therefore command you, 'Open your hand to the poor and needy neighbor in your land'" (NRSV, italics added).

This verse is part of a larger text that commands God's people to do some remarkable things. People should forgive their neighbors' debts every seventh year (Deut. 15:1). The text sets as the ideal that no one is in need (15:4), even as it's realistic about the enduring nature of poverty. The text continues:

> If there is among you anyone in need . . . , do not be hard-hearted or tight-fisted toward your needy neighbor. You should rather open your hand, willingly lending enough to meet the need, whatever it may be. Be careful that you do not entertain a mean thought . . . ; your neighbor might cry to the LORD against you, and you would incur guilt. Give liberally and be ungrudging when you do so, for on this account the LORD your God will bless you in all your work and in all that you undertake. (Deut. 15:7–10 NRSV)

The Old and New Testaments thus join in one chorus, singing that few things are more important than sharing possessions and caring for the poor.[26] This music, of course, clashes horribly with the jingles sung by modern society, which encourage greed, hoarding, and spending all we earn and then some on ourselves.

Tabernacle

Another key theme of the Torah is the *tabernacle*. It was Israel's portable sanctuary, used for sacrifice, worship, and housing the ark of the covenant.

---

25. Some interpreters connect "the least of these" with early missionaries who take on poverty for Jesus's sake (cf. Matt. 10:40–42; Hare, *Matthew*, 290). While early missionaries may be a subset of "the least of these," Jesus's language describes the poor in general.

26. On NT teachings about poverty (and wealth), see Matt. 5:3; 6:19–34; 11:5; 13:22; Mark 4:19; 12:38–44; Luke 6:20; 14:12–24; 16:13, 19–31; 19:8–9; 20:46–21:4; Acts 4:32; Gal. 2:10; James 1:27; 2:2–6; 5:1–5; cf. Rom. 15:26; 1 Cor. 11:17–22; 16:3; 2 Cor. 8:2. As Hoppe (*No Poor among You*, 143–65, esp. 164) puts it, "Despite the apocalyptic thrust of much of the New Testament, it does not suggest that poverty can be ignored or that its existence must be fatalistically accepted. Responding to Jesus' calls to repentance enables the disciples to hear the call for justice that comes from ancient Israel's prophetic tradition. It impels the disciples to sell what they have in order to give to the poor."

It's associated with the time from Moses to David. Solomon constructed a more permanent *temple* that closely resembled the tabernacle but stayed in one place.

Texts describing the tabernacle seem somewhat strange to many Western Protestants. Whereas Judaism, the Roman Catholic Church, the Eastern Orthodox Church, and Islam all see physical places as sacred, Western Protestants have tended not to do so. We have assumed that religion belongs to an alternate "spiritual" realm. We have stressed that our bodies are temples of the Holy Spirit and tended to view church buildings as mere gathering places. We have maintained that God is everywhere, failing to appreciate the biblical idea that sometimes God likes to show up in particular locations.

Parts of the Bible describing the tabernacle and temple suggest that we need to reflect on the theological importance of space. Buildings and structures communicate in powerful ways.[27]

Think for a moment about the mall in Washington, DC. Marble buildings and structures tower all around it. Near the center, the Washington Monument soars toward the heavens, with the Capitol, White House, and Lincoln Memorial each facing it from different directions. Dominating the landscape are neoclassical buildings like those from ancient Rome. Along the sides of the mall, one finds the Smithsonian Museums. Other monuments fill the surrounding and nearby landscape, such as the Vietnam War, Korean War, World War II, Roosevelt, and Jefferson Memorials.

These monuments, buildings, and structures inspire awe. They communicate that what happens in Washington has enormous significance. They suggest that the United States is a place that will endure for centuries. Visitors frequently experience a sense of wonder and patriotism. The structures remind Americans of their country's past while also giving them clues about what's valued in the future: courage, equality, and sacrifice.

The tabernacle and temple similarly communicated what really matters to the people of God. The construction of these buildings mirrored the creation of the world.[28] In the words of Jon Levenson, "The Temple represents the victory of God." It was the "moral center" of the world.[29] The tabernacle and temple suggested that God is nearby, eternal, precious, majestic, worthy of praise, and clothed in splendor.

Readers today can learn important things from biblical texts that show the tabernacle as adorned with color and covered with gold, silver, and copper.

27. For an example of work on this topic, see Dickinson, Blair, and Ott, *Places of Public Memory*.

28. See Balentine, *Torah's Vision of Worship*, 136–41.

29. Levenson, *Creation and the Persistence of Evil*, pt. 2, esp. 142–45, 172.

Haggai

The book of Haggai receives virtually no attention by preachers today. Yet few texts could be better for preaching during building campaigns. The prophet Haggai lived in a time when God's temple was in ruins and the people were slow to rebuild it. Haggai brought a short but powerful message to the people:

> Is it a time for you yourselves to live in your paneled houses, while [God's] house lies in ruins? Now therefore thus says the Lord of hosts: Consider how you have fared. You have sown much, and harvested little; you eat, but you never have enough; you drink, but you never have your fill; you clothe yourselves, but no one is warm; and you that earn wages earn wages to put them into a bag with holes. (Hag. 1:4–6 NRSV)

The people respond to Haggai with obedience. The temple is promptly rebuilt. What would happen if Christians today would respond similarly, rebuilding their churches and making them exciting, hospitable places where people can begin to imagine the wonders of our God?

After all, what Christians do every Sunday morning is more important than anything Congress has ever done. The nations are, as Isaiah tells us, a mere "drop in a bucket" (40:15, 17). When we gather around God's holy Word, we join in a practice thousands of years older than the United States.

Perhaps it's time that our church buildings reflect, if only in part, the majesty of our God. In particular, we can ask ourselves if new church buildings should be as bland as gymnasiums. We can ask if we are faithful when we spend thousands of dollars to renovate our homes while churches grow increasingly dilapidated. Run-down church buildings communicate to people that our faith is outdated, irrelevant, and obsolete. They suggest that what goes on inside the church merits as much attention as a dented folding chair. (See "Haggai.")

While there are differences between churches today and the tabernacle and temple of ancient Israel (like animal sacrifices), we nevertheless have much to learn about God's presence and sacred space by opening the pages of the Bible describing God's house.[30] The wonder and majesty of the tabernacle and temple are recurrent themes in the Old Testament, even beyond the Torah. Consider these psalms:

30. For more on sacred space in the OT, see Carvalho, "Finding a Treasure Map"; George, *Israel's Tabernacle as Social Space*; Sommer, *Bodies of God*, chaps. 4–5. On sacred space in the contemporary world, see Giles, *Re-pitching the Tent*; Rose, *Ugly as Sin*; cf. Jacobsen, *Space Between*.

> I love the beauty of your house, LORD;
>> I love the place where your glory resides. (Ps. 26:8)

> I have asked one thing from the LORD—
> it's all I seek—
>> to live in the LORD's house all the days of my life,
>> seeing the LORD's beauty
>> and constantly adoring his temple. (Ps. 27:4)

> I rejoiced with those who said to me,
>> "Let's go to the LORD's house!" (Ps. 122:1)

In the Old Testament, God's house befits the King of glory. It is a place of beauty that inspires worship.

Sacrifice

After a lengthy description of the tabernacle at the end of Exodus, Leviticus opens with a discussion of sacrifice. At first glance, the Bible's sacrificial system looks incredibly strange. It's something that today we associate with bizarre cults. Churchgoers would be horrified if their pastors started killing pigeons on altars to atone for unintentional sins. Yet, Leviticus 5 talks casually about such practices, as if they're commonplace. What's going on with these practices, and what theological insights might they hold for us today?

At the heart of many biblical sacrifices is the idea of fellowship with God.[31] (See "The Purposes of Sacrifice.") When you brought an animal for sacrifice, parts of the animal (sometimes all of it) were consumed by the fire. The idea was that God was present with you, eating the animal and enjoying the delicious smells (Lev. 21:6; Num. 28:2). Nowadays people often see sharing a meal together as a key to expressing friendship. The idea in the Old Testament was that through sacrifice, you became closer to God. In fact, sacrifices like the peace offering were community events—barbecues, if you will. God, the priests, and those who brought the offering (probably

---

31. Scholars debate the extent to which each element of a given sacrifice communicated something symbolically. They also disagree about whether symbolic interpretations of particular sacrifices were consistent among different groups across time. As Watts (*Ritual and Rhetoric*, 8) warns, "The power of a ritual for its participants may not necessarily depend on its symbolic interpretation, or at least on the participants' agreement on any one symbolic interpretation." While there's some reason for caution, it's also possible to discern why, within many biblical texts, sacrifices were made. For example, Abraham nearly sacrificed Isaac as an act of obedience (Gen. 22). On OT sacrifice, see Gorman, "Sacrifices and Offerings."

an extended family) had a worshipful celebration together as they all ate in one another's presence.[32]

Animal sacrifice no longer takes place in Judaism or Christianity. Such practices eventually died out after the Romans destroyed the Jerusalem temple in 70 CE. Nevertheless, both Jews and Christians celebrate times when they come together for feasts and understand God to be present among them. The feast of the Passover, the celebration of the Last Supper—perhaps even church potlucks—are important biblical practices. (See "Sacrifice and Communion.") Particularly in a society running on electronic communication and social media, people miss face-to-face contact.[33] When we share food together, however, we join in an age-old practice that builds community, overcomes loneliness, and celebrates God's presence among us.

Sacrifice is an important part of Old Testament ritual. People sometimes look at rituals with contempt, seeing them as empty practices that involve going through motions regardless of where our hearts actually are. While the Bible is aware that rituals can be abused (see Isa. 1:10–17; Hosea 6:6), it also emphasizes their importance. Biblical scholar Samuel Balentine gets at this idea:

> In short, rituals are never merely formal actions, offered simply for the sake of the acts themselves. They are a means of "world construction," a means of enacting, maintaining, and where necessary re-creating the world of God's design. . . .

The Purposes of Sacrifice

While I have chosen to emphasize how sacrifice brings people into fellowship with God, the Bible makes clear that other purposes also exist. People would make sacrifices in order to:

- show obedience or commitment to God,
- remember their dependence on God,
- mark their status and identity,
- give thanks,
- try to secure a blessing or desired answer to prayer,
- fulfill vows,
- cleanse themselves from impurities or sins,
- reinforce the tabernacle's or temple's sacredness, and
- turn away God's anger.

---

32. Klawans ("Ritual Purity, Moral Purity," esp. 26) criticizes those who read sacrificial regulations unsympathetically, pointing out, "The slaughterhouse is surely no more of a welcome place for an animal than an ancient temple. . . . Moreover, anyone familiar with the ways in which animal deaths are routinized in laboratories, hospitals, and biology classrooms can recognize that even if ritual sacrifice were entirely eliminated, one could certainly still question whether modernity has brought any improvements at all to the lives of animals."

33. On this topic, see Locke, *De-voicing of Society*; or more recently, Turkle, *Alone Together*.

In ritual activity, persons take a concrete stand in the world, and by engaging in very specific "flesh and blood" acts, they engage *mind and body* in a drama of teaching and learning.[34]

The value of ritual is also underscored by Evan Imber-Black and Janine Roberts:

> As you look at rituals in your life, you will find that they function in your individual development and in your interactions with others to enable *relating*, *changing*, *healing*, *believing*, and *celebrating*, which are, in fact, major themes in all human existence.[35]

Sacrifice and Communion

"Although animal sacrifices may appear primitive to some people today, it is important to remember that most of Israelite worship consisted of this sanctified meal. To be sure, sometimes the only one 'eating' was God (in the case of the whole burnt offering), but the food metaphor remained. 'Communion'—that is, encountering God—meant meeting God at the table. To lose sight of this means losing sight of the many images of sacrifice found in the New Testament—images that lie at the heart of the Eucharist, our sanctified meal with the Triune God."

Corrine L. Carvalho,
"Finding a Treasure Map," 128

Conclusion

For some, becoming friends with the Old Testament sounds like becoming friends with a legalistic do-gooder who knows little grace, who follows lists and lists of rules, and who takes everything much too seriously. It's more appropriate to think of the Old Testament as a law professor, who has extensive knowledge of different laws, rules, and customs in different places and times in Israel's history.

By spending time with this professor, we learn some interesting things. We encounter issues that beckon for serious theological reflection—matters like holiness, poverty, disgust, food, sacred space, and sacrifice. It would be easy for the church to overlook these issues, dismissing them as figments of an outdated religion. However, this law professor reminds us that God's law is alive and dynamic, changing as the living God interacts with the different needs of God's people. Carefully studying these Scriptures not only shows us similarities between biblical and modern culture; it also shows us what is most important to God and God's people, so that we might remain faithful even in a time much different from ancient Israel.

34. Balentine, *Torah's Vision of Worship*, 75–76.
35. Imber-Black and Roberts, *Rituals for Our Times*, 28. For more on how Christian worship draws on Old Testament and other Jewish ideas, see Beckwith, "Jewish Background," 68–80. For more on the importance of ritual, see Hogue, *Remembering the Future*, 116–52; Anderson and Foley, *Mighty Stories*.

For Further Study

Balentine, Samuel E. *The Torah's Vision of Worship*. Overtures to Biblical Theology. Minneapolis: Fortress, 1999.

This excellent study covers many of the topics above, but in greater depth. After reconstructing the Torah's historical background, the author argues that the Torah offers a transformative vision of worship that entails living in harmony with God's cosmic design.

Bechtel, Carol M., ed. *Touching the Altar: The Old Testament for Christian Worship*. Grand Rapids: Eerdmans, 2008.

This collection of essays provides several ways of connecting the Old Testament with worship today. For example, the article by Carvalho provides a studied account of how texts about the temple can illuminate our understanding of sacred space today.

Beck, Richard. *Unclean: Meditations on Purity, Hospitality, and Mortality*. Eugene, OR: Cascade, 2011.

This book provides excellent insights into the tension between purity and love throughout the Bible, drawing on a range of disciplines and offering useful wisdom about the role of disgust in the church today.

Douglas, Mary. *Leviticus as Literature*. Oxford: Oxford University Press, 1999.

For decades, Douglas used anthropological insight to study Leviticus, having a profound impact on biblical studies. This work represents one of her last and most comprehensive analyses.

Milgrom, Jacob. *Leviticus: A Book of Ritual and Ethics*. A Continental Commentary. Minneapolis: Fortress, 2004.

Throughout his career, Milgrom published extensively on the Torah, especially Leviticus. This volume offers a useful portal into the insights of one of the most influential biblical interpreters of the last generation. For those wanting to study his work in greater depth, he also has a three-volume commentary on Leviticus in the Anchor Bible. It's over 2,700 pages long.

Commentaries published by Abingdon, Baker Academic, Brazos, Eerdmans, Fortress, InterVarsity, Smyth & Helwys, Nelson, T&T Clark, Westminster John Knox, and university presses.

In the course of mentioning the importance of consulting others about perplexing passages (chap. 7), I suggested that readers check out what commentaries have to say. The publishers listed above frequently produce solid commentaries. While this list isn't exhaustive, it does begin to point readers in the right direction. Meanwhile, here are some useful study Bibles: *CEB Study Bible* (2013), *The New Oxford Annotated Bible* (4th ed., 2010), *The HarperCollins Study Bible* (rev., 2006), and *The New Interpreter's Study Bible* (rev., 2003).

The website www.MatthewSchlimm.com has additional resources, including group discussion questions.

9

Truth Is Many Sided

DOES THE OLD TESTAMENT CONTRADICT ITSELF?
How we answer this question matters deeply to the life of faith.
Many people have been driven to atheism by apparent contradictions in the biblical text.[1] Others have wanted to claim that the Bible is contradiction-free, but they have felt doubt gnawing away at their faith.

In this chapter I look at Old Testament texts that appear, at least initially, to exhibit some contradiction. There are many sorts of tension within the Bible. Sometimes these tensions pertain to small details, like the number of warriors David had (cf. 2 Sam. 24:9 and 1 Chron. 21:5). I don't see these inconsistencies as especially significant because good doctrine is never based on a single detail in Scripture. Biblical writers were not interested in the scientific precision that has become an idol today.[2]

There are, however, much bigger theological and ethical tensions in the Old Testament. Below, I suggest that these tensions within Scripture, and the many questions that confront us, may actually be very good things. (See "Greater Mystery.") Using three analogies from my own life, I talk about the complexity of Old Testament truth. This truth, I argue, is more like a conversation than a sales pitch. It's more like a work of art than a math equation. It's more like a tailor-made suit than a one-size-fits-all hospital gown. The Bible

1. Cf. Zuckerman, *Faith No More*, 33–39.
2. On tensions in the Bible, particularly how it "provides multiple witnesses to the same event," see Mark S. Smith, *Memoirs of God*, 162–68, esp. 164.

Greater Mystery

"As it was for Job, knowing God will immerse you in greater mystery, not solve the mysteries for you."

Jonathan Martin, Twitter, March 18, 2013

"It is better to limp along" reading the Bible "than to dash with all speed outside it."

John Calvin, *Institutes* 1.6.3 (trans. Battles)

"God's thoughts and works are characteristically vast, and maybe that is the best explanation for why the poetics of Scripture are habitually difficult: the biblical writers are inspired to mimic the Reality to which they witness. So instead of setting out straightforward moral lessons, they put their readers to work, confusing and unsettling us, raising questions where we might previously have imagined there was clarity. If we stick with these texts, submitting ourselves to the work the Holy Spirit is doing through them even now, in the midst of our own fresh difficulties, then in the end they may well complicate our thinking in useful ways—useful, at least, if the goal is to think more like God."

Ellen F. Davis, "Poetics of Generosity," 630

---

reflects the messy realities of our world, avoiding the sterile environments of scientific laboratories.

Sales Pitches versus Conversations

A couple of years ago, I was part of a task force at the university where I teach. We researched the technological needs of our school and how we could best meet those needs. At one point, we invited sales reps to campus to tell us how they could bolster our resources.

They began by telling us about all the wonderful things their products could do. After their spiels, we asked questions.

At certain moments with certain reps, it felt like they were physically incapable of answering candidly. Rather than being honest and naming the shortcomings of their products, they talked around the shortcomings. Instead of telling us what features they lacked, they just kept emphasizing the features they offered.

I left the meeting feeling like I had just spent time with a corrupt politician. I didn't want anything to do with their products because I felt as though I had been lied to. If they hadn't intentionally misled me, they certainly refused to be fully honest. They didn't give me the whole truth.

Sacred Conversation

"Scripture itself reflects and invites a sacred conversation between believers and God, and between believers and one another."

Karl Allen Kuhn, *Words with God*, 15

"There is not one voice in Scripture, and to give any one voice in Scripture or in tradition authority to silence other voices surely distorts the text and misconstrues the liveliness that the text itself engenders in the interpretive community."

Walter Brueggemann, in Brueggemann, Placher, and Blount, *Struggling*, 16

The Old Testament as a Friend We Love to Talk With

The Old Testament refuses to act like a half-honest sales rep. It doesn't give readers just one perspective. It shows things in different lights and from different angles. It doesn't present every viewpoint under the sun, but it does recognize the complexity of truth.[3]

In high school, I loved few things more than going to a coffee shop with close friends. We drank our mochas and, under the wonderful stimulation of espressos combined with frothy milk and hot chocolate, we had the deepest and most profound discussions of our lives. (At least they felt that way at the time.) We talked about why we were on earth. We talked about God. We talked about evil. Insight built upon insight. We challenged one another. We drew on one another's thoughts. Even when we disagreed and argued, we brought one another to deeper understandings of our world. We never would have reached such rich perspectives had we been sitting by ourselves. We needed one another. We needed conversation to reach enlightenment.

When readers engage the Old Testament as a whole, it's much more like joining a conversation than listening to a sales pitch. (See "Sacred Conversation.") As we bring together different passages, we arrive at complex truths about God, our world, one another, and ourselves. We begin to see how people can be *both* made in the image of God *and* sinful. We begin to understand why we should do the right thing *even though* it involves great personal sacrifice. We start to figure out how God can love us relentlessly *and* still grow angry over sin. The Old Testament is a friend who holds many diverse perspectives together in artful tension.

---

3. As elsewhere in this book, I here personify the OT, speaking of it in terms of a human who sees truth as complex. Others have suggested that the Holy Spirit, guiding what texts were included in the canon, helped the church to preserve the complexity of truth (Middleton and Walsh, *Truth Is Stranger*, 180; cf. Newsom, "Bakhtin, the Bible," esp. 297).

Example: Blessings and Curses

The Bible's diverse perspectives appear in many places.[4] Consider, for example, what the Old Testament says about rewards for faithful behavior in this life. Exodus, Leviticus, and Deuteronomy seem to make things perfectly clear: obey God, and blessings will follow. Disobey God, and hardship awaits.[5] Readers are often shocked at how vividly the Bible connects people's behaviors with what happens to them.

For example, Deuteronomy 28 begins, "Now if you really obey the LORD your God's voice . . . , then the LORD your God will set you high above all nations on earth." In the next dozen verses, the text concretely describes blessing after blessing—all pertaining to goodness in the here and now. Obedient people will have huge families. The land will be fertile. The economy will be booming. Enemies will flee like water dashed against rock. Other nations will be in awe of Israel. The chapter continues: "The LORD will open up for you his own well-stocked storehouse, the heavens, providing your land with rain at just the right time and blessing all your work" (Deut. 28:12).

> **A Fairer Day**
>
> Both the Old and New Testaments are aware that people don't always get what they deserve in this life. Together, they look toward a time when the moral order of the world will be set aright, when the innocent will suffer no longer and the wicked will get what they deserve (Jer. 31:29–30; Ezek. 18:1–32; Matt. 13:24–43).

It's not long, however, before the text turns to the consequences of disobedience: instead of abundant blessings, curses are everywhere. Neither people nor land has any fertility. Disobey God, and here's what will be next: "The LORD will send calamity, confusion, and frustration on you no matter what work you are doing until you are wiped out and until you disappear—it'll be quick! . . . The sky over your head will be as hard as bronze; the earth under your feet will be like iron. The LORD will turn the rain on your land into dust. Only dirt will fall down on you from the sky until you are completely wiped out" (Deut. 28:20, 23–24). As the chapter continues, the curses grow worse. The nations will not be in awe of Israel: they will be horrified at Israel. Illness of every type will strike. The people will be scattered across the world. The chapter ends by saying that the people will try to sell themselves into slavery, "but no one will want to buy you" (28:68). What could be worse?

---

4. See Goldingay, *Theological Diversity*, esp. 1–12.
5. See Exod. 23:20–32; Lev. 26; Deut. 27–28. Many prophetic works operate with similar logic (e.g., Amos 4:6).

The rhetoric of these texts is so powerful and unyielding that one could easily assume everything is settled and done. Obey God, and you'll receive blessings. Disobey God, and you'll receive curses.

Yet there are other Old Testament texts that present things in a very different light. Consider, for example, the book of Job. While some of Job's friends have perspectives like those found in Deuteronomy, the book as a whole, especially with its prologue, epilogue, and Job's speeches, tells readers that sometimes the innocent suffer even though they have done nothing wrong.[6]

The author of Ecclesiastes makes a similar point: "The righteous get what the wicked deserve, and the wicked get what the righteous deserve. I say that this too is pointless" (Eccles. 8:14).[7]

Other texts similarly emphasize that life isn't always fair. When punishment comes for sin, it's often delayed or incommensurate with the offenses. Psalm 73 makes clear that even if wickedness eventually catches up with people, it doesn't always do so immediately. (See "A Fairer Day.") Sometimes, the righteous suffer alongside the guilty (Ezek. 21:1–5). Other times, the guilty suffer more than they should for their sins (Isa. 40:2).

> ### A Compelling Bill of Goods
>
> "The appeal of prosperity theology is obvious. The faith movement sells a compelling bill of goods: God, wealth, and a healthy body to enjoy it. But it is the enjoyment, the feelings that lift believers' chins and square their shoulders, that is its fundamental achievement. The first step in accessing this good news is the belief that things *can* get better. The prosperity gospel's chief allure is simple optimism."
>
> Kate Bowler, *Blessed*, 232

Which set of texts is right? Do people get what's coming to them, as books like Deuteronomy emphasize? Or do the righteous suffer while the wicked prosper, as many other texts suggest?

The Bible doesn't give us just one answer. It refuses to say that things are just one way. It avoids the sales rep's technique of offering just one perspective. While it's possible to see the Old Testament's teachings on this topic as contradictory, it's also possible to see them as an ongoing dialogue about complex truths.

When taken as a whole, the Old Testament doesn't see truth as singular: either *A* or *B* is true. It instead sees truth as plural: both *A* and *B* have truth. It's not that the Old Testament thinks all truth is relative or that every opinion ever expressed is equally valid. Rather, the Old Testament refuses to present just one viewpoint and insist that this one viewpoint will work for everyone

6. Pope, *Job*, lxxvii–lxxix.
7. Interestingly, Eccles. 8:12b–13 gets closer to Deuteronomic thinking, though it's undermined by 8:10–12a.

in every circumstance. It instead offers several voices that together form a rich conversation about the complicated world we inhabit.

Unfortunately, a number of people have failed to see the Bible as a conversation about the results of obedience and disobedience. A powerful movement in America, sometimes called prosperity theology or the health-and-wealth gospel, has amplified some parts of the Bible while muting others. It emphasizes texts about psychological, physical, and material blessings following obedience to God—but it neglects texts that qualify these teachings in important ways. The sad result is a religious system that, at its worst, cherishes happiness, comfort, and worldly wealth—idolizing self-importance and money. At times it's little more than optimism walking around in Christian clothing.[8] (See "A Compelling Bill of Goods.")

Prosperity theology doesn't get everything wrong. There really *are* blessings that come in this life as a result of faith. (Friendship with other believers is a good example.) The problem is that this movement doesn't reflect the Bible's many perspectives on this topic. In a fallen world, right actions don't always translate into blessings.

Insulting God

"Preaching pie in the sky when you die is an insult to God."

Desmond Tutu,
God Is Not a Christian, 124–25

Some Christians have gone to the other extreme, losing sight of blessings in this life altogether. Sometimes called pie-in-the-sky theology, this way of thinking focuses on good things in heaven, rather than expecting much good to happen in the here and now. Put crudely, the basic sentiment is, "You'll get your pie in the sky (in heaven) even if you go hungry on earth now."[9] (See "Insulting God.") In its worst forms, this thinking

---

8. As Bowler (*Blessed*, 7–8, 125–27) points out, there's both a "hard" prosperity gospel that emphasizes worldly wealth and a "soft" prosperity gospel that emphasizes other sorts of benefits like psychological well-being. The latter can be seen, e.g., in Bruce Wilkinson's extremely popular *Prayer of Jabez*, which explicitly denounces those who expect God to give them luxury items, but then talks about tapping into "God's plenty" by using "the little prayer with the giant prize" (17–18). The soft (and even the hard) prosperity gospel is also seen in Joel Osteen's writing and preaching. He asserts, for example, that people who follow his steps "ultimately will be happier than ever before, living with joy, peace, and enthusiasm—not just for a day, or a week, but for the rest of your life!" (*Your Best Life Now*, viii).

9. The phrase "pie in the sky" is used in a parody of the hymn "Sweet Bye and Bye," which offered a harsh critique of preachers who wanted to save souls without feeding stomachs (J. Hill, "The Preacher and the Slave," in *Songs of Work and Protest*, 155–57, esp. 156):

Long-haired preachers come out ev'ry night,
Try to tell you what's wrong and what's right,
But when asked about something to eat,
They will answer with voices so sweet:
You will eat (you will eat), bye and bye (bye and bye),

Living with Tension

"Let the tensions stand. However acute the tension between two different [passages] may appear, it must not be resolved through exegetical distortion of the texts. The individual witnesses must be allowed their own voices."

Richard Hays, *Moral Vision*, 190

"Let the apparent tensions and inconsistencies in scripture stand as they are. God is not shaken from heaven. Christ is not stripped of authority. The gates of hell do not prevail against the church. The Bible, understood as what it actually is, still speaks to us with a divine authority. . . . If God did not feel the need to provide us, his church, with a fully harmonized version of biblical accounts, then we ought not to feel the need to impose one ourselves."

Christian Smith, *Bible Made Impossible*, 134

---

reduces Christianity to an otherworldly religion that someone like Abraham or Moses never would have recognized. It offers victims of oppression a mental escape but little more. It falls short of saying positive things about the blessings of Christianity in the here and now.

The Bible, on the other hand, refuses to take a one-sided approach to this-worldly blessings of our faith. It doesn't fully accept the prosperity gospel, just as it doesn't fully accept pie-in-the-sky theology. Instead, it gives readers many perspectives, pointing them to how complex the world really is. Reading the Bible faithfully means doing justice to its many points of view.[10] (See "Living with Tension.")

Math Problems versus Artwork

In addition to thinking about sales pitches and conversations, it's useful to think about basic mathematics in comparison with works of art. Growing up, I always loved mathematics. I come from a long line of engineers. One of my favorite high school subjects was calculus. I never did very well with sports, but "Mathlete" competitions were a different story.

In that glorious land in the sky (way up high).
Work and pray (work and pray), live on hay (live on hay),
You'll get pie in the sky when you die (that's a lie!).

10. Several works of biblical theology helpfully move in the direction of doing justice to the Bible's many perspectives. Preeminent among them is Crenshaw, *Defending God*, which deals with the wide variety of perspectives on suffering that the OT offers, rather than trying to collapse many viewpoints into one artificial system.

Figure 5. Detroit Industry, South Wall (Bottom-Right Portion). Diego Rivera, "South Wall of a Mural Depicting Detroit Industry, 1932–33 (Fresco)," *Bridgeman*, http://tinyurl.com/chb43lj.

I failed to appreciate literature. I loved the following "Deep Thought," by Jack Handey of *Saturday Night Live*: "Whenever you read a good book, it's like the author is right there, in the room, talking to you, which is why I don't like to read good books."[11] Stories and art seemed like fine pastimes for some people, but for the most part I didn't really see the point. I had many hobbies: canoeing, fishing, video games, watching sports, spending time with friends, and listening to music. Reading literature wasn't one of them.

I loved the realm of numbers, where things always made sense. Time after time, you could pinpoint the right answer. You could plug your initial answer back into the equation to make sure you were correct. There's a cleanliness to mathematics that I deeply appreciated, an assurance that things worked the way they should. I could complete a math problem and set it aside, knowing I did it right. It was completely unlike writing an essay, where it was never clear whether I had given a sufficient answer.

While in high school, I also took classes in Spanish. Along the way, we broke from studying Spanish to look at the great Spanish-speaking artists. It was there that I first experienced the artwork of Diego Rivera. Working in the middle of the twentieth century, Rivera created enormous murals, filled

11. Handey, *Deepest Thoughts*, 3.

with scenes of people working and laboring—typically in service of a wealthy few.

I was blown away by what I saw. I spent my summers shoveling dirt in a greenhouse. And in Rivera's work, I found the truest expression of what physical labor was really all about. For me, he captured part of human nature more vividly than anything else I had ever experienced.

A recurrent theme in Rivera's art is that masses working together could lead to great progress while, at the same time, dehumanize the workers themselves. Thus, in *Detroit Industry, South Wall*, viewers see the incredible nature of mass-producing automobiles, as Rivera depicts a factory with meticulous detail, filling the scene with enormous gears, belts, and pistons. At the same time, viewers also notice that, strikingly, nearly every member of the working class has a downcast or obstructed face: their humanity is hidden, even as they produce superhuman results. Supervisors, meanwhile, have faces that are easy to see. (See figure 5.)

Rivera communicated deep and conflicting truths that both in high school and even today are beyond what I could express with words. He captured the complexity of work: how it's necessary, how we all do it, and how those who work their bodies the hardest often get the least recognition or compensation. I could write at length about these topics, but in one mural, Rivera brings these and other ideas all together, vividly communicating them to viewers who, in a single moment, are confronted with the depth and fullness of the truth that he captures.

The novelist Iris Murdoch writes, "You may know a truth, but if it's at all complicated, you have to be an artist not to utter it as a lie."[12] Her idea is that some truths are very different from the simple truths we encounter in basic mathematics. Some truths are fraught with complexity and tension. And our words rarely do justice to them. (See "Bears and Stars.") As an incredible artist, Rivera artfully communicated a system of work that produced amazing results without giving workers all that they deserved.

The Old Testament as Artist

On the one hand, the Old Testament presents some truths with the certainty we would expect of simple mathematics. God is holy, and we should be

---

Bears and Stars

"Individuals can never state the exact measure of their needs, nor their ideas nor their sorrows; . . . human language is like a cracked kettle on which we beat out rhythms for bears to dance to, when what we want is to bring the stars themselves to tears."

Gustave Flaubert, *Madame Bovary*, 166 (alt. for gender inclusivity)

---

12. Murdoch, *Accidental Man*, 111.

too. This idea doesn't change. It's as reliable as π × (*radius of circle*)² = *area of circle.*

But on many topics, the Old Testament is less like a high school math teacher and more like a great artist. It captures truths that are far more complicated than any math equation.

Example: A King in Israel

Take, for instance, how the Old Testament presents the monarchy in ancient Israel. Most characters in 1 Samuel have conflicted positions about kings in Israel. *Both God and God's prophet Samuel* believe that God alone should rule over Israel—without a human counterpart (8:6–8; 10:18–19). However, after the people insist on having a king, God changes plans, allowing them to have one (8:9, 22). In fact, God plays an active role to ensure that Saul—and no one else—becomes Israel's first monarch (1 Sam. 9–10). Meanwhile, Samuel serves as God's instrument to install Saul as king (8:10–18; 10:1, 20–25; 11:14–15). Just a few chapters later, however, Samuel announces that God has changed God's mind about making Saul king (15:11, 35)—even though the immediate context says that God doesn't change God's mind (15:29).[13] The text could hardly be more confusing!

The text's taut tensions don't end there. *Saul himself* appears on the scene with no interest in becoming king. He doesn't seize power; he stumbles into the crown (1 Sam. 9–10). Saul doesn't seek the throne; he even hides when Samuel tries to announce that he will rule (10:22). Yet once he has power, Saul stubbornly refuses to let go, even though Samuel and God make clear that Saul's grip is constantly slipping. The man who once had no interest in the monarchy becomes obsessed with killing David, his chief rival to the throne (1 Sam. 16–30).

David, similarly, appears conflicted about the monarchy. Already in 1 Samuel 16, he lets himself be anointed as the next king by Samuel. He constantly forms alliances with Saul's children, positioning himself for power, making covenants with Saul's son Jonathan (18:3; 23:18; cf. 20:17) and marrying Saul's daughter Michal (18:17–30). However, David never opposes Saul directly. David has many chances to eliminate Saul, the only person standing in his way to the throne (chaps. 24; 26). Even when Saul seeks David's life, David never does the same to Saul. David severely scolds those who wish he would do otherwise (24:7).

---

13. Most English translations try to relax the tension between these verses. They tend to have 1 Sam. 15:11, 35 say that God "regretted making Saul king," but then they let 15:29 say that God "doesn't change his mind" (e.g., CEB; see also NRSV, NIV, NASB, NJPS). However, the same Hebrew word lies behind both "regretted" in 15:11, 35 and "change his mind" in 15:29.

Complexity and Truth

"The truth is rarely pure and never simple."

Oscar Wilde, *Importance of Being Earnest*, 258

"The truth about human nature, the world, and God *cannot* be uttered by a single voice but only by a community of unmerged voices, and that is what finds its artistic representation in the form of the [Bible's] Primeval History."

Carol Newsom, "Bakhtin, the Bible," 301

"Identifying the truth is an open-ended task at which we must constantly work along the way."

William Stacy Johnson, "Reading the Scriptures," 113

"The church has always maintained that, in principle, neither revelation nor reason lead to anything like complete knowledge. Much remains mysterious, especially when it comes to theology."[a]

Kenton L. Sparks, *Sacred Word*, 133

a. Cf. Goldingay, *Key Questions*, 72–73, 103.

The people of Israel similarly display tensions about the monarchy. In 1 Samuel 8, they demand a king, despite stern warnings from God and the prophet Samuel. Within a matter of chapters, however, they see their own desire for a monarchy as sinful (12:19).

It would be easy to dismiss 1 Samuel as thoroughly contradictory, especially when one looks at all the tensions as outlined above. Alternatively, it's easy to feel quite frustrated about this text, especially when we want clarity and assurance: Does God stand opposed to things like monarchies, or is God in favor of them? Couldn't God give us a clear-cut, easy-to-understand position that every Christian could adopt as an appropriate stance on human government?

No. With matters like these, the Old Testament doesn't offer the type of certainty that can be found in a field like basic mathematics. The truths that the Bible communicates are infinitely more complex than what high school students tackle in their math homework. (See "Complexity and Truth.")

Readers of 1 and 2 Samuel are given a story, one that takes them from the tumultuous period before the monarchy into the lives of Israel's first two kings. On the one hand, readers learn why a king would be necessary and why God would allow it. On the other hand, they learn why God would oppose a king

---

Agreement and Disagreement

"While there are many matters of which one can give straightforward explanations on which competent authorities can be expected to agree (characteristically, subjects studied by disciplines such as mathematics, geography, and the natural sciences), there are other realities (and questions about what lies behind the concerns of these disciplines), belonging more to the realm of the humanities, where straightforward explanations are rarer and disagreement among competent authorities is more common. What is a human being? What is right? What is the nature of Being? What is ultimate reality? Where is history going? Such questions are complex because the realities that they are seeking to grasp are complex, and it is not surprising if within a document such as the OT a variety of aspects of these complex wholes appears. If there were no tensions in the Bible, one might infer that it was too simple in its understanding of such questions."

John Goldingay, *Theological Diversity*, 14

---

from the outset, permit it only grudgingly, and eventually need to settle on working with very flawed individuals. The story is artfully told, filled with moments of suspense and danger as God works with a broken humanity.[14] Along the way, readers gain a sense of why God would oppose human government: there's something fundamentally wrong with an imperfect human being (which every leader is) having power over other human beings. Readers also learn the necessity of human government, even with all its problems: theocracy (where God is the ruler) quickly degenerates into anarchy (where there's no ruler). Thus 1–2 Samuel is a difficult and conflicted text because human government of any kind, including one that God helps to create, is intrinsically difficult and conflicted. (See "Agreement and Disagreement.")

One-Size-Fits-All versus Tailor-Made

A final metaphor may help us understand the Bible's approach to truth: many of us have had to wear a one-size-fits-all hospital gown. We look like fools in them, we would never wear them in public, and they are notorious for failing to cover our backsides. Yet they have value. Medical workers can easily pass them out to all patients. They don't need to measure or estimate a patient's size, which could waste valuable time in a hospital setting. Furthermore, the gowns are sanitary. They allow nurses and doctors easy access for IV fluids

14. Many works address both the artistry and ambiguities of 1 & 2 Samuel, including Alter, *David Story*; Miscall, *1 Samuel*.

or other injections. They are also thin enough that doctors and nurses can quickly listen to a patient's lungs or heart.

However, things are quite different when we have the pleasure of wearing clothes that fit us exceptionally well. They are neither too tight, causing discomfort, nor too loose, making us swim in their materials. Perhaps our favorite article of clothing is a tailor-made suit or an old, familiar T-shirt. It feels great, and we love putting it on.

These clothes that fit us well wouldn't work on most other people. Those with different builds would look bad in them—if they could put them on at all.

The Old Testament as Garment Maker

If we think of the Old Testament as a garment maker, it's clear that some of its truths can be likened to a one-size-fits-all outfit. We should love God with all we are (Deut. 6:5), and we should love our neighbors as ourselves (Lev. 19:18). These truths apply to everyone. Just as patients need hospital gowns, so Christians need these commandments.

However, it's a mistake to assume that the entire Old Testament functions like a one-size-fits-all hospital gown. Many of the Old Testament's truths are tailor-made. They work for certain people in certain situations. But they do not work for everyone on all occasions.[15] In fact, they may not work for some people at any point during their lives.[16] (See "From Contradiction to Atheism.")

Consider, for example, what's found in Proverbs 26:4–5:

> *Don't answer fools according to their folly,*
>   or you will become like them yourself.
> *Answer fools according to their folly,*
>   or they will deem themselves wise. (italics added)

If we assume that every verse of the Bible offers a one-size-fits-all presentation of truth, then we have a major contradiction on our hands. On the

---

15. As explained by Kort (*"Take, Read,"* chap. 1), Calvin's doctrine of reading Scripture bears great responsibility for the urge to apply individual texts to individuals' lives, though it did have antecedents, for example, in the monastic practice of *lectio divina*, a four-step approach to Bible study that involves reading, meditating, praying, and contemplating.

16. Jenson ("Snakes and Ladders") argues that Deuteronomy's commandments can be organized into three levels: (1) The Shema (Deut. 6:4–5) is the most general and comprehensive, corresponding to the one-size-fits-all category described in this chapter. (2) The Ten Commandments (Deut. 5:6–21) are more specific than the Shema but still not as specific as other commandments. (3) The detailed laws of Deut. 12–26 are the most specific and context-based. They correspond to the tailor-made suit described here.

From Contradiction to Atheism

The well-known atheist Christopher Hitchens talks about how the Bible contains many perspectives. He uses this fact to try to debunk the Bible's value: "Since all of these revelations, many of them hopelessly inconsistent, cannot by definition be simultaneously true, it must follow that some of them are false and illusory."[a]

Hitchens's point works only if we assume that everything the Bible says falls into a one-size-fits-all category of truth. Then, when tensions arise, readers may be driven to rejecting the Bible wholesale. However, if we see parts of the Bible as context-specific—tailored to particular situations—then we do not face the problem Hitchens claims to find.

The real problem here isn't the Bible. It's Hitchens's narrow view of truth.

a. Hitchens, *God Is Not Great*, 97.

---

other hand, it's possible to see these two proverbs as offering different words for different situations. As Peter Enns puts it, "There is more to wisdom than simply reading a *proverb*. One must also have the wisdom to read the *situation*, to know whether a proverb is fitting."[17]

Finding Clothes That Fit

If some texts are more tailored to particular life events, how can we tell which ones fit us and which ones don't? In other words, if we notice a tension between *Text A* and *Text B*, which one should exert the stronger influence on our lives?

The church maintains that God has given us not only the Bible, but also the Holy Spirit, fellow believers, the church's great traditions, and incredible minds.[18] Hopefully, we'll use all of these gifts, along with a healthy dose of humility, to understand the best relationships between the text and our lives.

Granted, we may still get things wrong. People misinterpret the Bible. We mistake our own wishes for the voice of the Holy Spirit. Our friends let us down. The church's traditions are filled with examples of when Christians sinned badly. Our sense of reason, experience, and emotion can easily be used

---

17. Enns, *Inspiration and Incarnation*, 74. This quotation is from a chapter on "The Old Testament and Theological Diversity," a useful supplement to this chapter. See also Prov. 25:11, as well as the discussion of knowing "the right time for a specific word or deed" in Crenshaw, *Old Testament Wisdom*, 10–11.

18. In the Wesleyan tradition, there's a strong emphasis on seeing the Bible as the primary source of theological authority, but also turning to tradition, reason, and experience (see Gunter et al., *Wesley and the Quadrilateral*).

toward selfish ends. While there's no foolproof approach, the following steps can move us in good directions:

First, we can ask, "Are my circumstances more like those in Text A or Text B?" We can investigate what circumstances gave rise to each text. Study Bibles and commentaries are especially useful with this task.[19] We can consider our own situations, asking whether our context is more like the one facing the audience of Text A or Text B. We can thoughtfully connect the most relevant text with our lives, relying on the Holy Spirit and other Christians to guide us. As I indicated in chapter 5, a text like Amos 1, which forbids war crimes, may have more to say to us today than texts like Joshua that commemorate the killing of Canaanites.[20]

Second, we can ask, "Who benefits from favoring one text over another?" If we're reading in ways that benefit only ourselves or our families, we're probably *not* doing a great job of following a God who demands complete allegiance and self-sacrifice. On the other hand, if we're reading the Bible and never sensing any joys or blessings of faith, then we're probably going too far the other direction, missing the whole point of God's love and grace. Reading the Bible should bear good fruit in our lives. If it doesn't, we need to reconsider how we're approaching the Bible.

Third, we can ask, "Even if I should embody the ideas of Text A, what does Text B still have to teach me?" If we claim that the entire Bible is God's Word, then even texts that are less relevant to our particular situations may still have much to teach us. For example, in Hosea, God says:

> For I desire goodness, not sacrifice;
> Obedience to God, rather than burnt offerings. (6:6 NJPS)

Many Christians relate easily to this text. We see Christ as the ultimate sacrifice (Heb. 10:10) and don't believe God wants us to make altars to burn animals to God.

However, we shouldn't entirely dismiss the Old Testament's teachings on sacrifice.[21] As indicated above, they can still connect with our lives in many ways. The Old Testament talks of sacrifices that atone: they restore harmony

19. See the end of chap. 8 for recommended study Bibles and commentaries.

20. As Goldingay, *Theological Diversity*, 37–39, 92–94, points out, sometimes, this step becomes complicated. We may know very little about the circumstances that gave rise to the text (e.g., many psalms are difficult to date). Or we may encounter texts with different viewpoints that come from nearly identical contexts. Other steps are necessary.

21. Indeed, while the prophets did critique sacrificial practices, they did so with hyperbole and exaggeration, such that they weren't calling for an end of sacrifice but rather a correction of abuses (G. Anderson, "Sacrifice and Sacrificial Offerings [OT]," 881–82).

with God (e.g., Lev. 4:20–35). Before we dismiss such texts, it's worth asking, "Are there sacrifices I should make that would restore harmony with God?"[22] While I don't advocate slaughtering animals, there may be other sorts of sacrifices that, in line with Old Testament sacrificial texts, would bring us peace with God.

Fourth, *we can put texts into dialogue with each other*, imagining conversations between authors and characters. The goal wouldn't necessarily be to resolve every difference. Rather, if we thoroughly ground such conversations in the biblical text itself, this sort of exercise can cause us to realize in fresh ways the different perspectives in the Bible.[23]

For example, Ezra is very opposed to the Israelites marrying foreigners,[24] yet the Moabite Ruth and the Israelite Boaz have a highly celebrated marriage (as we saw in chap. 6). If we could use a time machine so Ruth and Ezra meet up, what might they say to each other?[25]

RUTH: What you've done is evil in my eyes. You forced Israelite men to divorce and send away their foreign wives. You tore families apart. Even children had to leave [Ezra 10:44].

EZRA: Look! When I learned of those marriages, it made me sick. I was so upset I tore my clothes and pulled out my hair. I couldn't eat. When I prayed, I couldn't even look up toward heaven [Ezra 9:3, 5–6].

RUTH: What upset you so much: foreign marriages or foreign gods?

EZRA: Both. The two go hand in hand.

RUTH: No, they don't. I left behind the gods of Moab when I followed my mother-in-law to Israel [Ruth 1:16].

EZRA: Not everyone is like you.

22. Before Christians dismiss this idea by saying that Christ's sacrifice means we don't need to make sacrifices ourselves, we need to remember that even the NT upholds this idea (cf. Rom. 12:1). In Luke 19, Zacchaeus sacrifices half his belongings, giving them to the poor, and Jesus says, "Today, salvation has come to this household" (19:8–9).

23. Naturally, such conversations are interpretive acts and shouldn't be seen as having the same value as the Bible itself. Nevertheless, they can be illuminating, as pointed out by Newsom, "Bakhtin, the Bible," 304–6.

24. Much has been written about this topic. See the bibliography in Southwood, "The Holy Seed," 208–24.

25. The dialogue here imagines that both Ruth and Ezra have access to either the OT or at least the traditions that eventually became written down in the OT. Of course, the OT wasn't complete for either one of them, so my implying their knowledge of these texts is anachronistic. However, this entire imaginary dialogue is outside the bounds of time to begin with; it allows me to explore Ruth and Ezra not only as characters in themselves, but also as representatives of larger biblical traditions. For a similar treatment that also perceives a conversation between biblical voices, but not in terms of an outright dialogue as presented here, see Kuhn, *Having Words with God*, 48–70.

RUTH: If you made the same demands in my day, I would have been forced out of Israel. I would have taken my son Obed with me. He was King David's grandfather. Where would your nation have been without David's line [Ruth 4:17]?

EZRA: David's line took us into exile. It was David's son Solomon who invited other gods into our land when he married foreigners [1 Kings 11:1–11]. We abandoned the Lord for those other gods. After centuries of faithlessness, God's patience reached its end. Death and exile ensued. It all resulted from our failure to obey God's instruction, which strictly prohibits marriages with foreigners [Exod. 34:11–16; Deut. 7:1–5; Ezra 9:10–15].

RUTH: But elsewhere in our traditions, we learn that Abraham's great-grandson Joseph not only married an Egyptian—he also married the daughter of a pagan priest! Our traditions do nothing to condemn him for doing so. Instead, their children and descendants became two important tribes within Israel [Gen. 41:45, 50; 46:20].

EZRA: Joseph is no example to follow. He acted like the Egyptians, engaging in magic and stealing land from the hungry [Gen. 44:5, 15; 47:13–26]. Our God demands total faithfulness to himself and deep compassion for the poor and vulnerable [Deut. 6:5; 15:1–18].

RUTH: Sometimes foreigners are the poor and vulnerable [cf. Exod. 22:21]. Indeed, God has a habit of making exceptions for outsiders like me. Moses married a Cushite—and God punished Miriam and Aaron for opposing this marriage [Num. 12]. A generation later, Joshua spared the Canaanite Rahab but demanded the death of the Israelite Achan [Josh. 2:1–21; 6:17–25; 7:1–26].[26]

EZRA: Achan's problem was he didn't destroy every last relic of Canaanite belongings [Josh. 7:11]. We must be utterly set apart, undefiled from foreigners, different from the nations.

RUTH: God's plans are incomplete without other nations [cf. Isa. 45:1–4]. At times, God places Israel alongside Egypt and Assyria [Isa. 19:19–25]. Even you yourself have talked of God showing you grace in the sight of Persian kings [Ezra 9:8–9].

EZRA: Yes, but you know nothing about how desperate things were when I arrived in Jerusalem. We struggled to rebuild our homes, our temple, our city, our nation, and our identity. We faced threats from within and without. We were slaves to the empire, opposed by every neighboring people. Were it not for God's grace, things would have been utterly hopeless [Ezra 4:1–6:15; 9:8–9].

26. Davis, "Poetics of Generosity."

Survival

Ezra and Nehemiah's "policies are not born out of prejudice or paranoia. They are born of necessity. No *ethnie* [ethnic group] can survive if it fails to police its ethnic boundary; and ethnic boundaries are policed through attention to kinship, commensality, and religious cult—precisely the areas of life dealt with by Ezra and Nehemiah."

Neil Glover, "Your People," 306

Ezra and Nehemiah's "postexilic community shows signs of disintegration and trauma, to which they responded with attempts to shore up boundaries and remove economic or political temptations by pointing to their dire consequences in Israel's past. . . .

"Whatever objections modern readers may have with Ezra's tactics, one must also recognize that attending to issues of nonconformity and identity were essential to survival in Diaspora. The *concerns*, if not also the specific tactics, were genuine."

Daniel L. Smith-Christopher, *Theology of Exile*, 160, 162

RUTH: I know all too well about hopelessness. I have been a widow. I have been separated from my family, my home, and my people. I have faced famine. For me, God's grace came from being included with your people, not excluded from them [Ruth 1:5–6, 15–16; chaps. 2–4].[27]

EZRA: Neither the Israelites nor the Moabites were threatened with extinction in your day. In my day, it was unclear whether there would be any future for us as a people. We had to draw sharp lines between ourselves and surrounding peoples. The Jewish people would not have survived otherwise. (See "Survival.")

I would love for Ruth to convert Ezra to her more inclusive ways, but I doubt he would give up much ground—especially when ideas like hers make him physically sick.[28]

Furthermore, Ezra has a voice that I ought to hear, though I am tempted to mute him. He draws my attention to how vulnerable the people of God were when they returned from exile. He reminds me that the company we keep, whether spouses or even friends, profoundly affects us and our beliefs.

---

27. There's debate about whether Ruth actually becomes an Israelite. For a brief outline of different positions, see Glover, "Your People," 295. While one can engage this debate, the text makes clear that she comes to participate in Israelite society through her marriage to Boaz and her offspring becoming Israel's prototypical king.

28. See also the discussion in C. Hays, "Silence of the Wives," 79–80.

We live in a very different world than Ezra: faith doesn't necessarily go hand in hand with nationality. For this reason and countless others, I would never advocate division along nationalistic or ethnic lines.[29]

At the same time, Ezra makes me wonder about the wisdom of Christians marrying those with no sympathies to their faith. My natural inclination is to think that couples can work out even religious differences. But I know from my experiences in pastoral counseling that sometimes differences of faith are the source of greatest pain in marriages. In fact, it would be interesting to extend this conversation between Ruth and Ezra by adding the voice of the apostle Paul, who (1) worked relentlessly to include foreigners (gentiles) in the church, but (2) urged believers *not* to marry unbelievers, while (3) stopping short of telling believers to send away their unbelieving spouses (1 Cor. 7:12–16; 2 Cor. 6:14–18). Paul would likely side with Ruth at some moments but Ezra at other points.

God's truth about relating to foreigners and peoples with different faiths is quite complex. There isn't one word that works in every context. God doesn't hand out one-size-fits-all garments for everyone to wear. In our day, we can see why Ezra's teachings wouldn't fit us well. Foreigners may very well share our faith. Most of us in the Western world haven't faced traumas like exile. Christianity may be declining in the USA and Europe, but it's not on the verge of going extinct. Ruth's words fit us much better than Ezra's.

Yet I am thankful that at times the Jewish people followed Ezra's precedent while facing immense persecution. In doing so, they retained their identity, which is why they are around today. Meanwhile other people groups, like the Moabites, have vanished from the earth. I can appreciate what Ezra has to say, even if embodying his teachings would be like trying to put my adult body inside an infant's onesie.

Conclusion

Humans love shrinking the Bible down to a single concept. But God blows all our concepts

> ### A Prayer for Truth
>
> From the cowardice that shrinks from new truth,
> From the laziness that is content with half-truths,
> From the arrogance that thinks it knows all truth,
> O God of truth, deliver us.
>
> Elyse D. Frishman, ed.,
> *A Reform Siddur*, 43

---

29. Indeed, Willa M. Johnson, *Holy Seed Has Been Defiled*, passim, esp. 110, makes "the case against understanding Ezra 9–10 as a racist ideology, instead arguing that separation was a normative consequence of postexilic trauma." She argues, "The injunction against interethnic marriage in Ezra 9–10 is not so much a warning against race-mixing in the modern segregationist sense of the term, but a response to a complex confluence of economic, ethnic, gender- and class-related, and sexual concerns that emerged in the aftermath of the trauma of exile and the reconstruction of the identity of Yhwh's chosen people in their former land."

away. God is *transcendent*: beyond our ways of thinking and reasoning. As Paul Hanson writes, "It is idolatrous to claim that any human formulation can definitively describe the one true God."[30] In other words, God's truths are much bigger than we are, and certainly bigger than what our limited languages can nail down. God's truths are too much for our five senses to take in.

In her well-known poem "Tell All the Truth but Tell It Slant," Emily Dickinson writes:

> The Truth must dazzle gradually
> Or every man be blind.[31]

The Bible goes even further: it says that we must glimpse God only in bits and pieces or we will perish: "The LORD said, 'You can't see my face because no one can see me and live'" (Exod. 33:20). Instead of presenting all of God's fullness at once, the Old Testament presents fascinating conversations about who God is and what God wants from us.[32] These conversations continue, extending beyond the pages of Scripture into our own lives.[33]

Most of us have had the pleasure of talking late into the night with our closest friends. We eventually stop not because we want to, but because we dread how tired we'll be the next morning. The Old Testament is like that sort of friend. We can continue to talk with it late into the night. It always offers us more than we could consider on our own. We will find ourselves pondering some of the things it says, embodying other parts, and debating still other words. The deep truth it describes can only be plumbed, never encapsulated. (See "A Prayer for Truth.")

For Further Study

Goldingay, John. *Theological Diversity and the Authority of the Old Testament*. Grand Rapids: Eerdmans, 1987.

> Although this work is dated, it nevertheless represents an excellent account of contradictions in the Old Testament, how they might be classified, and approaches one can take to such contradictions.

Kuhn, Karl Allen. *Having Words with God: The Bible as Conversation*. Minneapolis: Fortress, 2008.

30. Hanson, *Diversity of Scripture*, 3.
31. E. Dickinson, "1129," *Complete Poems*, 507.
32. A. Heschel (*Man Is Not Alone*, 97) gets at a similar sentiment: "Definitions take the name of God in vain. We have neither an image nor a definition of God. We have only His name. And the name is ineffable."
33. Olson, "Biblical Theology as Provisional Monologization," 180.

This book insightfully develops the idea that the Bible itself is best seen as a conversation both among humans and between humans and God. It bears much in common with this chapter.

Newsom, Carol A. "Bakhtin, the Bible, and Dialogic Truth." *Journal of Religion* 76 (1996): 290–306.

This brilliant article inspired the chapter above. Newsom draws on the thinking of Russian literary critic Mikhail Bakhtin to describe dialogic ways of conceptualizing truth. Although her arguments are more philosophical, Newsom offers a host of generative suggestions.

The website www.MatthewSchlimm.com has additional resources, including group discussion questions.

10

Drowning in Tears and Raging at God

For many Christians, life with God means a life of *joy* and *peace*. Philippians 4:4 instructs readers to "rejoice in the Lord always" (NRSV). The reason for such joy is apparent in the following verses, which talk of God's peace surpassing all understanding (4:7). Such peace, we read elsewhere, should rule in our hearts (Col. 3:15).

The psalms speak repeatedly of praising God, of thanking our Creator for all the goodness that's in our lives. Psalm 9 reminds us that because of God's wonderful acts, celebration and songs of happiness should be hallmarks of our faith. Not once, not twice, but twenty-six times (!), Psalm 136 reminds readers that "God's faithful love lasts forever!"

For many of us, this emphasis on happiness and peace makes perfect sense. We have good news, and it naturally brings us deep joy.

However, people who have read the Bible carefully know that it doesn't always present the life of faith as one of joy and happiness. The Old Testament is filled with prayers that give voice to deep suffering. At times the hearts of God's people sink into utter despair. On other occasions, anger erupts, and people hurl insults at God. They dare to say that God is forgetful, unreliable, hidden, unresponsive, and the cause of suffering. Sometimes, people in the Bible even talk of God as their enemy.

Why are these expressions of sadness and anger in our Scriptures? How could they possibly be a good thing? Did the church forget to read what it was actually including in its Scriptures? This chapter looks at the raw emotion communicated to God through biblical prayer. After surveying what these prayers look like, this chapter shifts gears, asking what good they could bring to the life of faith.

The Depths of Sorrow

Job has a reputation for being *patient* after he loses property, children, and health. However, when we look at what the Bible actually says, we find that he isn't someone who waits quietly for things to get better. Instead, he wails:

> My groans become my bread;
>   my roars pour out like water.
> Because I was afraid of something awful, and it arrived;
>   what I dreaded came to me.
> I had no ease, quiet, or rest,
>   and trembling came. (3:24–26)

In desperation, Job later cries:

> I would choose strangling and death
>   instead of my bones.
> I reject life; I don't want to live long;
>   leave me alone, for my days are empty. (7:15–16)

These two passages are mere threads in a blanket; the book of Job is filled with similar words of anguish.

Although Job is sometimes seen as the key example of someone who suffers in the Bible, the Old Testament portrays suffering as a normal part of what it means to be human. The psalms in particular provide prayers for when life's tragedies strike. In Psalm 6:6, we read:

> I'm worn out from groaning.
> Every night, I drench my bed with tears;
> I soak my couch all the way through.

The Hebrew behind these words is even more vivid. Instead of simply saying that the bed is *drenched* with tears, the text literally reads, "I make my bed *swim* with tears." Rather than saying that the couch is *soaked*, the Hebrew evokes imagery of the couch being *dissolved*. It's as though the couch is a mere grain of salt in a tank of tears.

These words are a far cry from New Testament teaching about rejoicing always.[1] In fact, they're quite different from psalms where people can't stop praising God (e.g., Ps. 150). Yet these prayers of sorrow are surprisingly common, making up a large portion of the book of Psalms and showing up in other books of the Bible like Jeremiah. Scholars call these expressions of sorrow *psalms of lament*. They're one of the most common types of prayers in the book of Psalms, making up about a third of the book.[2]

> **The Book of Lamentations**
>
> "A more relentlessly brutal piece of writing is scarcely imaginable. This short biblical book affronts the reader with a barrage of harsh and violent images. . . . The reader is not so much engaged by the book of Lamentations as assaulted by it."
>
> Tod Linafelt,
> *Surviving Lamentations*, 2

Not surprisingly, the book of Lamentations is also filled with these sorts of prayers. The book is a response to the catastrophic events of 587 BCE, when the Babylonians invaded Judah and surrounded Jerusalem, slowly starving the inhabitants of the city until finally the city fell. Here are just a few of its verses that attempt to describe the totality of Jerusalem's grief.

> Cry out to my Lord from the heart, you wall of Daughter Zion;
>   make your tears run down like a flood all day and night.
> Don't relax at all;
>   Don't rest your eyes a moment.
> Get up and cry out at nighttime, at the start of the night shift;
>   pour out your heart before my Lord like water.
> Lift your hands up to him for the life of your children—
>   the ones who are fainting from hunger on every street corner.
> LORD, look and see to whom you have done this!
>   Should women eat their own offspring, their own beautiful babies?
>   Should priest and prophet be killed in my Lord's own sanctuary?
>   (Lam. 2:18–20)

Such a prayer is nearly incomprehensible to most of us. It's a far cry from our normal Sunday morning prayer concerns, which tend to focus on upcoming surgeries and "traveling mercies." Here in the Bible, however, raw grief meets honest prayer amid horrific events. (See "The Book of Lamentations.")

1. As Zenger (*God of Vengeance?*, 13–22) shows, some people recommend rejecting these psalms as "unchristian."
2. Cf. Murphy, *Gift of the Psalms*, 12–13.

Burning Anger

Like many Christians, I was taught to pray with my hands folded, my eyes closed, and my head bowed. My family's prayers were always polite, filled with words like *please* and *thank you*—nothing that might upset our Creator. In fact, we usually stuck to prayers we mechanically recited, presumably so we wouldn't accidentally let an irreverent word slip in.

When I study the prayers of the Bible, however, I find a very different way of communicating with God. People don't just express the depths of their sorrow. They shake their fists in rage at their Creator. They dare to hurl accusations at God. They fire piercing questions. (See "Israel's Faith.") Instead of affirming that God *protects* us in the worst of times, Old Testament prayers accuse God of *causing* the worst of times. If sorrowful prayers are *psalms of lament*, these angry prayers are *psalms of complaint*.

Most churchgoers are familiar with Psalm 23, which portrays God as a shepherd who cares for people, leading them to green pastures and still waters, protecting them even in the darkest valley. The previous psalm begins with a completely different characterization of God. *The Lord isn't nearby, but very far away*:

> **Israel's Faith**
>
> "Israel's faith is a probing, questioning, insisting, disjunctive faith."
>
> Walter Brueggemann,
> *Theology of the Old Testament*, 318

> My God! My God, why have you left me all alone?
>> Why are you so far from saving me—
>> so far from my anguished groans?
> My God, I cry out during the day,
>> but you don't answer. (Ps. 22:1–2)[3]

This image of God as being distant shows up several times in the Bible's prayers. Psalm 10 goes so far as to imply that God is a coward—*someone who hides from difficulty*:

> Why, O Lord, do you stand far off?
> Why do you hide yourself in times of trouble? (10:1 NRSV)[4]

Like many psalms of complaint, Psalm 10 moves on to speak in positive ways about God later in the prayer (see below). Nevertheless, the irreverence at the

---

3. Also see Pss. 42:9; 43:2; Jer. 14:9.
4. On the image of God hiding, see Pss. 10:11; 13:2; 27:9; 30:7; 69:17; 88:14; 89:46; 102:2; 104:29; 143:7; Isa. 45:15. For more on this biblical theme, see Balentine, *Hidden God*.

outset of this prayer is rather shocking, a sharp contrast to how many of us were taught to pray as children.

In other psalms of complaint, *God is accused of falling asleep on the job*, of failing at divine responsibilities:

> Rouse yourself!
>   Why do you sleep, O Lord?[5]
> Awake, do not cast us off forever!
>   Why do you hide your face?
>   Why do you forget our affliction and oppression? (44:23–24 NRSV)

Our churches frequently echo the refrain "God is good—all the time. All the time—God is good." These psalmists have very different ideas about God. Why did their words make it into the Holy Bible?

Many people would insist, contrary to the words in the above psalms, that God sees everything and knows everything (cf. Ps. 139:7–13). The author of Psalm 35 would likely agree, but then argue that God's seeing evil in no way excuses God. This psalmist dares to ask how God can witness suffering and *do nothing in response*:

> How long, O LORD, will you look on?
>   Rescue me from their ravages,
>   my life from the lions! (35:17 NRSV)[6]

Biblical prayers often contain questions with an accusatory tone. Those praying want to know how long God will allow evil people to triumph while good people suffer. They want to know why God hasn't yet intervened.[7]

I've often heard people say, "God always answers prayer—but it might not be the answer we're looking for." At the outset of the book of Habakkuk, however, the prophet avoids such platitudes—suggesting that God has *failed to hear our prayers* and has even *caused injustice*:

> LORD, how long will I call for help and you not listen?
>   I cry out to you, "Violence!" but you don't deliver us.
> Why do you show me injustice and look at anguish
>   so that devastation and violence are before me? (1:2–3)

5. Obviously there's tension between this verse and Ps. 121:4, which says that God "never sleeps or rests!" For more on theological tensions, see chap. 9.

6. Cf. Jer. 14:8.

7. Westermann, *Praise and Lament in the Psalms*, 176–78; Miller, *They Cried to the Lord*, 70–73; see also 73–79 for other ways complaints are made.

What would happen if Habakkuk showed up in our churches and prayed such a prayer? I, for one, would be uncomfortable. I can see myself interrupting him and saying, "Ah, before we pray any more, would you like to talk with us about what's bothering you? You and I can meet privately if you don't want to share with the group as a whole." I'd be afraid that his words would upset God. They're far from polite. They're far from thankful. Above all else, they're accusatory. They blame God—

> ### Unable to Reconcile
>
> Habakkuk "confessed an inability to reconcile what he had heard about God with actual experience. His questions, like Jeremiah's, address God with stark reality."
>
> James L. Crenshaw, "Human Dilemma," 242

and strangely enough, they're part of our holy Scriptures. (See "Unable to Reconcile.")

Another prophet, Jeremiah, accuses God of *being undependable*:

> Why am I always in pain?
>> Why is my wound incurable,
>> so far beyond healing?
> You have become for me as unreliable
>> as a spring gone dry! (15:18)[8]

As if Jeremiah's prayer isn't strange enough, *God's response is even weirder.* In the verses that follow, God doesn't strike Jeremiah down for his irreverence. Instead, God shows up, tells Jeremiah to say what's good, and promises to protect him. When Jeremiah returns to prophesying, God will make Jeremiah "a fortified wall of bronze" (15:20 NRSV). God pledges to be with Jeremiah, to save, deliver, and rescue the prophet when he's under attack (15:20–21). God doesn't always respond so positively to Jeremiah's prayers (e.g., 12:5), but here God offers to be with him.[9]

---

8. The book of Jeremiah contains several prayers (also called "confessions") that speak with brutal honesty to God: 11:18–23; 12:1–6; 15:10–21; 17:14–18; 18:18–23; 20:7–13, 14–18.

9. As Fretheim, *Jeremiah*, 241–42, explains, there's more than one way to interpret God's words in 15:19–21. While it's possible that God rebukes Jeremiah for lamenting, Fretheim convincingly argues that Jeremiah has *not* sinned. God does encourage Jeremiah to return to the work of prophesying, but that doesn't mean his lamentation was wrong. One should follow the NASB in translating the middle of 15:19 literally ("if you extract the precious from the worthless," which evokes images of both a remnant and bringing forth goodness from an otherwise corrupt society), rather than the paraphrases found in the NRSV and CEB ("If you utter what is worthwhile, not what is worthless" [CEB]). The Hebrew doesn't talk of "uttering" but of "bringing forth," and the Hebrew word for "worthless" refers to gluttony, freeloading, and being wishy-washy—things far removed from Jeremiah's lamentation (see Deut. 21:20; Prov. 23:20–21; 28:7; Jer. 2:36).

God has a relatively favorable response to accusations in the book of Job as well. Repeatedly Job speaks angrily about the world-shaking pain he faces. Job's friend Eliphaz, however, is highly uncomfortable with Job's emotions. He warns Job about the dangers of anger (5:2–5). He assures Job that God is compassionate and loving (5:9–11). He insists that Job can find ways to be happy and even laugh in the midst of difficulty (5:17, 22). It's reminiscent of how people today say, "God will never give you more than you can handle."

Despite how nice Eliphaz's words sound, Job is unfazed by them. (See "Job: The Rebel.") He responds by talking about *God as an enemy*:

> The Almighty's arrows are in me;
>   my spirit drinks their poison,
>   and God's terrors are arrayed against me. (6:4)[10]

Later, when Eliphaz wonders why Job can't find comfort in God (15:11), Job responds by saying:

> I've heard many things like these.
>   All of you are sorry comforters. (16:2)

If I were reading Job for the first time, I would expect that God would eventually side with Eliphaz. He has much in common with how Christians today think of faith and suffering.

Amazingly, at the end of the book, God prefers Job's red-faced accusations over his friends' "orthodox" theology:

> The Lord said to Eliphaz the Temanite: "My wrath is kindled against you and against your two friends; for you have not spoken of me what is right, as my servant Job has." (Job 42:7 NRSV)

God's words are outrageous. How are Job's words "right" when he angrily accuses God of terror?[11] How are the friends' words "not right" when they have defended God's ways? What's going on?

Job: The Rebel

Job's "way of praying is diametrically opposed to what [his friends] would deem appropriate and permissible. To the extent that one is to understand the friends as holding up traditional beliefs and practices, Job is portrayed as a rebel."

Samuel E. Balentine,
Prayer in the Hebrew Bible, 170

---

10. Job makes similar remarks on many other occasions; see, e.g., 10:16–19 and 16:7–17:1. Outside Job, God is portrayed as an enemy in texts such as Lam. 2:1–5; cf. Ps. 60:3; Jer. 14:19; Lam. 3:42–45.

11. Balentine (*Job*, 710–11) suggests that God deems Job's "prologue piety" to be right. It's also possible that Job's words of repentance in 42:1–6 are what God judges to be right.

A Terribly Cruel Notion

"The idea that Christians are supposed to have a deep inner joy all the time is a terribly cruel notion. . . . It turns people who wish to comfort the afflicted into tormentors. They want to help their suffering friends get the joy back, but in the process they insist their friends accept the idea that it's not normal for the Christian life to include deep suffering of heart. So in addition to their suffering, their friends are wounded by the suggestion that their affliction is due to some failure in their Christian life—as if there's something wrong with Christians who have a cross to bear."

Phillip Cary, *Good News*, 139

Similar questions come into our minds at the end of the book of Lamentations. The book concludes with questions, desperate pleas, and doubts about whether God will ever be gracious again. Addressing God, the text asks:

> Why have you forgotten us completely?
>> Why have you forsaken us these many days?
> Restore us to yourself, O LORD,
>> that we may be restored;
>> renew our days as of old—
> unless you have utterly rejected us,
>> and are angry with us beyond measure. (5:20–22 NRSV)

We expect the book to end with a positive conclusion: *suffering is bad now, but things will be better later.* Yet for the people uttering this prayer, the best they can do is ask for God's help and wonder if it will ever come.

What are these angry, sorrowful, and despairing texts doing in the Bible? Don't they contradict all the good things the Bible says about God?[12] No wonder people often ignore the Old Testament, especially when it contains words like the ones described in this chapter. These words seem opposed to every effort to evangelize: why would anyone want to follow a God accused of causing suffering, being unreliable, and falling asleep on the job?

However, several factors suggest that God sees Job's accusatory words in chaps. 3–31 as right. First, God speaks to Eliphaz, who doesn't appear at all in the prologue, making Balentine's suggestion unlikely. Second, Eliphaz's contrast with Job relates largely to whether Job should speak negatively about God. Thus God's siding with Job suggests that God favors honest accusations over superficial piety. Third, Job's accusations are not isolated, ambiguous examples but part of a broader biblical tradition that is comfortable with people making accusations of God. See Habel, *Book of Job*, 583.

12. For more on this topic, see Brueggemann, *Theology of the Old Testament*, esp. 317–403.

Impatient Protester

"God values the integrity of the impatient protester and abhors pious hypocrites who would heap accusations on a tormented soul to uphold their theological position."

Marvin H. Pope, *Job*, 350,
speaking of Job and his "friends"

"Dissent literature demonstrates Israel's basic honesty in dealing with theological questions. No issue was too delicate to ponder, no matter too dangerous to explore its merits. Indeed, its Lord openly invited expostulation, confident that his servants' devotion could endure fiery testing."

James L. Crenshaw,
"Human Dilemma," 258

Making Sense of Prayers of Complaint

Despite all of these difficulties, there are several reasons why these psalms of lament and complaint are actually very important to the life of faith.

The Pervasiveness of Tragedy

First, tragedy strikes us all. The opening chapters of the Bible make clear that we don't live in paradise any longer. We live in a world of thorns, pain, and death. We go through life, finding ourselves wronged by society, wronged by strangers, wronged by loved ones, and wronged by ourselves. No one is immune from life's tragedies.

Because we live in a fallen world, we need resources for dealing with tragedy. We don't need clichés or platitudes. We certainly don't need to be told we should smile in the face of tragedy because, all things considered, it's not really that bad. (See "A Terribly Cruel Notion.")

Sometimes life really is horrible. Psalms of lament and complaint give the church precisely what it needs to deal honestly with fierce emotion in our lives. These prayers give us permission to be open about what we're actually going through. They give us speech when suffering and injustices seem beyond words.[13]

The greatest dignity the church can give to people who suffer is to tell them that their cries of anguish are worthy of God's ear. The most shameful thing the church can do is tell people who suffer that there's something wrong with them for suffering. (See "Impatient Protester.")

---

13. Cf. Zenger, *God of Vengeance*, 85.

That's Cool

"As Peter Stearns has persuasively argued, between 1920 and 1950 a new emotional style began to emerge in America that has continued to the present day, one marked above all else by dispassion, or to use the term popular since the 1960s, by being 'cool.' With the growth of consumerism, corporate management, and the service-sector, the American middle class adopted an emotional style that places great stress on concealing emotional reactions, especially in the workplace where they could interfere with generating profits."[a]

Matthew Schlimm, *From Fratricide to Forgiveness*, 36

---

a. See Stearns, *American Cool*.

What's behind Sadness and Anger

American culture is highly uncomfortable with emotions like sadness and anger. (See "That's Cool.") While growing up, many of us were taught to see emotions as *childish*, *irrational*, *a sign of weakness*, *unreliable*, and *obstacles to getting what we really want*. Big boys don't cry.

All too often, Christians uncritically adopt societal attitudes about feelings, assuming that the life of faith gives people even more reasons to avoid sadness and anger. We speak of deep inner joy and abundant life, implying that Christianity gives people freedom from their most feared emotions.[14]

However, these so-called negative emotions like sadness and anger are actually quite valuable. Both sadness and anger stem from perceptions our bodies make about the world around us:

- Sadness comes from realizing that *something valuable has been lost*.
- Anger results from perceiving that *a wrongdoing has taken place*.

The only way to avoid sadness would be to go through life stubbornly refusing to see that anything of value is ever lost. Such a superficial existence requires continually denying the plain truth. It means we must pretend that we don't really care about shattered dreams, broken promises, or the six feet of cold dirt covering people we deeply loved. From cancer to mental illness, from war to poverty, tragedy randomly strikes people whether we want it to or not. The loss that comes with such events naturally causes sorrow, and we shouldn't feel bad for mourning. As my father-in-law said after my grandmother died, "Grief is the cost of deep love." (See "Coming to Church with Burdens.")

---

14. Cary, *Good News*, 138–39.

> **Coming to Church with Burdens**
>
> *"Not everyone who comes to church is full of joy and happiness.* There are many who come with great burdens, both physical and spiritual: sickness, marital problems, financial difficulties, pressure at work, even harassment and persecution. Old age brings all sorts of problems with it. Often people can see no way out, and they need to be allowed to cry out to God in their distress, just as Job did and Jesus himself did."
>
> Gordon J. Wenham,
> *Psalter Reclaimed*, 47
> (emphasis original)

Similarly, the only way to avoid anger would be to live as though wrongdoings never took place. Such a way of life is not only dishonest; it's also impossible. Everyone is a sinner, and everyone has been sinned against. When wrongdoings are committed against people we love or against ourselves, anger naturally occurs. The only way to be anger-free would be to have no sense of right and wrong.

At the same time, many of us are deeply afraid of sorrow or anger. We hate how these emotions feel, especially in a society that has taught us that we have nothing more important to do than pursue happiness. We fear that grief will take us into deep depression. We wonder if anger will make us cruel people. If we let these emotions into our lives, will they ever subside? We often prefer cool reason to the tumultuous landscape of emotion. (See "The Risk of Lament.")

Honest to God

Yet there's something deeply dishonest about acting happy or even detached when losses and injustices come our way.[15] We forget that God already knows

> **The Risk of Lament**
>
> "Lament is risky . . . because it abandons all pretense of excuse, denial, or cover-up."
>
> Scott A. Ellington, *Risking Truth*, 3

our innermost thoughts. We can remove the smile-covered masks. When we are sad, we can express that sadness directly to God, no matter how intense the emotion may be. Even when we are angry, we can rage at God. When we cannot find the words for either sorrow or rage, the Bible makes our mute tongues able to speak again. These prayers facilitate moments of holy honesty where we can articulate our darkest realities to God. (See "The Nature of Faith.")

Even Jesus found reason to pray with angry Psalms. On the cross, he uttered the opening of Psalm 22, "My God, my God, why have you forsaken me?!"

15. Tanner, *Psalms for Today*, 64.

The Nature of Faith

"Anyone who is repelled by the idea of complaining to God should rethink the meaning of faith, which is *not* stoicism."

Roland E. Murphy, *Gift of the Psalms*, 14

"The use of these 'psalms of darkness' . . . is an act of bold faith on the one hand, because it insists that the world must be experienced as it really is and not in some pretended way. On the other hand, it is bold because it insists that all such experiences of disorder are a proper subject for discourse with God. There is nothing out of bounds, nothing precluded or inappropriate. Everything properly belongs in this conversation of the heart. To withhold parts of life from that conversation is in fact to withhold part of life from the sovereignty of God."

Walter Brueggemann, *Message of the Psalms*, 52

(Matt. 27:46 NRSV; Mark 15:34). Anger and grief entered the lives of many other people in the Bible, including Abraham, Hagar, Moses, Ruth, Hannah, and the apostle Paul (Gen. 21:11, 16; 23:2; Num. 16:15; Ruth 1:9, 14; 1 Sam. 1:7–10; Acts 21:13; cf. John 11:35). We shouldn't expect freedom from emotions that our mothers and fathers in faith knew all too well.

Giving Up on God

Many people give up on God when tragedy strikes. They have grown up in the church. They have been told that God is always good. They have been showered with reminders of God's love. But the church's teachings quickly crumble when they stare death in the face or witness the senselessness of world events. In his book *Faith No More: Why People Reject Religion*, Phil Zuckerman explains, "When one's marriage falls apart, or when prayer fails to work, or when one experiences the tragic death of a loved one—all of these can lead to a loss of belief. . . . Such apostasy is often predicated upon a feeling of being forsaken, and seriously so."[16] The faith taught in churches today, which talks only of God's love, is often inadequate for facing real tragedy.

Ironically, the church has—in its own Scriptures—the very resources that allow people to deal honestly and prayerfully with feelings of abandonment by God. Although psalms of lament and complaint may be filled with doubt, they provide life-giving resources when everything else seems dead. (See "Faith and

16. Zuckerman, *Faith No More*, 40–55, esp. 52.

Doubt.") Sadly, the church has hidden these prayers away, overlooking them, failing to acknowledge their presence in our Bibles.[17] And so, people naturally give up on God because they cannot see how faith can persist in the face of evil.

Rather than abandoning faith, biblical writers took a very different approach. (See "Resuming the Journey of Faith.") They refused to give up on God.[18] Even if they had to hurl the worst accusations imaginable at their Creator, they kept speaking to God. Even if they erred on the side of accusing God of too much evil, they continued to pray: they wailed, they lamented, and they raged. Remarkably, they emerged from tragedy with their faith intact.

> **Faith and Doubt**
>
> There lives more faith in honest doubt,
> Believe me, than in half the creeds.[a]
>
> Alfred Lord Tennyson, "XCVI," in
> *In Memoriam*, 96–97
>
> a. Cf. Crenshaw, "Human Dilemma," 258.

We think that prayers of complaint will drive people away from church. After all, why would anyone want to worship a God accused of falling asleep on the job? Yet the counterintuitive truth is this: we need these prayers of complaint to prevent people from leaving the church. If these prayers became central to the church's practices, then

1. Christians would know that tragedy strikes us all.
2. Christians would know how to keep the lines of communication open between God and themselves when waves of sadness and anger came crashing down.
3. Christians could see how their faith could survive even in a world of disasters and catastrophes.

Uncomfortably Numb

Impression without expression leads to depression. In other words, when major life events happen, we need to express accompanying emotions or else we become hollow shells of ourselves, stumbling along as though we had a bad head cold, unable to experience the fullness of life. Repressed sadness and anger can lead to misplaced emotion, depression, and emotional numbness. (See "Anger and Expression.")

Therapist Marvin Allen discusses how an unwillingness to experience sadness leads to an inability to experience joy as well. He writes, "It's not possible to surrender part of the psyche and leave the rest intact. It's like going to the dentist

---

17. According to Murphy, *Gift of Psalms*, 12–13, the book of Psalms contains about 50 psalms of lament. About half of these (24) are omitted from the Revised Common Lectionary.
18. See Crenshaw, *Whirlpool of Torment*, 117–19.

> ### Resuming the Journey of Faith
>
> "Lament allows us to resume the journey of faith in the midst of profound loss and divine silence. Were we to either forsake our beliefs or deny our experience, it would be impossible to continue the journey. The cry of lament is not an embarrassing lapse of faith on Israel's part, but is a courageous act of risk-taking. Indeed to remain silent or, worse yet, to mouth praises into the silence, is a betrayal of faith, finding sufficiency as it does in a God who is distant and past. Lament is a profound and potent expression of faith."
>
> Scott A. Ellington, *Risking Truth*, 4

to have your tooth filled. In order to stop the pain of the one tooth, the dentist has to numb the whole side of your jaw."[19] People who make themselves numb to emotions like grief, Allen explains, will inadvertently blunt other emotions like happiness. Unexpressed emotions can become corrosive inside us. (See "What about Commands to Rejoice?")

> ### Anger and Expression
>
> I was angry with my friend;
> I told my wrath, my wrath did end.
> I was angry with my foe:
> I told it not, my wrath did grow.
>
> William Blake,
> "Poison Tree"

I pastored a church not long after the terrorist attacks of September 11, 2001. Following these attacks, both government leaders and Americans in general voiced the desire to "return to business as usual."[20] I told my church that we may instead need to spend time combining prayer, grief, and anger. On several occasions, we prayed Psalm 10. As mentioned above, it begins:

> Why do you stand so far away, LORD,
>   hiding yourself in troubling times? (10:1)

As the psalm proceeds, it urges God not to forget the afflicted. It summons God to "break the arms of those who are wicked and evil," to "seek out their wickedness until there's no more to find" (10:15). It ends with an assertion of confidence in God (10:17–18 NRSV, italics added):

> O LORD, you will hear the desire of the meek;
>   you will strengthen their heart, you will incline your ear
> to do justice for the orphan and the oppressed,
>   *so that those from earth may strike terror no more.*

19. Allen with Robinson, *Angry Men, Passive Men*, 15.
20. See, e.g., Myers and Schemo, "After the Attacks, . . . Business as Usual."

What about Commands to Rejoice?

In Philippians 4, readers find these words:

> Rejoice in the Lord always; again I will say, Rejoice. . . . Do not worry about anything. . . . And the peace of God . . . will guard your hearts and your minds. (Phil. 4:4, 6–7 NRSV)

What do we make of this text in light of biblical texts that show grief as a normal part of the life of faith?

First, we should remember that the Greek behind these commandments is plural, not singular. In other words, these commandments tell the church as a whole to rejoice—not individual believers.

Second, it's important to see these verses as one part of the Bible's conversation about emotions, not the last word. In Romans 12:15, Paul writes, "Rejoice with those who rejoice, weep with those who weep" (NRSV). Such words make clear that even for Paul, certain circumstances call for mourning.[a]

a. Phillip Cary, *Good News*, 139–40.

This prayer offered my church a way to be faithful in the aftermath of tragedy. It gave us permission to bare our hearts to God. We no longer needed to pretend that all was well when skyscrapers were crashing down. Rather than acting like nothing had happened, we could take our grief and anger to God, trusting in God (rather than flawed political leaders) to make the world right again.

Intimacy with God

People express emotions with those closest to them. A real relationship with God is bound to have something akin to lover's quarrels, tear-filled seasons, and even moments that feel hopeless. Perhaps these prayers of sorrow and anger show us what intimacy with God actually looks like: rather than hiding emotions, people approach God with such vulnerability and trust that they tell God all that they think and feel. Biblical authors didn't apologize for their emotions. They didn't give God the silent treatment, which is the functional equivalent of apostasy. Instead, they spoke directly to God about their feelings, much as they would with a close confidant. (See "All of Its Ugliness.")

God Shows Up

Perhaps the most amazing thing about these psalms of lament and complaint is that God responds to them. Most of the time, these prayers begin in

All of Its Ugliness

"What is clear from these cries to God is that there is nothing that should stop the conversation between God and God's people. The pain and hurt of life is to be brought before God in all of its ugliness, in all of its anger, and in all of its hurt. . . . These prayers for help prove that we do not have to dress up our words or even ourselves. God accepts our screams of pain. God accepts our accusations of a broken world. God accepts our true selves and our true emotions. We do not have to offer false praise when we feel otherwise."

Beth LaNeel Tanner, *Psalms for Today*, 66–67

the depths of despair, but they end with notes of highest praise.[21] Repeatedly the Bible portrays God as rushing to the needs of those who express their disappointment and anger over life's events.

At the middle point of Lamentations, something startling happens. Faith breaks through tears of anguish. Initially, Lamentations 3 talks of how God has made people's "teeth grind on gravel" and has caused people to forget "what happiness is" (3:16–17 NRSV). Readers expect this grief to continue. But then something happens that challenges the harsh realities all around:

> But this I call to mind,
>   and therefore I have hope:
> The steadfast love of the LORD never ceases,
>   his mercies never come to an end;
> they are new every morning;
>   great is your faithfulness.
> "The LORD is my portion," says my soul,
>   "therefore I will hope in him."
> The LORD is good to those who wait for him,
>   to the soul that seeks him.
> It is good that one should wait quietly
>   for the salvation of the LORD.
> It is good for one to bear the yoke in youth,
>   to sit alone in silence when the Lord has imposed it,
> to put one's mouth to the dust (there may yet be hope),
>   to give one's cheek to the smiter, and be filled with insults.
> For the Lord will not reject forever.

21. Following Westermann's lead, Patrick D. Miller ("Current Issues in Psalms Studies," 141) observes that the entire *book* of Psalms moves from a focus on lament to a focus on praise, which reflects on a macrolevel what takes place on the microlevel within particular psalms of lament.

Although he causes grief, he will have compassion
    according to the abundance of his steadfast love;
for he does not willingly afflict or grieve anyone.
    (Lam. 3:21–33 NRSV)

The Bible and Imagination

"The Bible . . . appeals to the imagination of its readers. It invites them to see the world differently—to see it *as* something different from the kind of world that it otherwise appears to be."

Garrett Green,
"Narrative and Scriptural Truth," 92

Amid the harshest of conditions, hope surfaces.[22]

The psalms function similarly. Even psalms with fierce accusations often contain notes of trust, hope, and thanksgiving.[23] One often finds a threefold pattern.[24] First, the people praying speak to God with brutal honesty about the struggles they face. Thus Psalm 13 begins:

How long, O Lord? Will you forget me forever?
    How long will you hide your face from me?
How long must I bear pain in my soul,
    and have sorrow in my heart all day long?
How long shall my enemy be exalted over me? (13:1–2 NRSV)

After raising accusing questions with their Maker, those praying urge God to act:

Look at me!
    Answer me, Lord my God!
Restore sight to my eyes!
    Otherwise, I'll sleep the sleep of death,
      and my enemy will say, "I won!"
    My foes will rejoice over my downfall. (13:3–4)

---

22. As observed in Parry, *Lamentations*, 92, recent interpreters tend to react negatively to the expression of hope in Lam. 3, seeing it as either (1) less authentic than the grief of Lam. 1–2 or (2) an attempt at orthodoxy that fails as hope slips away into despair in the following chapters. However, the presence of hope in many biblical psalms of lament suggests that Lamentations is part of a broader tradition that finds ways to express confidence in God, even as grief also surfaces. At the same time, one shouldn't understand my positive appraisal of Lam. 3 as an attempt to "tone down, expunge, or belittle the language of lament or anguish" found elsewhere in the book (to quote Linafelt, *Surviving Lamentations*, 2). Both the anguish and the hope need to be respected (cf. Westermann, *Lamentations: Issues*, 76–85).

23. The key exceptions would be Pss. 39; 44; 88, where there's little or no movement from accusation to praise. Perhaps these psalms are there for the harshest of occasions, when it's difficult even to imagine that God could show up.

24. Miller, *They Cried to the Lord*, 128–29; cf. Gunkel and Begrich, *Introduction to Psalms*, 177–86. Other elements may be present (e.g., a confession of sin; see the listing in Gerstenberger, *Psalms*, 1:12–13).

A Whole New Life

In his book *A Whole New Life*, Reynolds Price reflects on his experience of having cancer in his spinal cord. His advice bears a similarity to psalms of lament. He urges people to grieve, but then he also urges them to move on to new ways of thinking and being:

> Grieve for a decent limited time over whatever parts of your old self you know you'll miss. That person is dead as any teen-aged Marine drilled through the forehead in an Asian jungle; any Navy Seal with his legs blown off, halved for the rest of the time he gets; any woman mangled in her tenderest parts, unwived, unmothered, unlovered and shorn. Have one hard cry, if the tears will come. Then stanch the grief, by whatever legal means. Next find your way to be somebody else, the next viable you—a stripped-down whole other clear-eyed person, realistic as a sawed-off shotgun and thankful for air, not to speak of the human kindness you'll meet if you get normal luck.

Reynolds Price, *A Whole New Life*, 183

And then—much like in the middle of Lamentations—the tone suddenly changes. Those shaking their fists at God find comfort. They find reason to praise:

> But I have trusted in your faithful love.
>   My heart will rejoice in your salvation.
> Yes, I will sing to the LORD
>   because he has been good to me.
> (Ps. 13:5–6)

I don't know how to explain the sudden change of tone, other than to say that God shows up in the middle of these prayers. Amid these gut-wrenching wails, a way is made for rejoicing in God. It's as though those praying are invited to take a bold step of faith, engage their imaginations, and recognize that God has heard their plea and will work on their behalf in powerful ways. (See "The Bible and Imagination.") In fact, many scholars think that in ancient Israel, after a worshiper made laments and complaints, a priest or religious leader would offer a comforting word from God (called an *oracle of salvation*) that would lead to the note of praise found at the end of these prayers.[25]

---

25. Gunkel and Begrich, *Introduction to Psalms*, 180–84; cf. Brueggemann, *Psalms and the Life of Faith*, 72–74; Miller, *They Cried to the Lord*, 135–77.

Prayers of complaint don't just allow us to voice our agony to God. They also allow us to receive God's powerful self-revelation, which makes us smile even when tears are on our cheeks.[26] (See "A Whole New Life.")

Conclusion

Through many grief-filled seasons in my own life, I have found comfort in Psalm 126. Here's how it ends:

> Those who sow with tears
>   will reap with songs of joy.
> Those who go out weeping,
>   carrying seed to sow,
> will return with songs of joy,
>   carrying sheaves with them. (126:5–6 NIV)

Many prayers of complaint in the Bible reflect the movement seen here. There's an acknowledgment of the grief, anger, and anguish that normally accompany life. But there's also hope: that night shall end, and a brighter day shall arrive. (See "The Only Word That Matters.")

The Old Testament never envisions a life free from grief, anger, or anguish. Instead, it thoroughly incorporates these emotions into the life of faith.

As our friend in faith, the Old Testament is bolder than most of us when it comes to prayer. We have much to learn from this friend, who teaches us how to pray even when prayer is most difficult. Amid tragedy, we can speak with full honesty to God, and then wait as God shows up and gives us songs of joy.

For Further Study

Ellington, Scott A. *Risking Truth: Reshaping the World through Prayers of Lament.* Princeton Theological Monograph Series. Eugene, OR: Pickwick Publications, 2008.

> This outstanding survey of lament in the Christian Bible speaks with great clarity, explaining scholarship and offering creative insights. It's a treasure box for those wanting to think more deeply about biblical lament.

Tanner, Beth LaNeel. *The Psalms for Today.* Louisville: Westminster John Knox, 2008.

26. In Numbers, the Israelites' complaints are seen very negatively. When one views the canon as a whole, it appears that part of the problem may have been that they remained entrenched in their complaints and did not move to praise.

This book provides a highly accessible introduction to the Psalms. It includes a chapter focusing on psalms of lament.

Wolterstorff, Nicholas. *Lament for a Son*. Grand Rapids: Eerdmans, 1987.

This book isn't a commentary on the laments of the Bible. Rather, it's a lament itself that bears many points of continuity with biblical psalms of laments. The author is one of the most respected philosophical theologians of the last generation, and he wrote this book after his son fell to his death in a mountain-climbing accident.

The website www.MatthewSchlimm.com has additional resources, including group discussion questions.

> ## The Only Word That Matters
>
> "There where the human condition is at its worst and no mortal can sufficiently help, where people are terribly frightened, God speaks the only word that matters: you don't have to be afraid."
>
> Patrick D. Miller,
> *They Cried to the Lord*, 174

11

Great and Terrible Is the Wrath of the Lord

I T'S ONE THING TO ACCEPT THAT *WE* CAN BE ANGRY AT G*OD*.
It's a very different thing to accept that *God* is angry at *us*. The dominant message of Christianity today is simple: God loves us. We've exalted John 3:16 ("For God so loved the world . . . ") above all other Bible verses. For a great number of us, it's nearly inconceivable that this loving, caring, compassionate, forgiving God would also be angry with us.

Yet throughout the Bible, and especially in the prophetic books of the Old Testament, readers find a very frightening message: *the people have sinned blatantly, filling God with rage.* The following text from Ezekiel is similar to what can be found in many other prophetic texts:[1]

> Therefore, as surely as I live, this is what the LORD God says: Because you made my sanctuary unclean with all your disgusting practices and detestable things, . . . one-third of you will die of plague and waste away by famine among you. One-third will fall by the sword all around you. And one-third I will scatter to all the winds, letting loose a sword to pursue them. My anger will be complete. I will exhaust my wrath against them and take my revenge. Then they will know that I, the LORD, have spoken against them in my zeal and consumed them in my wrath. (Ezek. 5:11–13)

1. For an account of divine discipline in the OT (an obvious result of divine anger), see Boda, *A Severe Mercy*, passim, esp. 519–23.

Most of us hate it when another person is mad at us. The thought of God's anger can be overwhelming.

God's Wrath and Popular Thinking

During the mid-eighteenth century, many people became quite enthusiastic about their faith as part of a movement called the Great Awakening. Jonathan Edwards helped to lead this movement in America, urging his audiences to "flee the wrath to come." In "Sinners in the Hands of an Angry God"—perhaps the most famous sermon in American history—Edwards doesn't shy from God's anger. If anything, he amplifies it:

> How awful are those Words, Isai. 63. 3. which are the Words of the great God, *I will tread them in mine Anger, and will trample them in my Fury; and their Blood shall be sprinkled upon my Garments.* . . . [God] will know that you can't bear the Weight of Omnipotence treading upon you, yet he won't regard that, but he will crush you under his Feet without Mercy; he'll crush out your Blood, and make it fly, and it shall be sprinkled on his Garments. . . . He will not only hate you, but he will have you in the utmost Contempt; no Place shall be thought fit for you, but under his Feet, to be trodden down as the Mire of the Streets.[2]

Remarkably, many people responded earnestly to messages like this one. They sought to change the course of their lives, fleeing God's wrath through holier living.

Living with Wrath

Times have changed, and sermons like Edwards's are quite rare. Yet the image of an angry God persists in many people's minds. Indeed, some Christians live in crippling fear of God's wrath. For them, God's anger looms so large that it blocks any glimpses of God's compassion. The life of faith has become a life of guilt. T. S. Matthews speaks this way in his memoir *Under the Influence*:

> Try as I may, I cannot altogether shake off my habitual awe of the Church nor completely dissociate it from the far more fearful God to whom the Church makes its ritual obeisances. I still think of God . . . as a watchful, vengeful, enormous, omniscient policeman, instantly aware of the slightest tinge of irreverence in my innermost thought, always ready to pounce (though with ominous patience

2. Edwards, "Sinners in the Hands of an Angry God," 359 (emphasis original).

he might hold his hand for a time) if I curse, if I mention him in anger, fun or mere habit, if I (O hell-fire and horror!) blaspheme his holy name.[3]

One can see how thinking about God as wrathful can cause all sorts of problems, from overwhelming feelings of guilt, to fear of God, to abandoning religion.

Placing God's Wrath on Other People

Not surprisingly, preachers nowadays have backed away from preaching about divine wrath. Preachers who *do* talk about damnation usually suggest that God's wrath is aimed at people very different from themselves.

Thus, after the September 11, 2001, terrorist attacks, Pat Robertson of the *700 Club* and fellow televangelist Jerry Falwell asserted that the attacks were at least partially the result of God's anger at pagans, gays, civil liberties groups, and people who have had abortions.[4] About a decade later, Robertson suggested that a massive earthquake in Haiti resulted from a slave revolt in 1791 where, he claimed, Haitians formed "a pact to the devil."[5] Significantly, I've never heard Robertson talk about God's wrath falling on himself for his failing to give away his fortune to help the poor (Matt. 19:16–30; Mark 10:17–31; Luke 18:18–30), even though Robertson's reported net worth is $100 million.[6]

Exposing a Contradiction

Rob Bell exposes the contradiction in evangelical beliefs that God is (a) very loving, but also (b) willing to punish anyone with eternal damnation who happens to die without accepting the faith in the right way. He writes:

> If something is wrong with your God,
> if your God is loving one second and
>   cruel the next,
> if your God will punish people for all of
>   eternity for sins committed in a few
>   short years,
> no amount of clever marketing
> or compelling language
> or good music
> or great coffee
> will be able to disguise
> that one, true, glaring, untenable, un-
>   acceptable awful reality.

Rob Bell, *Love Wins*, 175

---

3. T. S. Matthews, *Under the Influence*, 343. My attention was originally drawn to this quotation by Fretheim, *Suffering of God*, 1.
4. Harris, "God Gave U.S."
5. Marquand, "Pat Robertson Haiti Comments."
6. "Pat Robertson Net Worth." See also Finley, "A Moralist Who Loves Racing," which reports that Robertson once purchased a race horse for $520,000.

Questioning Wrath

Many Christians shun Robertson's logic; thoughts of God's anger toward *anyone* do not sit well with them. As mentioned above, the dominant note in most churches today is God's love, not God's wrath. In fact, Pastor Rob Bell—named by *Time Magazine* as one of the world's one hundred most influential people—wrote a book in 2011 called *Love Wins*, which found itself number 2 on the *New York Times* bestseller list as soon as it was published.[7] In the book, Bell challenges traditional notions about God's wrath and eternal damnation. Like many Christians today, Bell believes that in the end, God's love wins out over God's anger. (See "Exposing a Contradiction.")

Rejecting Parts of the Bible

When Christians encounter Old Testament passages that talk about God's wrath, they often shift gears to Jesus, insisting that "the God of the New Testament is just so much more loving than the angry God of the Old Testament." Such thinking obviously degrades the Old Testament. Sometimes these thoughts are more developed. People assume:

1. Jesus died on the cross for our sins.
2. Therefore, we no longer have any reason to fear God's judgment on our lives. The Old Testament's tales of a wrathful God no longer apply.

This type of sentiment is often found among all sorts of Christians.

Mennonite pastor Ryan Dueck recently described how his eleven-year-old son, after reading of Sodom and Gomorrah, said to him, "Sometimes I'm afraid of God." Pastor Dueck described how difficult it was to respond to his son's remark, eventually concluding, "I really do believe that when I come across horrifying passages in the OT, that rather than trying to rationalize or spin or defend, my only recourse is to turn to the Crucified One who shows me, in the truest and most complete way, what God is like—who shows me that we do not have to be afraid."[8]

Dueck is not alone. Retired Episcopalian bishop John Shelby Spong moves in the same direction, but more aggressively. He rejects much of the Old Testament. In particular, he laments that "the Bible, again and again, portrays a wrathful God's intention to punish the chosen people."[9] This tendency to abandon the Old Testament because of discomfort with divine wrath isn't

7. Meacham, "Rob Bell"; "Hardcover Advice & Misc."
8. Dueck, "Sometimes I'm Afraid of God."
9. Spong, *Sins of Scripture*, 170.

new. As I mentioned in chapter 1, it's been taking place at least since the time of Marcion.[10]

Rejecting Faith

Images of God's anger cause some people to reject not just the Old Testament, but their entire faith in God. The famous atheist Richard Dawkins writes, "The God of the Old Testament is arguably the most unpleasant character in all fiction." Dawkins claims there are many reasons why the Old Testament God is this way. Among them are what he calls God's "maniacal jealousy" and "characteristic fury."[11]

We don't live in a world where Christianity is the only religious option. When confronted with the Bible's portraits of an angry God, many people find it easier to give up their faith than to live with guilt and fear. (See "From Fearing God to Leaving Church.")

From Fearing God to Leaving Church

"Many of the people I interviewed, particularly those who had been raised in conservative Protestant denominations or strongly Catholic households, had been taught to fear Satan and hell. And they did. And this fear remained an ugly, damaging, disturbing element of their lives for many years. As they got older, they began to resent it, hate it, and eventually question it. Such teachings and beliefs can, for some people, produce long-term negative feelings, entrenched discomfort, and prolonged despair. And some people with such experiences, at some point, just want to get away from the source of those feelings, namely their religion."

Phil Zuckerman, *Faith No More*, 162

What Are We Missing?

Are there any alternatives to living with crippling fear, condemning people unlike ourselves, rejecting the Bible, or rejecting faith? When we closely study the Bible's accounts of God's anger, is there anything we are missing? Is there something that might help us better understand why Jewish and Christian communities would—for thousands of years—be willing to claim that biblical texts speaking of an angry God are inspired and sacred?

Divine Anger in Both Testaments

This chapter tackles these questions, but first it's important to notice that divine anger isn't just an Old Testament problem. Contrary to popular perception,

10. Tertullian, *Against Marcion* 1:24–27 (*ANF* 3:289–93).
11. Dawkins, *God Delusion*, 51, 278, 279.

it's actually a biblical problem. People who associate the Old Testament with wrath and the New Testament with grace have not spent much time carefully reading either Testament.

The Old Testament contains countless texts that speak of God's mercy, compassion, forgiveness, and steadfast love. As Psalm 103:12 puts it,

> As far as east is from west—
>> that's how far God has removed our sin from us.

The prophet Joel similarly emphasizes God's forgiveness:

> Return to the LORD your God,
>> for he is merciful and compassionate,
> very patient, full of faithful love,
>> and ready to forgive. (Joel 2:13)

The idea that God was unforgiving until Jesus died on the cross simply doesn't match what the Bible itself says. Although the Old Testament contains plenty of texts that speak of God's anger, it repeatedly describes God's undying compassion for Israel.

Furthermore, divine wrath isn't confined to the Old Testament. Jesus brings messages of woe and doom like Old Testament prophets before him (e.g., Matt. 23:13–29; Luke 6:24–26; 13:1–5). Jesus tells many parables where the character representing God becomes intensely angry and even violent (e.g., Mark 12:9; Luke 14:21; 19:27). Mark 3:5 says specifically that Jesus became angry, and there are other passages that portray him as acting or speaking in anger (e.g., Matt. 21:12–13; 23:13–29; Luke 6:24–26; 11:42–52). Much like texts in the Old Testament, Jesus speaks specifically of the "wrath to come" (Matt. 3:7 NRSV; Luke 3:7; cf. Luke 21:23). The rest of the New Testament continues these sorts of ideas found with Jesus.[12]

Hell and the Bible

The Old Testament does not speak of a hell. It uses the word "Sheol" quite frequently, but that word is different. "Sheol" means the underworld, the grave, the place of the dead, or even death itself.

The New Testament, however, speaks about "a hell of fire," a place where the ungodly receive eternal punishment (Matt. 5:22; 18:9; cf. Mark 9:43; James 3:6).

In fact, despite the Old Testament's haunting imagery, one can easily argue that divine wrath in the New Testament is even more disturbing. While the Old

---

12. As, e.g., in Rom. 1:18; 2:5, 8; 12:19; Rev. 6:16–17; 11:18; 14:10, 19; 15:1, 7; 16:1, 19; 19:15.

Testament talks about punishments coming in this lifetime, the New Testament describes eternal punishment. As John Wenham describes, of the Old and New Testaments, "the New Testament is the more terrible, for the Old Testament seldom speaks of anything beyond temporal judgments."[13] It's Jesus himself who speaks the most about everlasting damnation, whether it's "eternal fire" or "hell" itself.[14] (See "Hell and the Bible.")

God's anger is an issue that must be engaged by all readers of the Bible. It simply doesn't work to relegate divine wrath to the Old Testament.

God and Metaphor

"It has been rightly stated that virtually all of the language used in the Bible to refer to God is metaphorical; the word 'God' would be an exception. Occasionally such language is drawn from the natural world, both animate (God is an eagle, Deut. 32:11) and inanimate (God is a rock, Ps. 31:2–3). The vast majority of the metaphors for God in the OT, however, are drawn from the sphere of the human: (a) form, with its function (mouth, speaking, Num. 12:8); (b) emotional, volitional and mental states (rejoicing, Zeph. 3:17); (c) roles and activities, within the family (parent, Hos. 11:1) or the larger society (shepherd, Ps. 23:1)."

Terence E. Fretheim, *Suffering of God*, 5–6

Metaphors for God

Given the pervasiveness of God's anger, how should we understand it? To begin, it's important to keep in mind that *the Bible typically talks about God by using metaphors*. A metaphor is when one thing is spoken of in terms of something else, such as, PREACHERS ARE PILOTS. We all know there are many differences between people who give sermons and those who fly airplanes. Yet this metaphor suggests that there are interesting similarities between these two vocations. Both preachers and pilots try to take people somewhere different from where they started. Ideally, pastors move people's hearts, bringing them farther along in their journey of faith. Meanwhile, pilots move people's bodies, bringing them to new physical locations. When sermons or flights take too long, it's a miserable experience that leaves no one happy.

When it comes to language for God, the Bible uses metaphorical language so frequently that we don't always notice it. Biblical images for God speak powerfully about who God is, but they also break down, failing to encapsulate or define God's identity. (See "God and Metaphor.")

---

13. J. Wenham, *Goodness of God*, 16.
14. On "eternal fire," see Matt. 18:8; 25:41. On "hell" itself, see Matt. 5:22–30; 10:28; 18:9; 23:33; Mark 9:43–47; Luke 12:5.

Consider this image: GOD IS OUR KING. This metaphor comes from the Bible (e.g., Ps. 145:1), and it sheds light on how God should rule over the covenant people. Yet this image breaks down. For example, God may be king, but the Bible doesn't extend this metaphor to talk about a queen to whom God is married.[15]

Or consider this image: GOD IS A ROCK. Again, this metaphor comes straight out of the Bible (e.g., Ps. 18:2). Yet we can see how it both works and doesn't work. It vividly illustrates God's stability and trustworthiness, even in the storms of life. It suggests that God will not be shaken. At the same time, we all know that rocks aren't living—unlike God. So, the metaphor breaks down.

In a similar way, we need to think about GOD IS ANGRY as metaphorical language. It uses the human experience of anger and applies it to God. In doing so, it speaks valuable information about God, but as we'll see, there are also places where this image for God doesn't work. Human anger often reflects human limitations, so divine anger is naturally different.

The Workings of Divine Anger

What, then, is it about the metaphor GOD IS ANGRY that makes sense? Why do biblical authors return to it again and again?

As mentioned in the last chapter, anger arises when someone perceives that a *wrongdoing* has taken place. Furthermore, this emotion often means that the angry person wants to see *justice*, correction, or punishment come to the wrongdoer.[16]

With these two key components in mind, it becomes obvious why the Bible would portray God as angry:

1. God perceives wrongdoings.
2. Repulsed by evil, God wants to execute justice.

God knows the evil that takes place in the world. Because God is good, God wants to stop that evil and prevent it from recurring. The metaphor GOD IS ANGRY captures these central ideas of the Bible.

The Metaphor Breaks Down

While we can thus begin to see why the metaphor GOD IS ANGRY works, we need also to be mindful of how this metaphor breaks down.

---

15. See Frymer-Kensky, *In the Wake of the Goddesses*, 151–61, esp. 158, on the debate over whether some ancient Israelites thought of Asherah as God's consort, even if their perspectives are not promoted by biblical texts.

16. See Schlimm, *From Fratricide to Forgiveness*, esp. chap. 4.

One of the most significant differences between divine and human anger pertains to human limitations, imperfections, and sins: humans have trouble getting anger right. (See "The Difficulty of Anger.") All too often, people

- become angry for the wrong reasons,
- overreact in anger,
- make biased judgments while angry,
- remain angry for far too long,
- fail to become angry over real injustices,
- fail to use their anger constructively, and
- do something wrong while angry.

As Terence Fretheim puts it, "Most human expressions of anger are 'infected' with sin."[17]

Obviously, God is different from humanity. God doesn't have the shortcoming, limitations, and sinfulness that we do. God grows angry over the right things. (See "A Drastic Difference.") God alone sees our hearts with clarity. No one but God is in a position to judge who deserves mercy and who deserves punishment. Far more than any human, God knows how to exercise anger in ways that bring about good for all involved.[18] Unlike with short-tempered humans, it often takes centuries to make God mad. In Hosea, while God is portrayed as passionately angry (11:5–7), the text's tone suddenly changes (11:8–9), and we read:

> I won't act on the heat of my anger;
>   I won't return to destroy Ephraim;
> *for I am God and not a human being*, the holy one in your midst;
>   I won't come in harsh judgment. (Hosea 11:9; italics added;
>   cf. Isa. 55:8–9)

Human anger helps us to begin to see what God's anger is like. Yet God may not follow through with anger the way humans so often do. We commit grave errors when we assume that divine anger reflects all our interpersonal experiences of it.

One of the most common experiences of human anger is communication breakdowns. When two people are mad at each other, they often talk past each other, failing to hear what the other actually says. In contrast, the book of Exodus suggests that God hears what people say, even in the midst of divine rage. Thus, in Exodus 32, the Israelites create a golden calf and worship it. God

17. Fretheim, "Wrath of God," esp. 6.
18. See Davis, *Imagination Shaped*, 64.

is furious, muttering to Moses, "Now leave me alone! Let my fury burn and devour them. Then I'll make a great nation out of you" (32:10). Moses boldly refuses to grant God's wish. Instead of leaving God alone, Moses confronts this angry deity: "Lord, why does your fury burn against your own people, whom you brought out of the land of Egypt with great power and amazing force? . . . Calm down your fierce anger. Change your mind about doing terrible things to your own people" (32:11–12). Readers might expect Moses to get zapped for confronting an angry God

> ### The Difficulty of Anger
>
> "Anybody can become angry—that is easy . . . but to [do this] to the right person, and to the right amount, and at the right time, and for the right purpose, and in the right way—this is not within everybody's power and is not easy; so that to do these things properly is rare, praiseworthy, and noble."
>
> Aristotle,
> *Nicomachean Ethics* 2.9.2
> (trans. Rackham)

this way. Instead, God hears what Moses says and changes plans (32:14). This God is far different from humans who become blind (and deaf) with rage, insisting on their own way.

The Bible's images of divine wrath need to be taken seriously, and they ought to cause some fear in us. They should jolt us out of complacency with evil. At the same time, these images shouldn't become so dominant that we overlook (1) God's patience, (2) the value of divine anger, or (3) God's love persisting beyond expressions of anger. The rest of this chapter examines these three themes.

> ### A Drastic Difference
>
> "Humanity's sense of injustice is a poor analogy to God's sense of injustice. The exploitation of the poor is to us a misdemeanor; to God it is a disaster. Our reaction is disapproval; God's reaction is something no language can convey.
>
> "Just as God is absolutely different from humanity, so is divine anger different from human anger."
>
> Abraham Joshua Heschel, *Prophets*,
> 2:64–65, 74 (alt. for gender inclusivity)

Slow to Anger

No concept is more helpful to thinking about God's anger than this: *God is slow to anger.*

Many biblical theologians have suggested that the clearest picture of God in the Old Testament is found in Exodus 34:6–7.[19] (See "Defining God's

---

19. See G. E. Wright, *God Who Acts*, 85–86; Brueggemann, *Theology of the Old Testament*, 215–16; Goldingay, *Old Testament Theology*, 338, 828; Fretheim, *God and World*, 333, n. 6; Childs, *Biblical Theology*, 354; Boda, *A Severe Mercy*, 522–23; Crenshaw, *Defending God*, 3–4, 93.

Character.") There, God passes before Moses. Readers expect a physical description of God. Instead, they learn about God's compassion and patience:

> The LORD passed before [Moses], and proclaimed, "The LORD, the LORD, a God merciful and gracious, *slow to anger*, and abounding in steadfast love and faithfulness, keeping steadfast love for the thousandth generation, forgiving iniquity and transgression and sin, yet by no means clearing the guilty, but visiting the iniquity of the parents upon the children and the children's children, to the third and the fourth generation." (NRSV, italics added)

These verses clearly affirm the reality of God's anger, especially at the end. But they also make clear that God abounds in loyal love and compassion. God's scales tilt toward forgiveness. Verses throughout the Old Testament echo this description.[20]

In fact, the books of 1–2 Kings can be read as one long story that illustrates the same point: God is slow to anger. These books span around four hundred years. Throughout this time, the people of Israel and Judah are described as very sinful. King after king does what's evil in the eyes of the Lord. Yet punishment for sin does not come immediately. It's only after generations of idol worshiping that God's judgment comes and the people are sent into exile. In 722 BCE, the Assyrians attack and conquer Israel, and in 587 BCE the Babylonians do the same thing with Judah. The Bible never says that this punishment came the moment one person said a bad word or broke a single commandment. Instead, despite the people's nearly continual lack of faithfulness, God's anger took centuries to materialize.

> **Defining God's Character**
>
> "This listing of qualities stands as one of the most important definitions of the character of God in the entire Bible."
>
> Dennis Olson,
> "Exodus," 143–44 OT,
> commenting on Exod. 34:6–7

The idea that God is slow to anger corrects two of the most problematic ideas among Christians today. The first mistaken notion is that *God will never get angry*. This idea is problematic because it doesn't match the Bible, it suggests that God doesn't oppose evil, and it promotes religion without morality. God becomes reduced to a puppy dog. Seeing God as unmoved by our sins only encourages us to dive deeper into wrongdoing.

The other mistaken notion is that *God will pounce on us for the slightest spiritual mistake*. This second idea is problematic because it doesn't match the Bible either, it suggests that God is cruel, and it entraps people in cages of guilt and fear. If we adopt this view of God, then God becomes a tormenting monster.

20. Num. 14:18; Neh. 9:17; Pss. 86:15; 103:8; 145:8; Joel 2:13; Jon. 4:2; Nah. 1:3.

If we adhere to the simple idea that God is slow to anger, then we avoid both pitfalls. We can then affirm that God is forgiving and merciful, even as we also affirm that God is just and opposed to evil.

The idea that God is slow to anger can be stated another way: God's anger arises in response to sin that is marked by three characteristics. *First, this sin is unwavering.* In the prophets, God's anger doesn't arise simply because the people sin. It arises because people sin without ceasing. Aside from a few rare exceptions, leaders and nations tend to plunge further and further into wickedness.[21] Eventually God's patience runs its course. Only then does divine wrath take form.

Second, this sin is pervasive. The prophets are more concerned with an entire society that has gone amuck than with one person's transgressions.[22] Thus the prophets bring their words against the people as a whole. Or they focus on leaders and those who have power and influence over the people as a whole (like King David, 2 Sam. 12:1–15).

Third, this sin is horrendous. The prophets don't care about small sins or trite transgressions. For example, they never say that the Babylonians will crush Jerusalem because of someone's foul language.[23] The prophets instead condemn things that are especially horrendous. Amos blasts those who commit massive crimes against humanity, slaughtering the innocent (1:11–12).[24] Repeatedly, prophets denounce child sacrifice (Isa. 57:5; Jer. 7:31–32; 32:35; Ezek. 16:20–21, 36; 20:31). Time and again, the prophets cry out against idolatry because people are forsaking the very God who rescued them from slavery. The prophets express God's fury over the exploitation of the poor, needy, and vulnerable—things that should upset us all.

Why It's Good That God's Angry

Odd as it sounds, there truly are good things about God's anger. Consider the alternative: a God who never grew angry over the worst atrocities, a God who heard the cry of the needy but refused to respond with justice, a God who told Pharaoh "I love you" instead of "Let my people go." (See "A God Whom Hitler Would Love.")

21. Two exceptions are Josiah in 2 Kings 23:25 and the Assyrians in Jon. 3:6–10.
22. Earlier in the canon, one finds examples of God's punishment of an individual's sins (e.g., Gen. 12:17–19; Num. 15:32–36; Josh. 7). However, by the time one gets to the literary prophets, the focus is more on the sins of the nation and its leaders.
23. To the contrary, the prophets themselves felt compelled to use bad words at times. The Hebrew of Ezek. 23 is far more explicit than most English translations admit.
24. Schlimm, "Teaching the Hebrew Bible: . . . Amos 1:3–2:3."

Would such a God be worthy of our praise? Could we honestly worship such a deity? Is it fair to ask people who suffer injustice to sing hymns to a God who remains detached from the affairs of humanity? Should I tell my students from East Africa, who have lost half of their family members to war, that God has no anger toward those who killed their loved ones? (See "God Isn't Hallmark.")

The church father Tertullian, responding to Marcion, observed that if God failed to punish unrepentant wickedness, then God would be letting it go free, essentially condoning it. The Creator of the universe would be reduced to a wimp unable to fight evil.[25]

In the book of Jeremiah, God describes people's sins and asks what the proper response should be:

> Criminals are found among my people;
>   they set traps to catch people,
>   like hunters lying in wait.
> Like a cage full of birds,
>   so their houses are full of loot.
> No wonder they are rich and powerful
>   and have grown fat and sleek!
> To be sure, their evil deeds exceed all limits,
>   and yet they prosper.
> They are indifferent to the plight of the orphan,
>   reluctant to defend the rights of the poor.
> Shouldn't I punish such acts? declares the LORD.
>   Shouldn't I repay that nation for its deeds? (Jer. 5:26–29)

> **God Isn't Hallmark**
>
> "I don't think it should bother us that [God] is no Hallmark greeting card. If God is to be God the Creator of all, he must be utterly beyond our comprehension—and, therefore, awfully scary."
>
> Thomas Cahill,
> *Gifts of the Jews*, 245

Here God denounces the way that people exploit the weak, poor, and vulnerable. God thinks it's wrong when some people become gluttons while others starve. God thinks it's wrong when the rights of poor are neglected in court. God thinks it's wrong when people are cheated out of what little money they have. We should feel the same way.

Martin Luther King Jr. observed that few things were worse than seeing injustice and doing nothing in response. As he puts it, "Those who passively accept evil are as much involved

25. Tertullian, *Against Marcion* 1.27 (ANF 3:292).

A God Whom Hitler Would Love

A former nun writes, "It is wonderful not to have to cower before a vengeful deity, who threatens us with eternal damnation if we do not abide by his rules."[a]

Religion scholar Conor Cunningham responds, "Imagine if Hitler rather than an ex-nun had written those words."[b] Cunningham then refers his readers to Czesław Miłosz, who writes, "A true opium for the people is a belief in nothingness after death—the huge solace of thinking that our betrayals, greed, cowardice, and murders are not going to be judged."[c]

a. Armstrong, *A History of God*, 378.
b. Cunningham, *Darwin's Pious Idea*, 235.
c. Miłosz, "Discreet Charm of Nihilism."

---

in it as those who help to perpetuate it. Those who accept evil without protesting against it are really cooperating with it." For King, remaining silent in the face of injustice was even more deplorable than blatant evil. Elsewhere he writes:

> If the moderates of the white South fail to act now, history will have to record that the greatest tragedy of this period of social transition was not the strident clamor of the bad people, but the appalling silence of the good people.[26]

Unlike complacent humans, the God of the Bible will not sit by idly while rampant evil flourishes. This God refuses to remain silent while people harm one another or creation. This God will not passively accept evil. Evil angers God. We wouldn't want it any other way. (See "Humanity's Infernal Cruelty.")

Reading the Text Closely

When we study the Bible closely, we find other pictures emerging alongside God's anger. At times, for example, we find God less angry and more grieved by the people's continual rejection:

> Have I been a wasteland to Israel
>   or a land of dense darkness?
> Why then do my people say,
>   "We have wandered far away;
>   we'll come to you no longer"?

26. King, *Testament of Hope*, 429, alt. for gender inclusivity; 475.

Humanity's Infernal Cruelty

"The destructiveness of God's power is not due to God's hostility to humanity, but to His concern for righteousness, to His intolerance of injustice. . . . God's anger is fierce because humanity's cruelty is infernal."[a]

Abraham Joshua Heschel,
Prophets, 1:80 (alt. for gender inclusivity)

a. Heschel may be alluding to the Holocaust. This work was dedicated "to the martyrs of 1940–45" (1:v).

> Does a young woman forget her jewelry
>   or a bride her wedding dress?
> Yet you have forgotten me days without end! (Jer. 2:31–32)

Biblical scholar Terence Fretheim has shown that God suffers not only because of the people's rejection. God also suffers alongside the people as they suffer—even if the people's pain is due to their own sin.[27] This suffering by God in the Old Testament foreshadows what comes with Jesus in the New Testament.[28]

Even though prophetic writings contain some of the most frightening images of God's wrath, they also contain some of the most hopeful images of God's love, which endures even on the other side of God's punishment. Divine anger rarely has the last word in the Bible. Because God is merciful, the prophets bring not only doom-filled words about the future. They also resound with oracles of hope. Earlier I mentioned that God's anger took centuries to reach fruition with the Babylonians conquering Jerusalem. The Old Testament repeatedly offers hope on the other side of this catastrophic event. As God says in Isaiah 54:

> For a brief moment I abandoned you,
>   but with great compassion I will gather you.
> In overflowing wrath for a moment
>   I hid my face from you,
> but with everlasting love I will have compassion on you,
>   says the LORD, your Redeemer. . . .
> For the mountains may depart
>   and the hills be removed,
> but my steadfast love shall not depart from you,
>   and my covenant of peace shall not be removed,
>   says the LORD, who has compassion on you. (54:7–8, 10 NRSV)

27. Fretheim, *Suffering of God*, chaps. 7–8.
28. Cf. ibid., 6–7, 166; Brueggemann, *Theology of the Old Testament*, 302.

Sadly, people who use the Bible to condemn others rarely follow the prophets' example of reassuring people that even on the other side of punishment, God's love will persist in abundance.

The book of Amos, which continually hurls accusations and forecasts destruction, nevertheless ends with a note of hope:

> I will restore the fortunes of my people Israel,
>> and they shall rebuild the ruined cities and inhabit them;
> they shall plant vineyards and drink their wine,
>> and they shall make gardens and eat their fruit. (Amos 9:14 NRSV)[29]

On the other side of catastrophe, one finds visions of a good life, even here on earth.

When people read the prophets, they too often ignore God's wrath or ignore God's comfort. The Bible we have, however, intertwines the two. As the psalms put it:

> For [God's] anger is but for a moment;
>> his favor is for a lifetime.
> Weeping may linger for the night,
>> but joy comes with the morning. (Ps. 30:5 NRSV)

The Old Testament is acutely aware of how bad decisions have terrible consequences. It's also aware that God's love persists before, during, and after those consequences.[30]

Conclusion

At first glance, it may seem that becoming friends with the Old Testament is like befriending a person with warped ideas of the divine—someone who delights in the idea of an angry God. However, when we learn more, we discover that the Bible speaks of God's anger in complicated and intricate ways. The Old Testament reveals a God who is deeply concerned about evil and firmly opposed to it—but also slow to anger. We discover that God's anger exists in uneasy tension with love.[31] (See "Anger in Tension.")

29. Many scholars suggest that this epilogue wasn't original to the book (e.g., Jeremias, *Book of Amos*, 5, 9). In any event, the text as it has been transmitted refuses to omit any sense of hope.

30. As I explain in Schlimm, "Different Perspectives," 693, even some of God's most wrathful statements have glimpses of God's grace alongside them (cf. Jer. 12:8 and 12:15).

31. Brueggemann (*Theology of the Old Testament*, 267–313, esp. 268, 295–96) talks about similar tensions within God, speaking of disjunctions between "unlimited sovereignty

Understanding God's anger requires keeping several things straight. Looking at the Old Testament as a whole, we see the following:

1. God's anger is real.
2. God's anger needs to be taken seriously.
3. God is slow to anger.
4. This anger does not endure.

Anger in Tension

"Despite its tragic necessity, . . . anger is not depicted as an emotion God delights in; instead, it grieves God to be angry (Lam. 3:33) and God would prefer to avoid it altogether (Isa. 27:2–3; Hos. 11:9)."[a]

Gary A. Herion,
"Wrath of God (OT)," 995

a. Also Isa. 28:21 suggests that anger is not the normal way God interacts with people.

If we get any of these points wrong, we end up with a skewed picture of God. If we neglect number 1 and number 2, then God becomes a puppy dog who lets us do anything we want, failing to oppose grave evil. If we neglect number 3 and number 4, then God becomes a cruel presence in our lives, a monster seeking to destroy us.

Neither of these twisted pictures matches what the Bible as a whole says about the Divine. God's anger is both like human anger and unlike human anger.

One of my favorite college professors said that heresy is not so much the embrace of blatant lies. It's failing to get the right priorities—minoring on the majors and majoring on the minors.[32] Unfortunately, Christians today tend to minor on some of the four points above, and they end up with an unbiblical picture of God.

Other parts of this book have stressed the importance of reading the Bible alongside other Christians. When it comes to texts about God's anger, it's especially helpful to read with other faithful people. Our sisters and brothers in Christ can help us avoid the extremes of envisioning God as incapable or only capable of anger.

For Further Study

Brueggemann, Walter. *Theology of the Old Testament: Testimony, Dispute, Advocacy.* Minneapolis: Fortress, 1997. Esp. 267–313.

---

and risky solidarity" and between "Yahweh's self-regard" and "Yahweh's commitment to Israel."

32. Victor Hamilton shared this insight in many of his classes at Asbury College (now Asbury University).

Fretheim, Terence E. "Theological Reflections on the Wrath of God in the Old Testament." *Horizons in Biblical Theology* 24 (December 2002): 1–26.

Heschel, Abraham. *The Prophets.* 2 vols. Peabody, MA: Prince, 1999.

Schlimm, Matthew R. "Different Perspectives on Divine Pathos: An Examination of Hermeneutics in Biblical Theology." *Catholic Biblical Quarterly* 69, no. 4 (2007): 673–94.

> Brueggemann, Fretheim, and Heschel are prominent interpreters who have carefully studied God's wrath and passionate involvement with the world. My article explains the differences between these authors, showing, for example, that Brueggemann closely connects human and divine anger, whereas Heschel strongly differentiates the two, while Fretheim finds middle ground.

The website www.MatthewSchlimm.com has additional resources, including group discussion questions.

12

The Old Testament's Authority

A QUESTION HAS BEEN LURKING JUST BELOW THE SURFACE of all the preceding discussions: How should we think of the Old Testament's authority? Christians often talk of the Bible as *the word of God*, *inspired*, and *God's revelation*. However, is it possible to be more specific? How should we see the Old Testament's power over our lives? This final chapter explores different models of biblical authority, searching for the best ways to think about the Old Testament.

What Is an Authority?

It's useful to begin by thinking about what an *authority* is. Many types of people function as authorities. A *drill sergeant* certainly does. Soldiers are expected to obey every command that's issued without question. They face severe consequences for failing to do so.

Bosses are also authority figures. Some of us have great bosses. Others of us have terrible ones. Whether they are good or not, however, our workplace superiors exert some level of control over how we do our jobs.

Teachers are also authorities. They know more than we do, but they share their knowledge and help to make us better people.

At times people talk about authorities who are further removed from their lives. For example, I may watch a television show about dinosaurs that features a leading authority on paleontology. The idea here is that this *expert* would be a trustworthy source. Similarly, a *book* about dinosaurs written by this scientist would be considered an authority. (In fact, the word *authority* is related to the word *author*.)

This brings up an important point. People often use *authority* for *something that isn't human*. A judge's ruling, for example, may be considered authoritative for future court cases.

Nowadays, much authority is suspect. Since the seventeenth century (the so-called Age of Enlightenment), pivotal thinkers have been extremely suspicious of traditional forms of authority. You could even say that it's now a tradition to reject tradition.

Furthermore, many of us live in countries that celebrate our nation's independence from another nation's control. We love freedom, especially freedom from other people telling us what to do. We cherish liberty, whether that means we are our own authorities or we get to decide which authorities influence our lives.

Biblical Authority: Different Views

Just as there are many ways of thinking about authority in general, there are many ways of thinking about the Old Testament's authority in particular.

No or Limited Authority

On one end of the spectrum, people reject the Bible's authority altogether. Obviously, many atheists take such a stance. As we saw in chapter 1, Marcion and his disciples also followed this approach, throwing out the Old Testament's sacred status.

Others claim that the Old Testament has limited authority as a historical relic from the ancient world. Even then, there's debate about how reliable it is as a historical manuscript, given the biased nature of these writings that don't hesitate to speak of the supernatural.

Or, people might say that the Bible is important because it has shaped modern culture, especially in the Western hemisphere. However, this position is still far removed from saying that the Old Testament *should* shape our own lives in definitive ways today.

The Drill-Sergeant Model

Among those who accept the Old Testament as an authority in their lives, extremists sometimes have the loudest voices. Many see the Bible as something like a drill instructor: it tells us what to do, and we do it. No questions asked. As a popular saying puts it, "God said it. I believe it. That settles it. Forever."

This saying can be a source of comfort to people wrestling with doubt or needing assurance. More broadly, the drill-sergeant model of biblical authority may work for some, especially those comfortable with military models of authority.

However, many people have problems when this type of authority becomes their primary basis for thinking about the Bible's power in our lives. For example, if the God of the Bible loves us, then why would the Bible function more like a drill sergeant than a gentle teacher?

Another problem with this model of authority: New Testament Christians didn't follow it. As noted in chapters 7 and 8, the Old Testament commands circumcision and food restrictions. If the earliest church saw the Old Testament as a drill sergeant, they never would have deviated from these commands. Instead, the church met and worked with the Holy Spirit to discern that God was doing a new thing.

The drill-sergeant model of biblical authority is also susceptible to misuse. In faith communities where the Bible must be accepted without question, leaders too often use their own (sometimes quite bad) interpretations of Scripture to manipulate others to do their bidding. To avoid unhealthy images of dominance and submission, most of us do well to look beyond this model of biblical authority.[1]

The Inerrant-Infallible Model

Another approach sees the Bible less as someone who shouts commands and more as a completely accurate speaker. This model claims that the Bible is *inerrant* (free from errors) and *infallible* (incapable of letting readers down).[2]

This sort of language suggests that the Bible is something like a trustworthy dictionary that gives definitions of God, humanity, and the world. The Bible nails everything down, defining who God is.

Or, to those more scientifically minded, words like "infallible" imply that the Bible is something akin to *a math formula for life*: you just need to apply

1. Lancaster, "Authority and Narrative," 84. Also see Lancaster, *Women and the Authority of Scripture*, esp. chap. 7. On 166–77, she discusses seeing "The Bible as Teacher." While I like the teacher metaphor far more than seeing the Bible as a drill sergeant, it may not work for people who haven't been deeply inspired by teachers. This metaphor also breaks down rather quickly: the OT is intimate with its readers, sharing everything from sexual activities in Song of Songs to raw, unrestrained anger in many psalms. Obviously teachers with healthy boundaries don't share such aspects of their personal lives with students.

2. While many authors perceive a difference between inerrancy and infallibility, those differences can vary from writer to writer (Thorsen and Reeves, *What Christians Believe about the Bible*, 165–79; cf. Plummer, *40 Questions about Interpreting*, 38).

this formula (the Bible) to the right numbers (your life), and you'll get the right answer (what you should do) every time.

Or, to those of us who like history, words like "inerrancy" suggest that every detail in the Bible will always check out by modern historical standards.

Many have found the language of *inerrancy* and *infallibility* appealing. Insofar as their main concern is to say that the Bible as a whole is reliable when it comes to thinking about God, humanity, and creation, I don't have a bone to pick with them. However, many problems can arise when words like "inerrant" set the tone for how we think about the Bible. (See "Where the Bible Is Mute.")

First, the language of "inerrancy" suggests that we are dealing with the type of sentences that can have either a true or a false value. However, the Bible refuses to be confined to declarative sentences that can be classified as fact or lie. Some of the best parts of the Bible are not its statements, but its questions, commands, and exclamations. Most of these cannot be assessed according to a simple true-or-false scheme. Yet these questions, commands, and exclamations can shape our lives in powerful ways. Where would we be if we didn't

> **Where the Bible Is Mute**
>
> "Nowhere does the Bible speak of inerrancy."
>
> William Abraham,
> *Divine Inspiration*, 31

have the freedom ask honest questions in prayer (see chap. 9)? Where would we be without commands to love God with all we are? Where would we be without exclamations like the following?

> LORD, our Lord, how majestic
>   is your name throughout the earth! (Ps. 8:1)

Second, language like "inerrancy" causes readers of the Bible to focus on the wrong things. In addition to dictionaries and math formulas, the language of inerrancy suggests something like an accurate historical account or a precise scientific description. Yet, as we saw in chapters 2 and 3, we can easily miss the main points of biblical texts if we approach them while thinking their goal is to convey historical or scientific information.

Third, if "inerrancy" is the primary way we should think about the Bible, then we need to wrestle with odd ancient expressions like "the four corners of the earth" (Isa. 11:12; Ezek. 7:2; Matt. 24:31; Mark 13:27; Rev. 7:1) and whether such expressions are error-free. We suddenly need to fret over the tiniest of details, like whether Ahaziah became king of Judah when Joram was in his eleventh or twelfth year of reigning over Israel (2 Kings 8:25; 9:29). We should be focusing on more important matters, like the salvation of the world. (See "Diverting Energy.")

Diverting Energy

"The stress on inerrancy does not contribute to taking the text of scripture itself with great seriousness. It tends to divert energy from the task of interpreting scripture to a preoccupation with harmonization, which hinders rather than helps an understanding of particular texts."[a]

John Goldingay, *Models for Scripture*, 277

a. On "the idolatry of history," see Mark S. Smith, *Memoirs of God*, 164–65.

Fourth, the language of "infallibility" can suggest that the Bible will never let people down. Yet we know that people are finite and sinful. We know that the church has misinterpreted Scriptures, sometimes for centuries. (See "Moses's Horns.") We know that even the devil can quote Scripture (Matt. 4:1–11). We know that we need other people and the Holy Spirit to make adequate sense of the Bible, and even then we may come up short. Perhaps all these problems lie more with us as sinful humans than with the Bible itself. Yet what good does it do to talk about the Bible as infallible if we as humans can't use it infallibly?[3] We know that people in the Bible sometimes felt that God had let them down (see chap. 9). We'd be mistaken to think that we will never feel the same way about the Bible.

Finally and most damning, the only writings that can be considered error-free and failsafe are those that are boring. If you want to fall asleep, read something that recounts only dry facts, can be proved true in a laboratory, and never makes any audacious claims. But do not read the Bible. Avoid its memorable accounts of creation, its R-rated stories, its groundbreaking claims about gender, its peculiar laws, its brutally honest prayers, and its tales of a wrathful deity.

Figure 6. Moses's Horns. *Wikimedia Commons,* http://commons.wikimedia.org/wiki /File:Moses_San_Pietro_in_Vincoli.jpg.

3. People sometimes try to argue that while there may be errors in the surviving ancient manuscripts of the Bible, the original manuscripts (called "autographs") were inerrant. However, we don't have those original manuscripts, so the argument makes little real difference.

Moses's Horns

A good example of interpreters misunderstanding the Bible shows up in Michelangelo's statue of Moses. (See figure 6.) You'll notice that Moses has horns sticking out of his head. Exodus 34:29–35 says that Moses didn't know his face radiated after he spent time speaking with God. However, the Hebrew word for *radiate* is similar to the Hebrew word for *horn*. So when Jerome translated the text into Latin in the fourth century, he mistakenly wrote, "Moses didn't know that his face was horned." This mistake seems funny today, but it illustrates how the church has sometimes made significant mistakes in translating and interpreting the Bible.

Stick to safer literature! Crack open a dictionary and see how far you can make it before your eyes move over the words without anything registering in your mind. Spend some time with a philosophy textbook. Peruse historical accounts that stick only to the bare facts, with minimum interpretation. Study the first one thousand digits of π. But don't read the Bible itself, paying close attention to the oddities, wonders, and surprises therein.

A Way of Becoming Closer to God

Christians have proposed a variety of other models of biblical authority. Many of these models stress that the Bible is not God—just a way to become closer to God.[4] Thus theologian Karl Barth says that the Bible is like *an earthen vessel containing heavenly treasures*. It has its limitations and weaknesses, and yet we can marvel that God shows up even amid the shortcomings of the text.[5]

Others assert that the Bible is *merely a finger pointing to God*. We as Christians need to focus on God more than the finger, or we miss the whole point.[6] (See "Imprisoning God.") John Calvin

---

Imprisoning God

The Christian Bible "can only become and be the Word of God so long as we do not seek to imprison God within it; for this would be to make it a substitute for the God who addresses us and makes claims upon us."

Ernst Käsemann,
"Canon of the New Testament," 105–6

---

4. See McKnight, *Blue Parakeet*, 87–88.

5. Barth, *Church Dogmatics*, vol. 3, pt. 1:93–94. Barth's metaphor here is part of his broader idea that Jesus is the Word of God, and the Bible serves as a witness to this Word (see, e.g., idem, *Evangelical Theology*, 36). Cf. Sparks, *Sacred Word*, 156–57.

6. Weems, *Battered Love*, 119; Yang, "Word of Creative Love, Peace, and Justice."

Demand versus Invitation

Sociologist Christian Smith talks about two types of authority. One type involves *power over others*: forcing people to do what they may not want to. The other type is *power to get things done*, which involves transforming people to act differently. He suggests that we think of biblical authority less in terms of forcefulness and more in terms of transformative power.[a]

New Testament scholar Joel Green gets at a similar idea: "The authority of Scripture is less demand and more invitation to come and live this story, to inhabit the narrative of God's ongoing and gracious purpose for his people."[b]

a. C. Smith, *Bible Made Impossible*, 164–65.
b. J. Green, *Seized by Truth*, 170; cf. Pregeant, *Reading the Bible*, 32; Lancaster, *Women and the Authority of Scripture*, chap. 6.

---

made a similar suggestion, likening the Bible to *a pair of glasses that allow us to see who God is*. It lets us see God, but it shouldn't be equated with God's presence in the world.[7]

These images provide important reminders that our ultimate focus is God, not the Bible itself. Yet when these images become our primary ways of thinking about the Bible, they fall flat. First, they imply that the Bible is all about God. While God is the dominant character in the Bible, the Bible has much to teach us about creation, other people, and ourselves. These metaphors don't do justice to how the Bible has much to tell us about these other things.

Second, none of these metaphors capture how strange the Bible is. The Bible upsets our expectations. It's filled with complexity. It shocks its readers. By comparison, a piece of pottery, a pointing finger, a pair of spectacles—these images are too boring to capture the challenges and the joys of reading the Bible.

A Better Model

The church today needs a better model of biblical authority, one that reflects the living nature of God's Word, one that makes better sense of all parts of the Bible, not just true-or-false sentences. We need a way of approaching Scripture that entails respect and honor, while still giving us room to admit that some texts make very little sense to us today. We need a model

---

7. Calvin, *Institutes* 1.6.1. See also Kort, *"Take, Read,"* 31. Bloesch, *Holy Scripture*, 59, joins Calvin in using an optical metaphor, saying that the Bible is like a lightbulb.

that doesn't come from ideas of authority that can be easily abused, one that has less to do with drill sergeants or inerrancy and more to do with healthy relationships.[8]

Throughout this book, I have argued that THE OLD TESTAMENT IS OUR FRIEND IN FAITH. This metaphor suggests that however old the Old Testament may be, it's still alive—something that can speak to us in powerful ways today. Like a friend you love to be with, the Old Testament is playful, exciting, honest, passionate, and full of life.

Seeing the Old Testament as our friend in faith explains how we can be firmly committed to Scripture, even as we express questions, doubts, and possible disagreements with it. The same thing happens with our friends. We respect them. We honor them. We take what they say with great seriousness, even if we sometimes question or doubt what they say.

Some will say that we need a more forceful model of biblical authority, one that evokes more power and control. Yet who has more power over us than our closest friends? Who influences us more than the company we keep? (See "Demand versus Invitation.")

As I observed in chapter 6, there have been times when my closest friends have said to me, "Matt, I think you're making a huge mistake." In those moments, they spoke to me with a transformative power that reached to the core of who I am. My friends changed the course of my life. They made me a better person. (See "Speaking Painful Truth.")

We may give lip service to rulers and complete our boss's assignments, but our friends are the ones who change us in profound ways. We turn to our companions when we need someone the most. We take their words more seriously than anyone else's. We let the words of our closest friends into our hearts, and they make us better people.

Of all our friends in faith, the Old Testament is easily the quirkiest. This friend is from another culture and speaks with a thick Hebrew accent. There's also quite a generation gap—one that spans over two thousand years.

> **Speaking Painful Truth**
>
> "To love others [so much] that you cannot bear to see the stain of sin upon them, and to speak painful truth through loving words,—that *is* friendship."
>
> Henry Ward Beecher,
> *Life Thoughts*, 81–82, alt.

As soon as the Old Testament begins to speak, our minds fill with questions.

Yet we need this oddball of a companion precisely because the Old Testament shatters our expectations and forces us to think about things in new and

8. Cf. McKnight, *Blue Parakeet*, 84–86, 89–93.

creative ways. The Old Testament ensures there will always be more to learn about God, God's desires, and God's creation.

Conclusion

Just what kind of friend in faith is the Old Testament? It's more like someone you'd meet in a bar than someone you'd meet in a church. It's rough around the edges. It speaks with brutal honesty. It doesn't sugarcoat much of anything. It doesn't mind sharing its sorrow, its anger, or its secrets. The Old Testament is not at all what we expect the Bible to be. It doesn't match its reputation very well.

We hear that this friend is opposed to science—even to the point of denying the greatest areas of consensus in the scientific community. However, when we get to know the Old Testament better, we learn that it loves to speak in moving, symbolic stories about the fundamentals of humanity and the world. We also discover that the Old Testament has a critical openness about the world's origins. It's fairly open to what people think about the dawn of time, but it refuses to use accounts of the world's origins to excuse violence or inequality.

We're stunned to find the Old Testament talking frankly about topics avoided in polite company. The Old Testament speaks openly about scandals, sex, violence, and gore. And while its favorite topics initially strike us as odd, just the opposite of what we think God would want us talking about, we soon realize that the Old Testament addresses the times in life when we need a friend the most. It deals with our sinfulness and violence because scars from wrongdoing cover our fallen world.

We worry that the Old Testament is a male chauvinist from a patriarchal culture far removed from our own. Certainly it often reflects such a culture. Yet when we study it carefully, we see that there are moments when it breaks free from the constricting biases of its day. In its foundational statement about gender, it daringly affirms that women and men share in the image of God. As it proceeds, it surprises us repeatedly in how it affirms the worth of women though its surrounding culture did not.

We're tempted to disregard the Old Testament as a legalistic prude. However, as we spend more and more time with the Old Testament, we find that it's actually more like a law professor who knows different laws that, on close study, have much to teach us today.

The Old Testament strikes us as a very confused individual who has great difficulty keeping things straight and speaks in contradictory ways. Yet the closer we get to the Old Testament, the more we realize that it actually has very complex conceptions of truth, ones that are entirely appropriate for talking about an infinitely complex God.

We are shocked, even offended, at the raw intensity with which the Old Testament prays: how it hides nothing in its heart, how it screams in both rage and sorrow, how it asks God questions that are piercing if not insulting. We deem it wrong to pray likewise, until it dawns on us that anger and grief are tearing holes in our own hearts while we pray with a superficial politeness that bears only the slightest resemblance to how we really feel.

We fear that the Old Testament has warped ideas about God—especially when it comes to God's anger. We much prefer a supreme being who matches our definitions of love, rather than a wrathful deity we cannot control. Yet as our friendship with the Old Testament deepens, we realize that God's wrath is an extension of God's goodness. We learn that God is slow to anger. When this anger materializes, it's in the face of horrendous evils that anyone with half a conscience would want to see ended. We find that the Old Testament tells us the truth about God. It refuses to talk of a God complacent with evil, a God who's a wimp in the face of the world's great evils, a deity who would make Hitler smile.

The Old Testament has a bad reputation. Our first impressions of it aren't good ones. But as we read it, reread it, and read it yet again, we learn that it's a friend who possesses the realism we need for an authentic life of faith.

The Old Testament isn't just engaging literature. It's not simply useful for the life of faith. As our friend, the Old Testament also offers an irresistible invitation to a richer, fuller, and more faithful life than we could ever manage on our own.[9]

For Further Study

Brown, William P., ed. *Engaging Biblical Authority: Perspectives on the Bible as Scripture*. Louisville: Westminster John Knox, 2007.

This excellent collection of essays provides a variety of perspectives on the Bible's authority. It looks for middle ground between the extremes of seeing the Bible as having inerrant authority and having no authority.

Enns, Peter. *Inspiration and Incarnation: Evangelicals and the Problem of the Old Testament*. Grand Rapids: Baker Academic, 2005.

In this book, Enns advances the argument (which others have made but not in the same way) that just as Jesus was fully divine and fully human, so is the Bible. He does so by tackling three

9. I here intentionally allude to Booth, *Company We Keep*, 223, who uses nearly identical language to describe the literary friendships he has formed with the great classics of literature.

key issues: (1) how the Old Testament relates to its ancient Near Eastern environment, (2) how the Old Testament is exceptionally diverse, and (3) how the Old Testament is interpreted in New Testament writings.

Goldingay, John. *Models for Interpretation of Scripture*. Grand Rapids: Eerdmans, 1995.

———. *Models for Scripture*. Grand Rapids: Eerdmans, 1994.

In these volumes, Goldingay usefully discusses four common ways of thinking about the Bible: as witnessing tradition, authoritative canon, inspired word, and experienced revelation. He explains that each model primarily relates to part of the Bible: narrative, Torah, prophecy, and apocalypse, respectively. Additionally, he explores the extent to which it's appropriate to relate each model to the entirety of Scripture. These are great books for studying biblical inspiration.

Lancaster, Sarah Heaner. *Women and the Authority of Scripture*. Harrisburg, PA: Trinity, 2002.

This book provides a thoughtful, scholarly account of how one can endorse the Bible's authority in light of concerns raised by feminist scholars.

Smith, Christian. *The Bible Made Impossible: Why Biblicism Is Not a Truly Evangelical Reading of Scripture*. Grand Rapids: Brazos, 2011.

In this book, sociologist Christian Smith analyzes popular conservative assumptions about the Bible's authority. While remaining committed to the Bible's sacred worth, Smith challenges common assumptions that don't match the Bible itself, such as the notion that the Bible's authority is like a police officer's authority.

The website www.MatthewSchlimm.com has additional resources, including group discussion questions.

Appendix

A Literal Translation of Genesis 2:4b–4:16

M̲Y TRANSLATION BELOW FOLLOWS THE HEBREW more closely than most modern translations. Hebrew words are given in brackets to draw attention to features like repetition.

^{2:4b} In the time when the LORD God made land [*erets*] and skies:

⁵ No plant of the field was yet on the land [*erets*].
   No vegetation of the field had yet sprouted.

For the LORD God had not sent rain on the land [*erets*],
   and there was no earthling [*adam*] to work the earth [*adamah*].
⁶ A stream [*ed*] went up from the land [*erets*],
   and it watered the entire [*kol*] face of earth [*adamah*].

⁷ So, the LORD God formed the earthling [*adam*]
   from the dust [*apar*] of the earth [*adamah*].
He breathed into his nostrils the breath of life [*hay*].
   Thus the earthling [*adam*] became a creature that lived [*hay*].

⁸ Then the LORD God planted a garden [*gan*] in Delight [*eden*], in the east.
   There [*sham*] he set [*sim*] the earthling [*adam*] that he formed.
⁹ Then the LORD God made sprout from the earth [*adamah*]
   every [*kol*] tree [*ets*] pleasing for sight and good for eating [*maakal*].
The tree [*ets*] of life [*hay*] was in the middle of the garden [*gan*],
   along with the tree [*ets*] of experiencing good and evil. (See "Experiencing Good and Evil.")

Experiencing Good and Evil

Most translations speak of "the tree of knowledge of good and evil." However, the Hebrew word in 2:9 can refer not only to knowledge in an abstract sense, but also experience in a concrete and vivid sense of knowing something firsthand or being acquainted with it.

"Experiencing" makes better sense in the context. When Adam and Eve disobey God's commandment not to eat from the tree, they experience the categories of good and evil in a way that they did not previously, discovering firsthand what it means to do good and evil.

¹⁰ A river goes forth from Delight [*eden*] to water the garden [*gan*].
From there [*sham*], it is divided and becomes four headwaters.
¹¹ The name [*shem*] of one is Pishon.
It encircles the entire [*kol*] land [*erets*] of Havilah,
where there [*sham*] is gold.

Alliteration

Genesis 2:14 contains a dozen words in Hebrew. Most of these words prominently feature an "h" sound:

veshem hannahar hashelishi hiddeqel hu haholek qidmat ashur vehannahar harebii hu perat.

Repeating consonant sounds is called *alliteration*.

¹² The gold of that land [*erets*] is good.
There [*sham*] is also bdellium and the carnelian stone.
¹³ The name [*shem*] of the second river is Gihon.
It encircles the entire [*kol*] land [*erets*] of Cush.
¹⁴ The name [*shem*] of the third river is Tigris.
It flows east of Assyria.
The fourth river is Euphrates. ("See Alliteration.")

¹⁵ The Lord God took the earthling [*adam*]
and caused him to rest in the Garden [*gan*] of Delight [*eden*],
by working it and watching over it. (See "Oxymoron.")

¹⁶ The Lord God commanded the earthling [*adam*]:
"From every [*kol*] tree [*ets*] of the garden [*gan*]—eat [*akal*]—you will eat [*akal*]!
¹⁷ But from the tree [*ets*] of experiencing good and evil—
Do not eat [*akal*] from it!
For in the time of your eating [*akal*] from it—die [*mut*]—you will die [*mut*]!"

Oxymoron

An *oxymoron* is a contradictory figure of speech, like "awfully good." Verse 2:15b contains an obvious example of an oxymoron. Most translations say that the Lord God "set" the human in the Garden of Eden. However, the Hebrew literally means "caused him to rest." On the surface of things, this literal meaning seems incongruent with the following words "by working it and watching over it." Yet it appears that this idea of resting serves to qualify the type of work envisioned: it is different from both the sweat-inducing work of 3:17–19 and the work imposed on humanity by deities in other myths of the ancient world (like the Babylonian *Enuma Elish*).

---

[18] The Lord God said,

"It's not good that the earthling [*adam*] is alone.
I will make her for him: a helper as his counterpart." (See "Assonance.")

[19] So the Lord God formed from the earth [*adamah*]
every [*kol*] living [*hayyah*] thing in the field
and every [*kol*] bird in the skies.
Then he brought each to the earthling [*adam*]
to see what he would call it.
Whatever [*kol*] the earthling [*adam*] called a living [*hay*] creature,
that was its name [*shem*].
[20] The earthling [*adam*] called out names [*shem*] for every [*kol*] beast,
for every [*kol*] bird in the skies,[1]
and for every [*kol*] living [*hayyah*] thing in the fields.
But for the earthling [*adam*], he could not find a helper as his
counterpart.

[21] So the Lord God made a deep sleep
fall over the earthling [*adam*]. He
slept.
Then he took one of his ribs,
and he enclosed flesh [*basar*] in its
place.
[22] The Lord God constructed—
with the rib that he took from the
earthling [*adam*]—a woman [*ishah*].

Assonance

Assonance means the repetition of vowel sounds. In the Hebrew, the end of Genesis 2:18 displays this literary feature. It's dominated by the "e" sound:

e'eseh-lo ezer kenegdo

---

1. The word for "every" in this line likely dropped out due to a scribal error. Other ancient manuscripts contain it.

He brought her to the earthling [adam].
²³ The earthling [adam] said,
    "This time, it's right—
    Bone [etsem] of my bones [etsem].
    Flesh [basar] of my flesh [basar].
This one will be called Woman [ishah],
    because from Man [ish] this one was taken."
²⁴ For this reason a man [ish] will leave his father and his mother.
    He will cling to his woman [ishah].
    They will become one flesh [basar].

²⁵ Both of them were unclothed in plain sight [arom],
    the earthling [adam] and his woman [ishah], but they felt no shame.
³:¹ Now the snake was more insightful [arum]
    than any [kol] living [hayyah] thing of the field
    that the Lord God made.
It said to the woman [ishah],
    "What next? God is saying,
    'Do not eat [akal] from any [kol] tree [ets] of the garden [gan]!'"
² The woman [ishah] said to the snake,
    "From the fruit of the trees [ets] of the garden [gan], we can eat [akal].
³ But from the fruit of the tree [ets] that is in the middle of the garden
    [gan],
    God said, 'Do not eat [akal] from it!
    Do not touch it! Or you will die [mut].'"
⁴ The snake said to the woman [ishah],
    "No death [mut]—you will not die [mut]!
⁵ For God knows that in the time of your eating [akal] from it,
    your eyes will be opened.
You will be like God, knowing good and evil firsthand."

⁶ The woman [ishah] saw that the tree [ets] was delicious for food
    [maakal],
    and that it was beautiful for the eyes.
    The tree [ets] was desirable for success.
So she took some of its fruit, and she ate [akal].
She also gave to her man [ish] beside her, and he ate [akal].

⁷ The eyes of both of them were opened.
    They knew that they were naked [erom].
They stuck fig leaves together.
    They made small coverings for themselves.

⁸ Next, they heard the sound of the Lord God
    walking in the garden [gan] during the evening breeze.

So the earthling [*adam*] and his woman [*ishah*] hid themselves
    away from the LORD God in the trees [*ets*] of the garden [*gan*].
⁹ The LORD God called to the earthling [*adam*].
    He said to him, "Where are you?"
¹⁰ He replied, "Your sound—I heard it in the garden [*gan*].
    I was afraid because I am naked [*erom*], so I hid."
¹¹ He said, "Who told you that you are naked [*erom*]?
    From the tree [*ets*] that I commanded you not to eat [*akal*]—
    did you eat [*akal*] from it?!"
¹² The earthling [*adam*] said, "The woman [*ishah*] whom you gave to be
    with me—
    she herself gave to me from the tree [*ets*], so I ate [*akal*]."
¹³ The LORD God said to the woman [*ishah*],
    "What is this you have done?"
The woman [*ishah*] said, "The snake—it tricked me, so I ate [*akal*]."
¹⁴ Then the LORD God said to the snake,
    "Because you did this,
    you shall be more cursed than any [*kol*] beast,
        more than any [*kol*] living [*hayyah*] thing in the field.
    On your belly—that is how you shall go.
    Dust [*apar*]—that is what you shall eat [*akal*]
        all [*kol*] the times of your life [*hay*].
¹⁵ Hatred—that is what I set between you and the woman [*ishah*],
    between your offspring and her offspring.
    Her offspring—that is who shall strike your head.
    You—that is who shall strike the offspring's heel."
¹⁶ To the woman [*ishah*], he said,
    "Multiplying—I shall multiply your pains in pregnancy.
    In pain—that is how you shall give birth to children.
        Still, to your man [*ish*]—that shall be your desire.
    He—that is who shall rule over you."
¹⁷ To the earthling [*adam*], he said,
    "Because you obeyed your woman [*ishah*],
    and you ate [*akal*] from the tree [*ets*] that I commanded you
    saying,
        'Do not eat [*akal*] from it!'—
    the earth [*adamah*] shall be cursed because of you.
    In pain—that is how you shall eat [*akal*] from it
        all [*kol*] the times of your life [*hay*].
¹⁸ Thorns and thistles—that is what it shall sprout for you
        when you eat [*akal*] the vegetation of the field.
¹⁹ With sweat on your face—that is how you shall eat [*akal*] food
    until you return to the earth [*adamah*].

Indeed, from it—that is where you were taken.
Indeed, you are dust [apar].
    To dust [apar] you shall return."

²⁰ The earthling [adam] named [shem] his woman [ishah] Life [havvah],
    for it was she who was the mother of all [kol] life [hay].

²¹ The LORD God made
    for the earthling [adam] and his woman [ishah]
    leather clothes, and he dressed them.

²² Then the LORD God said, "Look!
    The earthling [adam] has become like one of us,
        knowing good and evil firsthand.
    What if he now reaches his hand out
        and also takes from the tree [ets] of life [hay]
        and eats [akal] and lives [hayah] forever?!"
²³ So the LORD God sent him away from the Garden [gan] of Delight
    [eden]
    to work the earth [adamah] from which he was taken.
²⁴ He drove out the earthling [adam],
    and he stationed east of the Garden [gan] of Delight [eden]
the heavenly beings and the flame of the sword
    that twists and turns to protect the way to the tree [ets] of life [hay].

⁴:¹ The earthling [adam] had an experience with Life [havvah], his
    woman [ishah],
    and she conceived, and she gave birth to Spear [qayin].
    She said, "I have secured [qanah] a man [ish] with the LORD."
² Again, she gave birth to his brother, Fleeting Breath [hebel].
    Fleeting Breath [hebel] was a shepherd of the flock.
    Spear [qayin] was a worker of the earth [adamah].

³ It happened at the end of some days,
    that Spear [qayin] brought
    some fruit of the earth [adamah] as a gift for the LORD.
⁴ But Fleeting Breath [hebel], for his part, brought
    some of the firstborn of his flock and some of the choicest meat.
The LORD paid attention to Fleeting Breath [hebel] and to his gift.
⁵ But to Spear [qayin] and to his gift, he did not pay attention.
    So Spear [qayin] grew very angry. His face fell.
⁶ The LORD said to Spear [qayin],
    "Why are you angry? Why has your face fallen?
    ⁷ Is this not true that if you do good, a lifting?²

2. In the immediate context, this "lifting" refers to Cain's face, which the previous verse describes as being fallen (or downcast) from anger. For more on how this line relates to the rest of Genesis, see Schlimm, *From Fratricide to Forgiveness*, 137–38, 178–79, 183–84.

Inclusio

Sometimes biblical texts contain similar material at their beginning and ending. This literary device goes by many names. It can be called an *inclusio*, a *frame*, *bookends*, or an *envelope structure*. The idea is that the text offers a sense of closure by returning to a key idea found at the beginning of the text. Here Genesis 4:16 (like 3:23–24) makes mention of Eden (or "Delight"). This name appeared early in the passage, at 2:8. The text returns full circle to where we began, causing readers to realize how much things have changed: humanity is forced out of paradise into a world of wandering and violence.

But if you avoid good, at the entryway to sin,[3] something crouches down.
Its desire is for you. You yourself—that is who must rule over it."

[8] Spear [*qayin*] said to Fleeting Breath [*hebel*], his brother,
"Let's go to the field."[4]
It happened when they were in the field.
Spear [*qayin*] arose toward Fleeting Breath [*hebel*] his brother,
and he killed him.

[9] Then the LORD said to Spear [*qayin*],
"Where is Fleeting Breath [*hebel*] your brother?"
He said, "I do not know.
Am I my brother's protector?"
[10] He said, "What have you done?!
The voice of your brother's blood
cries to me from the earth [*adamah*]!

[11] So now, you shall be cursed away from the earth [*adamah*],
which opened its mouth to take your brother's blood from your
hand.
[12] When you work the earth [*adamah*],
it shall no longer give its power to you.
A vagrant [*na*] and a vagabond [*nad*][5]—that is what you shall be in
the land [*erets*]."
[13] Spear [*qayin*] said to the LORD,
"My punishment is too great to lift.

---

3. This rendering is explained in Schlimm, "At Sin's Entryway."
4. This line of the translation is missing in Hebrew but present in other ancient manuscripts. Most likely it fell out due to a scribal error.
5. This rendering is used in Gowan, *From Eden to Babel*, 71.

¹⁴ Think about it—you have driven me out today
    away from the face of the earth [*adamah*].
    Away from your face, I will be hidden.
I will be a vagrant [*na*] and a vagabond [*nad*] in the land [*erets*].
    Anyone [*kol*] who finds me will kill me."
¹⁵ The LORD said to him,
    "Not so. Anyone [*kol*] who kills Spear [*qayin*]
    will be avenged seven times over."
Thus the LORD established a sign for Spear [*qayin*],
    so that anyone [*kol*] finding him would not strike him down.
¹⁶ Then Spear [*qayin*] went away from the LORD.
He lived in the land [*erets*] of Vagrancy [*nod*], east of Delight [*eden*].
    (See "Inclusio.")

Works Cited

Abraham, William J. *The Divine Inspiration of Holy Scripture*. Oxford: Oxford University Press, 1981.

Aharoni, Yohanan, and Michael Avi-Yonah. *The Macmillan Bible Atlas*. 3rd ed. New York: Macmillan, 1993.

Albright, William F. "The Location of the Garden of Eden." *American Journal of Semitic Languages and Literatures* 39 (1922): 15–31.

Allen, Marvin, with Jo Robinson. *Angry Men, Passive Men: Understanding the Roots of Men's Anger and How to Move beyond It*. New York: Fawcett Columbine, 1993.

Alter, Robert. *The Art of Biblical Narrative*. New York: Basic Books, 1981.

———. *The David Story*. New York: Norton, 1999.

Ancient Egyptian Literature. Edited by Miriam Lichtheim. 2nd ed. 3 vols. Berkeley: University of California Press, 2006.

Anderson, Bernhard W. *The Living Word of the Bible*. Philadelphia: Westminster, 1979.

Anderson, Gary A. "Sacrifice and Sacrificial Offerings [OT]." Pages 870–86 in vol. 5 of *Anchor Bible Dictionary*. Edited by D. N. Freedman. 6 vols. New York: Doubleday, 1992.

Anderson, Herbert, and Edward Foley. *Mighty Stories, Dangerous Rituals*. San Francisco: Jossey-Bass, 1998.

Ante-Nicene Fathers. Edited by Alexander Roberts and James Donaldson. 1885–87. 10 vols. Repr. Peabody, MA: Hendrickson, 1994.

Aquinas. *See* Thomas Aquinas

Aristotle. *Nichomachean Ethics*. Translated by H. Rackham. Loeb Classical Library 73. Cambridge, MA: Harvard University Press, 1926.

Armstrong, Karen. *A History of God: The 4,000-Year Quest of Judaism, Christianity and Islam*. 1993. Repr. New York: Random House, 2011.

Astley, Jeff. "Evolution and Evil: The Difference Darwinism Makes in Theology and Spirituality." Pages 163–80 in *Reading Genesis after Darwin*. Edited by Stephen C. Barton and David Wilkinson. Oxford: Oxford University Press, 2009.

Augustine. *On Genesis*. The Works of Saint Augustine I/13. Edited by John E. Rotelle. Translated by Edmund Hill. Hyde Park, NY: New City, 2002.

Avalos, Hector. *Fighting Words: The Origins of Religious Violence*. Amherst, NY: Prometheus, 2005.

———. "The Letter Killeth: A Plea for Decanonizing Violent Biblical Texts." *Journal of Religion, Conflict, and Peace* 1 (2007). http://www.religionconflictpeace.org/volume-1-issue-1-fall-2007 /letter-killeth.

Axworthy, Lloyd. "Opening Remarks by the Honourable Lloyd Axworthy, Minister of Foreign Affairs of Canada, to the 1999 Post-Ministerial Conference ASEAN-Canada 'Ten-Plus-One' Dialogue, Singapore, July 27, 1999." http://www.asean.org/communities/asean-political -security-community/item/opening-remarks-by-the-honourable-lloyd-axworthy-minister-of -foreign-affairs-of-canada-to-the-1999-post-ministerial-conference-asean-canada-ten-plus-one -dialogue-singapore-july-271999-2.

Babylonian Talmud. See Neusner

Bader, Barbara. *Aesop and Company*. New York: Houghton Mifflin, 1991.

Bakhtin, Mikhail. *Problems of Dostoevsky's Poetics*. Minneapolis: University of Minnesota Press, 1984.

Bal, Mieke. "Dealing/With/Women: Daughters in the Book of Judges." Pages 317–33 in *Women in the Hebrew Bible: A Reader*. Edited by Alice Bach. New York: Routledge, 1999.

Balentine, Samuel E. *The Hidden God: The Hiding of the Face of God in the Old Testament*. Oxford: Oxford University Press, 1983.

———. *Job*. Macon, GA: Smyth & Helwys, 2006.

———. *Prayer in the Hebrew Bible: The Drama of Divine-Human Dialogue*. Overtures to Biblical Theology. Minneapolis: Fortress, 1993.

———. *The Torah's Vision of Worship*. Overtures to Biblical Theology. Minneapolis: Fortress, 1999.

Barr, James. *The Concept of Biblical Theology: An Old Testament Perspective*. Minneapolis: Fortress, 1999.

———. "Old Testament and the New Crisis of Biblical Authority." *Interpretation* 25 (1971): 24–40.

———. *The Semantics of Biblical Language*. London: Oxford University Press, 1961.

Barth, Karl. *Church Dogmatics*. 4 vols. in 13 pts. Edinburgh: T&T Clark, 1936–69.

———. *Evangelical Theology: An Introduction*. Grand Rapids: Eerdmans, 1979.

Barton, John. *Ethics and the Old Testament*. 2nd ed. London: SCM, 2002.

———. *Understanding Old Testament Ethics: Approaches and Explorations*. Louisville: Westminster John Knox, 2003.

Barton, Stephen C. "'Male and Female He Created Them' (Gen. 1:27): Interpreting Gender after Darwin." Pages 181–201 in *Reading Genesis after Darwin*. Edited by Stephen C. Barton and David Wilkinson. Oxford: Oxford University Press, 2009.

"Bas-Relief from Palace of Tiglath-Pileser III, 746–727 B.C." Minneapolis Institute of Arts. https://collections.artsmia.org/index.php?page=detail&id=1337.

Bauckham, Richard. "Reading Scripture as a Coherent Story." Pages 38–53 in *The Art of Reading Scripture*. Edited by Ellen F. Davis and Richard B. Hays. Grand Rapids: Eerdmans, 2003.

Bauer, W., F. W. Danker, W. F. Arndt, and F. W. Gingrich. *Greek-English Lexicon of the New Testament and Other Early Christian Literature*. 3rd ed. Chicago: University of Chicago Press, 2000.

Bechtel, Carol M., ed. *Touching the Altar: The Old Testament for Christian Worship*. Grand Rapids: Eerdmans, 2008.

Bechtel, Lyn M. "What If Dinah Is Not Raped? (Genesis 34)." *Journal for the Study of the Old Testament* 62 (1994): 19–36.

Beck, Richard. *Unclean: Meditations on Purity, Hospitality, and Mortality*. Eugene, OR: Cascade, 2011.

Beckwith, Roger T. "The Jewish Background to Christian Worship." Pages 68–80 in *The Study of Liturgy*. Edited by Cheslyn Jones, Edward Yarnold, Geoffrey Wainwright, and Paul Bradshaw. Rev. ed. London: SPCK, 1992.

Beecher, Henry Ward. *Life Thoughts*. Google ebook. London: James Blackwood, 1858. http://books.google.com/books/about/life_thoughts.html?id=1iuAxwQdMS0C.

Bell, Rob. *Love Wins: Heaven, Hell, and the Fate of Every Person Who Ever Lived*. New York: HarperOne, 2011.

Bellis, Alice Ogden. *Helpmates, Harlots, and Heroes: Women's Stories in the Hebrew Bible*. Louisville: Westminster John Knox, 1994.

Bellis, Alice Ogden, and Joel S. Kaminsky, eds. *Jews, Christians, and the Theology of the Hebrew Scriptures*. Society of Biblical Literature Symposium Series. Atlanta: Society of Biblical Literature, 2000.

Benjamin, Walter. "The Storyteller: Reflections on the Works of Nikolai Leskov." Pages 83–109 in *Illumination*. Edited by Hannah Arendt. Translated by Harry Zohn. New York: Harcourt, Brace & World, 1968.

Berlin, Adele. "Introduction to Hebrew Poetry." Pages 301–15 in vol. 4 of *New Interpreter's Dictionary of the Bible*. Edited by Katharine Doob Sakenfeld. 5 vols. Nashville: Abingdon, 2009.

Berry, Wendell. *Bringing It to the Table: On Farming and Food*. Berkeley: Counterpoint, 2009.

———. "The Pleasures of Eating." *Ecoliteracy*. www.ecoliteracy.org/essays/pleasures-eating.

———. *What Are People For?* San Francisco: North Point, 1990.

Bettelheim, Bruno. *The Uses of Enchantment: The Meaning and Importance of Fairy Tales*. New York: Alfred A. Knopf, 1976.

Binz, Stephen J. *Women of the Torah: Matriarchs and Heroes of Israel*. Grand Rapids: Brazos, 2011.

Black, M. C., K. C. Basile, M. J. Breiding, S. G. Smith, M. L. Walters, M. T. Merrick, J. Chen, and M. R. Stevens. *The National Intimate Partner and Sexual Violence Survey (NISVS): 2010 Summary Report*. Atlanta: National Center for Injury Prevention and Control, Centers for Disease Control and Prevention, 2011. http://www.cdc.gov/violenceprevention/pdf/nisvs_report2010-a.pdf.

Blake, William. "A Poison Tree." *Poetry Foundation*. http://www.poetryfoundation.org/poem/175222.

Bloesch, Donald. *Holy Scripture*. Downers Grove, IL: InterVarsity, 1994.

Bloom, Harold. *The Book of J*. New York: Grove Weidenfeld, 1990.

Boda, Mark J. *A Severe Mercy: Sin and Its Remedy in the Old Testament*. Siphrut: Literature and Theology of the Hebrew Scriptures 1. Winona Lake, IN: Eisenbrauns, 2009.

Bonhoeffer, Dietrich. *The Cost of Discipleship*. New York: Touchstone, 1959.

Booth, Wayne C. *The Company We Keep: An Ethics of Fiction*. Berkeley: University of California Press, 1988.

———. *The Rhetoric of Fiction*. Chicago: University of Chicago Press, 1961.

Bowler, Kate. *Blessed: A History of the American Prosperity Gospel*. New York: Oxford University Press, 2013.

Brett, Mark G. "Motives and Intentions in Genesis 1." *Journal of Theological Studies* 42 (1991): 1–16.

Briggs, Richard S. *The Virtuous Reader: Old Testament Narrative and Interpretive Virtue*. Studies in Theological Interpretation. Grand Rapids: Baker Academic, 2010.

Brooks, Roger, and John J. Collins, eds. *Hebrew Bible or Old Testament? Studying the Bible in Judaism and Christianity*. Notre Dame, IN: University of Notre Dame Press, 1990.

Brown, William P., ed. *Engaging Biblical Authority: Perspectives on the Bible as Scripture*. Louisville: Westminster John Knox, 2007.

Brueggemann, Walter. *The Covenanted Self: Explorations in Law and Covenant*. Minneapolis: Fortress, 1999.

———. *Divine Presence amid Violence: Contextualizing the Book of Joshua*. Eugene, OR: Cascade, 2009.

———. *The Message of the Psalms*. Minneapolis: Augsburg, 1984.

———. *The Psalms and the Life of Faith*. Minneapolis: Fortress, 1995.

———. *Theology of the Old Testament: Testimony, Dispute, Advocacy*. Minneapolis: Fortress, 1997.

Brueggemann, Walter, William C. Placher, and Brian K. Blount. *Struggling with Scripture*. Louisville: Westminster John Knox, 2002.

Bultmann, Rudolf. "The Significance of the Old Testament for the Christian Faith." Pages 8–35 in *The Old Testament and Christian Faith*. Edited by Bernhard W. Anderson. New York: Harper & Row, 1963.

Bunyan, John. *The Pilgrim's Progress*. 1678. Repr. New York: Holt, Rinehart & Winston, 1949.

Burke, Kenneth. "Literature as Equipment for Living." Pages 253–62 in *The Philosophy of Literary Form*. Rev. ed. New York: Vintage, 1957.

———. *The Rhetoric of Religion*. Boston: Beacon, 1961.

Cahill, Thomas. *The Gifts of the Jews: How a Tribe of Desert Nomads Changed the Way Everyone Thinks and Feels*. New York: Nan A. Talese, 1998.

Calvin, John. *Calvin: Institutes of the Christian Religion*. Edited by John T. McNeill. Translated by Ford Lewis Battles. 2 vols. Louisville: Westminster John Knox Press, 2011.

Carroll R., M. Daniel. *Christians at the Border: Immigration, the Church, and the Bible*. Grand Rapids: Baker Academic, 2008.

———. Introduction to *Theory and Practice in Old Testament Ethics*, by John Rogerson. London: T&T Clark, 2004.

Carvalho, Corrine L. "Finding a Treasure Map: Sacred Space in the Old Testament." Pages 123–53 in *Touching the Altar: The Old Testament for Christian Worship*. Edited by Carol M. Bechtel. Grand Rapids: Eerdmans, 2008.

Cary, Phillip. *Good News for Anxious Christians*. Grand Rapids: Brazos, 2010.

Cassuto, Umberto. *A Commentary on the Book of Genesis: Part I*. Translated by Israel Abrahams. Jerusalem: Magnes, 1961.

Chapman, Stephen B. "Ban, The." Page 89 in *The Dictionary of Scripture and Ethics*. Edited by Joel Green. Grand Rapids: Baker Academic, 2011.

———. "Holy War." Pages 369–70 in *The Dictionary of Scripture and Ethics*. Edited by Joel Green. Grand Rapids: Baker Academic, 2011.

Charlesworth, James H., ed. *Old Testament Pseudepigrapha*. 2 vols. Peabody, MA: Hendrickson, 1983–85.

Childs, Brevard. *Biblical Theology of the Old and New Testaments*. Minneapolis: Fortress, 1993.

Clabeaux, John J. "Marcion." Pages 514–16 in vol. 4 of *Anchor Bible Dictionary*. Edited by D. N. Freedman. 6 vols. New York: Doubleday, 1992.

Collins, John J. *Does the Bible Justify Violence?* Minneapolis: Fortress, 2004.

Context of Scripture, The. Edited by W. W. Hallo. 3 vols. Leiden: Brill, 1997–2003.

Copan, Paul. *Is God a Moral Monster? Making Sense of the Old Testament God*. Grand Rapids: Baker, 2011.

Cosgrove, Charles. *Appealing to Scripture in Moral Debate: Five Hermeneutical Rules*. Grand Rapids: Eerdmans, 2002.

Cowles, C. S., Daniel L. Gard, Stanley N. Gundry, and Eugene H. Merrill. *Show Them No Mercy: Four Views on God and Canaanite Genocide*. Grand Rapids: Zondervan, 2003.

Crenshaw, James L. *Defending God: Biblical Responses to the Problem of Evil*. Oxford: Oxford University Press, 2005.

———. "The Human Dilemma and Literature of Dissent." Pages 235–58 in *Tradition and Theology in the Old Testament*. Edited by Douglas A. Knight. Philadelphia: Fortress, 1977.

———. *Old Testament Wisdom: An Introduction*. Rev. ed. Louisville: Westminster John Knox, 1998.

———. *A Whirlpool of Torment: Israelite Traditions of God as an Oppressive Presence*. Overtures to Biblical Theology. Philadelphia: Fortress, 1984.

Crouch, Carly Lorraine. *War and Ethics in the Ancient Near East: Military Violence in Light of Cosmology and History*. Beihefte zur Zeitschrift für die alttestamentliche Wissenschaft 407. Berlin: Walter de Gruyter, 2009.

"Cuneiform Tablet: Atra-hasis, Babylonian Flood Myth." *The Metropolitan Museum of Art*. http://www.metmuseum.org/collections/search-the-collections/30000627?img=1.

Cunningham, Conor. *Darwin's Pious Idea: Why the Ultra-Darwinists and Creationists Both Get It Wrong*. Grand Rapids: Eerdmans, 2010.

Curtis, Val, Robert Aunger, and Tamer Rabie. "Evidence That Disgust Evolved to Protect from Risk of Disease." *Proceedings of the Royal Society of London* B (Supplement) 271 (2004): S131–33.

Daniels, Kevin, and Paul Archibald. "The Levitical Cycle of Health: The Church as a Public Health Social Work Conduit for Health Promotion." *Social Work and Christianity* 38 (2011): 88–100.

Darr, Katheryn Pfisterer. *Far More Precious Than Jewels: Perspectives on Biblical Women.* Louisville: Westminster John Knox, 1991.

Darwin, Charles. *The Descent of Man: And Selection in Relation to Sex.* 2 vols. New York: P. F. Collier & Son, 1905.

———. *Origin of Species by Means of Natural Selection, or, The Preservation of Favored Races in the Struggle for Life.* New York: P. F. Collier & Son, 1902.

Davidsohn, A. S. "Soap and Detergent." *Encyclopaedia Britannica Online.* http://www.britannica.com/EBchecked/topic/550751/soap.

Davies, Eryl W. *The Immoral Bible: Approaches to Biblical Ethics.* London: T&T Clark, 2010.

Davis, Ellen F. *Getting Involved with God: Rediscovering the Old Testament.* Cambridge, MA: Cowley, 2001.

———. *Imagination Shaped: Old Testament Preaching in the Anglican Tradition.* Valley Forge, PA: Trinity, 1995.

———. "Losing a Friend: The Loss of the Old Testament to the Church." Pages 83–94 in *Jews, Christians, and the Theology of the Hebrew Scriptures.* Edited by Alice Ogden Bellis and Joel S. Kaminsky. Society of Biblical Literature Symposium Series. Atlanta: Society of Biblical Literature, 2000.

———. "The Poetics of Generosity." Pages 626–45 in *The Word Leaps the Gap: Essays on Scripture and Theology in Honor of Richard B. Hays.* Edited by R. Wagner, K. Rowe, and A. K. Grieb. Grand Rapids: Eerdmans, 2008.

———. *Scripture, Culture, and Agriculture: An Agrarian Reading of the Bible.* Cambridge: Cambridge University Press, 2009.

———. *Wondrous Depth: Preaching the Old Testament.* Louisville: Westminster John Knox, 2005.

Davis, Ellen F., and Richard B. Hays, eds. *The Art of Reading Scripture.* Grand Rapids: Eerdmans, 2003.

Dawkins, Richard. *The God Delusion.* Kindle ed. Boston: Mariner, 2008.

Day, John. *Yahweh and the Gods and Goddesses of Canaan.* Sheffield Academic Press, 2000.

Day, Troy, Andrew Park, Neal Madras, Abba Gumel, and Jianhong Wu. "When Is Quarantining a Useful Control Strategy for Emerging Infectious Diseases?" *American Journal of Epidemiology* 163 (2006): 479–85.

Delitzsch, Friedrich. *Die grosse Täuschung.* 2 vols. Stuttgart: Deutsche Verlags-Anstalt, 1920–21.

Dickinson, Emily. "1129 (Tell All the Truth but Tell It Slant)." Pages 506–7 in *The Complete Poems of Emily Dickinson.* Edited by Thomas H. Johnson. Boston: Little, Brown, & Co., 1960.

Dickinson, Greg, Carole Blair, and Brian L. Ott, eds. *Places of Public Memory: The Rhetoric of Museums and Memorials.* Tuscaloosa: University of Alabama Press, 2010.

Dik, Bryan. "Why the Bill Nye vs. Ken Ham Debate Makes Me Sad." *Acculturated: Pop Culture Matters.* February 12, 2014. http://acculturated.com/why-the-bill-nye-vs-ken-ham-debate-makes-me-sad.

Dikkers, Scott, ed. *Our Dumb Century.* New York: Three Rivers, 1999.

Donne, John. "Devotions upon Emergent Occasions." *The Anglican Library.* HTML ed. 2000. http://www.anglicanlibrary.org/donne/devotions/devotions19.htm.

Douglas, Mary. "The Forbidden Animals in Leviticus." *Journal for the Study of the Old Testament* 59 (1993): 3–23.

———. "Holy Joy: Rereading Leviticus, the Anthropologist and the Believer." *Conservative Judaism* 46 (1994): 3–14.

———. *Leviticus as Literature*. Oxford: Oxford University Press, 1999.

———. *Purity and Danger: An Analysis of Concepts of Pollution and Taboo*. New York: Praeger, 1966.

Dueck, Ryan. "Sometimes I'm Afraid of God." *Christian Century*. February 20, 2013. http://www.christiancentury.org/blogs/archive/2013-02/sometimes-im-afraid-god.

Duggan, Michael. *The Consuming Fire: A Christian Introduction to the Old Testament*. San Francisco: Ignatius, 1991.

Dunn, James D. G. *The New Perspective on Paul*. Rev. ed. Grand Rapids: Eerdmans, 2005.

———. *Romans 1–8*. Word Biblical Commentary 38A. Dallas: Word, 1988.

Edwards, Jonathan. "Sinners in the Hands of an Angry God." Pages 347–64 in *American Sermons*. Edited by Michael Warner. New York: Library of America, 1999.

Ellington, Scott A. *Risking Truth: Reshaping the World through Prayers of Lament*. Eugene, OR: Pickwick Publications, 2008.

Enns, Peter. *The Evolution of Adam: What the Bible Does and Doesn't Say about Human Origins*. Grand Rapids: Brazos, 2012.

———. *Inspiration and Incarnation*. Grand Rapids: Baker Academic, 2005.

"Equal Pay." United States Department of Labor. www.dol.gov/equalpay.

Evans, Rachel Held. *A Year of Biblical Womanhood*. Nashville: Nelson, 2012.

Exum, J. Cheryl. "'You Shall Let Every Daughter Live': A Study of Exodus 1.8–2.10." Pages 37–61 in *A Feminist Companion to Exodus to Deuteronomy*. Edited by Athalya Brenner. Sheffield: Sheffield Academic Press, 1994.

Feder, Yitzhaq. "Between Contagion and Cognition: Bodily Experience and the Conceptualization of Pollution (ṭumʾah) in the Hebrew Bible." *Journal of Near Eastern Studies* 72 (2013): 151–67.

Finley, Bill. "A Moralist Who Loves Racing." *New York Times*. April 22, 2002. http://www.nytimes.com/2002/04/22/sports/horse-racing-a-moralist-who-loves-racing.html.

Flaubert, Gustave. *Madame Bovary*. Translated by Raymond N. MacKenzie. Indianapolis: Hackett, 2009.

Fontaine, Carole R. "The Abusive Bible: On the Use of Feminist Method in Pastoral Contexts." Pages 84–113 in *A Feminist Companion to Reading the Bible: Approaches, Methods, and Strategies*. Edited by Athalya Brenner and Carole Fontaine. Sheffield: Sheffield Academic Press, 1997.

Fortey, Stuart. *Collins German-English, English-German Dictionary*. 4th ed. Glasgow: HarperResource, 2003.

Fretheim, Terence E. *About the Bible: Short Answers to Big Questions*. Rev. ed. Minneapolis: Augsburg, 2009.

———. *God and World in the Old Testament: A Relational Theology of Creation*. Nashville: Abingdon, 2005.

———. *Jeremiah*. Macon, GA: Smyth & Helwys, 2002.

————. *The Suffering of God: An Old Testament Perspective*. Overtures to Biblical Theology. Philadelphia: Fortress, 1984.

————. "Theological Reflections on the Wrath of God in the Old Testament." *Horizons in Biblical Theology* 24 (December 2002): 1–26.

Fretheim, Terence E., and Karlfried Froehlich. *The Bible as Word of God in a Postmodern Age*. Minneapolis: Fortress, 1998.

Frishman, Elyse D., ed. *Mishkan T'filah: A Reform Siddur*. New York: Central Conference of American Rabbis, 2007.

Frykholm, Amy. *Rapture Culture: "Left Behind" in Evangelical America*. Oxford: Oxford University Press, 2004.

Frymer-Kensky, Tikva. *In the Wake of the Goddesses: Women, Culture, and the Biblical Transformation of Pagan Myth*. New York: Fawcett Columbine, 1992.

————. *Reading the Women of the Bible: A New Interpretation of Their Stories*. New York: Schocken, 2002.

Fuchs, Esther. "Men in Biblical Feminist Scholarship." *Journal of Feminist Studies in Religion* 19 (2003): 93–114.

————. "Reclaiming the Hebrew Bible for Women." *Journal of Feminist Studies in Religion* 24 (2008): 45–65.

————. *Sexual Politics in the Biblical Narrative: Reading the Hebrew Bible as a Woman*. Journal for the Study of the Old Testament: Supplement Series 310. Sheffield: Sheffield Academic Press, 2000.

"Geneva Conventions." *Legal Information Institute*. Cornell University Law School. http://www.law.cornell.edu/wex/geneva_conventions.

George, Mark K. *Israel's Tabernacle as Social Space*. Atlanta: Society of Biblical Literature, 2009.

Gerstenberger, Erhard S. *Psalms*. 2 vols. Grand Rapids: Eerdmans, 1987.

Gervais, Ricky. "Humpty Dumpty from Politics." *YouTube*. http://youtu.be/hYytaZ06Hco.

Giles, Richard. *Re-pitching the Tent: Re-ordering the Church Building for Worship and Mission*. Rev. ed. Norwich, UK: Canterbury, 1999.

Glover, Neil. "Your People, My People: An Exploration of Ethnicity in Ruth." *Journal for the Study of the Old Testament* 33 (2009): 293–313.

Goddu, André L. "Science and the Bible." Pages 681–84 in *The Oxford Companion to the Bible*. Edited by Bruce M. Metzger and Michael D. Coogan. New York: Oxford University Press, 1993.

Goitein, Shelomo Dov. "Women as Creators of Biblical Genres." *Prooftexts* 8 (1988): 1–33.

Goldin, Judah, ed. *The Living Talmud: The Wisdom of the Fathers and Its Classical Commentaries*. Chicago: University of Chicago Press, 1957.

Goldingay, John. *Approaches to Old Testament Interpretation*. Toronto: Clements, 1990.

————. *Key Questions about Biblical Interpretation: Biblical Answers*. Grand Rapids: Baker Academic, 2011.

————. *Models for Interpretation of Scripture*. Grand Rapids: Eerdmans, 1995.

————. *Models for Scripture*. Grand Rapids: Eerdmans, 1994.

————. *Old Testament Theology: Israel's Gospel*. Downers Grove, IL: InterVarsity, 2003.

———. *Theological Diversity and the Authority of the Old Testament*. Grand Rapids: Eerdmans, 1987.

Gorman, Frank H. "Sacrifices and Offerings." Pages 20–32 in vol. 5 of *New Interpreter's Dictionary of the Bible*. Edited by Katharine Doob Sakenfeld. 5 vols. Nashville: Abingdon, 2009.

Gossai, Hemchand. "The Old Testament: A Heresy Continued?" *Word and World* 8 (1988): 150–57.

Gowan, Donald E. *From Eden and Babel: A Commentary on the Book of Genesis I–II*. International Theological Commentary. Grand Rapids: Eerdmans, 1988.

Green, Garrett. "'The Bible as . . . ': Fictional Narrative and Scriptural Truth." Pages 79–96 in *Scriptural Authority and Narrative Interpretation*. Edited by Garrett Green and Hans Frei. Philadelphia: Fortress, 1987.

Green, Joel B. "The Authority of Scripture." Pages 527–31 in *CEB Study Bible*. Nashville: Common English Bible, 2013.

———. *Seized by Truth: Reading the Bible as Scripture*. Nashville: Abingdon, 2007.

Greenstein, Edward. "Biblical Law." Pages 83–103 in *Back to the Sources*. Edited by Barry W. Holtz. New York: Summit, 1984.

Grossman, Jonathan. *Esther: The Outer Narrative and the Hidden Reading*. Siphrut: Literature and Theology of the Hebrew Scriptures 6. Winona Lake, IN: Eisenbrauns, 2011.

Gunkel, Hermann, and Joachim Begrich. *Introduction to Psalms: The Genres of the Religious Lyric of Israel*. Macon, GA: Mercer University Press, 1998.

Gunter, W. Stephen, Ted A. Campbell, Scott J. Jones, Randy Maddox, and Rebekah L. Miles. *Wesley and the Quadrilateral: Renewing the Conversation*. Nashville: Abingdon, 1997.

Habel, Norman C. *The Book of Job*. Old Testament Library. Philadelphia: Westminster, 1985.

Haidt, Jonathan, Clark McCauley, and Paul Rozin. "Individual Differences in Sensitivity to Disgust: A Scale Sampling Seven Domains of Disgust Elicitors." *Personality and Individual Differences* 16 (1993): 701–13.

Ḥakham, Amos, and Israel V. Berman. *Psalms with the Jerusalem Commentary*. 3 vols. Jerusalem: Mosad Harav Kook, 2003.

Hamilton, Victor. "One on One." *Ambassador* 39, no. 1 (Spring 2012): 6–8.

Handey, Jack. *Deepest Thoughts: So Deep They Squeak*. New York: Hyperion, 1994.

Hanson, Paul D. *The Diversity of Scripture: A Theological Interpretation*. Overtures to Biblical Theology. Philadelphia: Fortress, 1982.

———. "The Theological Significance of Contradiction within the Book of the Covenant." Pages 110–31 in *Canon and Authority: Essays in Old Testament Religion and Authority*. Edited by George W. Coats and Burke O. Long. Philadelphia: Fortress, 1984.

———. "War and Peace in the Hebrew Bible." *Interpretation* 38 (1984): 341–62.

"Hardcover Advice & Misc." *New York Times*. April 3, 2011. http://www.nytimes.com/best-sellers-books/2011-04-03/hardcover-advice/list.html.

Hardy, Barbara. "Towards a Poetics of Fiction: (3) An Approach through Narrative." *Novel: A Forum on Fiction* 2 (1968): 5–14.

Hare, Douglas R. A. *Matthew*. Interpretation: A Commentary for Teaching and Preaching. Louisville: John Knox, 1993.

Harlow, Daniel C. "After Adam: Reading Genesis in an Age of Evolutionary Science." *Perspectives on Science and Christian Faith* 62 (2010): 179–95.

Harmless, William, ed. *Augustine in His Own Words*. Washington, DC: The Catholic University of America Press, 2010.

Harnack, Adolf von. *Marcion: The Gospel of the Alien God*. Translated by J. E. Steely and L. D. Bierma. Durham, NC: Labyrinth, 1990.

Harrelson, Walter J. *The Ten Commandments for Today*. Louisville: Westminster John Knox, 2006.

Harrington, Hannah K. "Clean and Unclean." Pages 681–89 in vol. 1 of *The New Interpreter's Dictionary of the Bible*. Edited by Katharine Doob Sakenfeld. 5 vols. Nashville: Abingdon, 2006.

Harris, John F. "God Gave U.S. 'What We Deserve,' Falwell Says." *Washington Post*. September 14, 2001, C3.

Hauerwas, Stanley. *After Christendom?* Nashville: Abingdon, 1991.

———. *Unleashing the Scripture*. Nashville: Abingdon, 1993.

———. *War and the American Difference*. Grand Rapids: Baker Academic, 2011.

Hauerwas, Stanley, and William H. Willimon. *Resident Aliens*. Nashville: Abingdon, 1989.

———. *The Truth about God: The Ten Commandments in Christian Life*. Nashville: Abingdon, 1999.

Hawk, L. Daniel. "The God of the Conquest: The Theological Problem of the Book of Joshua." *The Bible Today* 46 (2008): 141–47.

Hays, Christopher B. *Death in the Iron Age II and in First Isaiah*. Forschungen zum Alten Testament 20. Tübingen: Mohr Siebeck, 2011.

———. "The Silence of the Wives: Bakhtin's Monologism and Ezra 7–10." *Journal for the Study of the Old Testament* 33 (2008): 59–80.

Hays, Richard B. "Can the Gospels Teach Us How to Read the Old Testament?" *Pro ecclesia* 11 (2002): 402–18.

———. *The Moral Vision of the New Testament*. San Francisco: HarperSanFrancisco, 1996.

Herion, Gary A. "Wrath of God (OT)." Pages 989–96 of vol. 6 in *Anchor Bible Dictionary*. Edited by D. N. Freedman. 6 vols. New York: Doubleday, 1992.

Heschel, Abraham Joshua. *Man Is Not Alone*. New York: Jewish Publication Society, 1951.

———. *The Prophets*. 2 vols. Peabody, MA: Prince, 1999.

Heschel, Susannah. *The Aryan Jesus: Christian Theologians and the Bible in Nazi Germany*. Princeton: Princeton University Press, 2008.

Hess, Carol Lakey. *Caretakers of Our Common House: Women's Development in Communities of Faith*. Nashville: Abingdon, 1997.

Hettema, Theo L. *Reading for Good: Narrative Theology and Ethics in the Joseph Story from the Perspective of Ricoeur's Hermeneutics*. Kampen: Kok Pharos, 1996.

Hill, Edmund, ed. *On Genesis*. The Works of Saint Augustine I/13. Hyde Park, NY: New City, 2002.

Hill, Joe. "The Preacher and the Slave." Pages 155–57 in *Songs of Work and Protest*. Edited by Edith Fowke and Joe Glazer. New York: Dover, 1973.

Hitchens, Christopher. *God Is Not Great: How Religion Poisons Everything*. New York: Twelve, 2007.

Hogue, David A. *Remembering the Future, Imagining the Past*. Cleveland: Pilgrim, 2003.

Hoppe, Leslie J. *There Shall Be No Poor among You: Poverty in the Bible*. Nashville: Abingdon, 2004.

Horn, Stephan Otto, and Siegfried Wiedenhofer, eds. *Creation and Evolution: A Conference with Pope Benedict XVI in Castel Gandolfo*. San Francisco: Ignatius, 2008.

Imber-Black, Evan, and Janine Roberts. *Rituals for Our Times*. Northvale, NJ: Jason Aronson, 1998.

Jacob, Benno. *The First Book of the Bible: Genesis*. Translated by Ernest I. Jacob and Walter Jacob. New York: Ktav, 1974.

Jacobs, A. J. *The Year of Living Biblically: One Man's Humble Quest to Follow the Bible as Literally as Possible*. New York: Simon & Schuster, 2007.

Jacobs, Mignon R. *Gender, Power, and Persuasion: The Genesis Narratives and Contemporary Portraits*. Grand Rapids: Baker Academic, 2007.

Jacobsen, Eric O. *The Space Between: A Christian Engagement with the Built Environment*. Grand Rapids: Baker Academic, 2012.

Janzen, Waldemar. *Old Testament Ethics: A Paradigmatic Approach*. Louisville: Westminster John Knox, 1994.

Jenkins, Philip. *Laying Down the Sword: Why We Can't Ignore the Bible's Violent Verses*. New York: HarperOne, 2011.

Jenson, Philip P. "Snakes and Ladders: Levels of Biblical Law." Pages 187–207 in *Ethical and Unethical in the Old Testament: God and Humans in Dialogue*. Edited by Katharine J. Dell. New York: T&T Clark, 2010.

Jeremias, Jörg. *The Book of Amos*. Translated by Douglas W. Stott. Old Testament Library. Louisville: Westminster John Knox, 1998.

Johnson, Luke Timothy. "The Bible's Authority for and in the Church." Pages 62–72 in *Engaging Biblical Authority: Perspectives on the Bible as Scripture*. Edited by William P. Brown. Louisville: Westminster John Knox, 2007.

Johnson, Willa M. *The Holy Seed Has Been Defiled: The Interethnic Marriage Dilemma in Ezra 9–10*. Sheffield: Sheffield Phoenix, 2011.

Johnson, William Stacy. "Reading the Scriptures Faithfully in a Postmodern Age." Pages 109–24 in *The Art of Reading Scripture*. Edited by Ellen F. Davis and Richard B. Hays. Grand Rapids: Eerdmans, 2003.

Käsemann, Ernst. "The Canon of the New Testament and the Unity of the Church." Pages 95–107 in *Essays on New Testament Themes*. Translated by W. J. Montague. Naperville, IL: Alec R. Allenson, 1964.

Kazen, Thomas. *Emotions in Biblical Law: A Cognitive Science Approach*. Sheffield: Sheffield Phoenix, 2011.

———. *Jesus and Purity Halakhah: Was Jesus Indifferent to Impurity?* Coniectanea biblica: New Testament Series 38. Stockholm: Almqvist & Wiksell, 2002.

Kelle, Brad E. "Dealing with the Trauma of Defeat: The Rhetoric of the Devastation and Rejuvenation of Nature in Ezekiel." *Journal of Biblical Literature* 128 (2009): 469–90.

King, Martin Luther, Jr. *A Testament of Hope: The Essential Writings and Speeches of Martin Luther King, Jr.* Edited by James M. Washington. San Francisco: HarperSanFrancisco, 1986.

Kirk, J. R. Daniel. "Does Paul's Christ Require a Historical Adam?" *Fuller Theology, News & Notes* (Spring 2013). http://cms.fuller.edu/TNN/Issues/Spring_2013/Does_Paul_s_Christ_Require_a_Historical_Adam.

Klawans, Jonathan. "Concepts of Purity in the Bible." Pages 2041–47 in *The Jewish Study Bible*. Edited by Adele Berlin and Marc Zvi Brettler. Oxford: Oxford University Press, 2004.

———. *Impurity and Sin in Ancient Judaism*. Oxford: Oxford University Press, 2000.

———. "Ritual Purity, Moral Purity, and Sacrifice in Jacob Milgrom's *Leviticus*." *Religious Studies Review* 20 (2003): 19–28.

Knowles, Melody D., John Pawlikowski, Esther Menn, and Timothy J. Sandoval, eds. *Contesting Texts: Jews and Christians in Conversation about the Bible*. Minneapolis: Fortress, 2007.

Kort, Wesley A. *"Take, Read": Scripture, Textuality, and Cultural Practice*. University Park: Penn State University Press, 1996.

Kraeling, Emil G. *The Old Testament since the Reformation*. New York: Harper & Brothers, 1955.

Kuhn, Karl Allen. *Having Words with God: The Bible as Conversation*. Minneapolis: Fortress, 2008.

LaCocque, André. *Onslaught against Innocence: Cain, Abel, and the Yahwist*. Eugene, OR: Cascade, 2008.

Lamb, David T. *God Behaving Badly: Is the God of the Old Testament Angry, Sexist and Racist?* Downers Grove, IL: InterVarsity, 2011.

Lancaster, Sarah Heaner. "Authority and Narrative." Pages 81–89 in *Engaging Biblical Authority: Perspectives on the Bible as Scripture*. Edited by William P. Brown. Louisville: Westminster John Knox, 2007.

———. *Women and the Authority of Scripture*. Harrisburg, PA: Trinity, 2002.

Lapsley, Jacqueline. *Whispering the Word: Hearing Women's Stories in the Old Testament*. Louisville: Westminster John Knox, 2005.

LeMon, Joel M. "Saying Amen to Violent Psalms: Patterns of Prayer, Belief, and Action in the Psalter." Pages 93–109 in *Soundings in the Theology of Psalms: Perspectives and Methods in Contemporary Scholarship*. Edited by Rolf A. Jacobson. Minneapolis: Fortress, 2011.

Lesser, Harry. "'It's Difficult to Understand': Dealing with Morally Difficult Passages in the Hebrew Bible." Pages 292–302 in *Jewish Ways of Reading the Bible*. Journal of Semitic Studies Supplement 11. Edited by George J. Brooke. Oxford: Oxford University Press, 2000.

Lessl, Thomas M. *Rhetorical Darwinism: Religion, Evolution, and the Scientific Identity*. Waco: Baylor University Press, 2012.

Levenson, Jon D. *Creation and the Persistence of Evil: The Jewish Drama of Divine Omnipotence*. San Francisco: Harper & Row, 1988.

Levine, Amy-Jill. "Jewish-Christian Relations from the 'Other Side': A Response to Webb, Lodahl, and White." *Quarterly Review* 20 (2000): 297–304.

Lewis, C. S. *An Experiment in Criticism*. London: Cambridge University Press, 1961.

———. *The Lion, the Witch and the Wardrobe*. New York: HarperCollins, 2000.

Linafelt, Tod. *Surviving Lamentations: Catastrophe, Lament, and Protest in the Afterlife of a Biblical Book*. Chicago: University of Chicago Press, 2000.

Locke, John L. *The De-voicing of Society: Why We Don't Talk to Each Other Anymore*. New York: Simon & Schuster, 1998.

Luther, Martin. *Luther's Works*. 55 vols. St. Louis: Concordia, 1955–76.

Lyotard, Jean-François. *The Postmodern Condition: A Report on Knowledge*. Translated by Geoff Bennington and Brian Massumi. Minneapolis: University of Minnesota Press, 1984.

MacDonald, Nathan. "Deuteronomy." Pages 259–324 OT in *CEB Study Bible*. Nashville: Common English Bible, 2013.

———. *What Did the Ancient Israelites Eat? Diet in Biblical Times*. Grand Rapids: Eerdmans, 2008.

Magallanes, Hugo. "Preferential Option for the Poor." Pages 618–20 in *Dictionary of Scripture and Ethics*. Edited by Joel Green. Grand Rapids: Baker Academic, 2011.

Marquand, Robert. "Pat Robertson Haiti Comments: French View Theory with Disbelief." *Christian Science Monitor*. January 14, 2010. http://www.csmonitor.com/World/Europe/2010/0114/Pat-Robertson-Haiti-comments-French-view-theory-with-disbelief.

Marriott, William K. "Biographical Note: Nicolò Machiavelli 1469–1527." Pages ix–x in *Great Books of the Western World 21: Machiavelli, Hobbes*. Edited by Mortimer J. Adler. 2nd ed. Chicago: Encyclopaedia Britannica, 1990.

Martin, Jonathan (@renovatuspastor). Twitter. August 17, 2012. https://twitter.com/renovatuspastor/status/236573520790945793.

———. Twitter. March 18, 2013. https://twitter.com/renovatuspastor/status/313834245464399873.

Matthews, Thomas Stanley. *Under the Influence*. London: Cassell, 1977.

Matthews, Victor H. *A Brief History of Ancient Israel*. Louisville: Westminster John Knox, 2002.

———. *Judges and Ruth*. New Cambridge Bible Commentary. Cambridge: Cambridge University Press, 2004.

"May 21, 1901: Connecticut Enacts First Speed-Limit Law." *This Day in History*. http://www.history.com/this-day-in-history/connecticut-enacts-first-speed-limit-law.

McBride, William T. "Esther Passes: Chiasm, Lex Talio, and Money in the Book of Esther." Pages 211–23 in *"Not in Heaven."* Edited by Jason P. Rosenblatt and Joseph C. Sitterson Jr. Bloomington: Indiana University Press, 1991.

McFague, Sallie. *Models of God*. Philadelphia: Fortress, 1987.

McGrath, Alister E. *Darwinism and the Divine: Evolutionary Thought and Natural Theology; The 2009 Hulsean Lectures, University of Cambridge*. Oxford: Wiley-Blackwell, 2011.

McKnight, Scot. *The Blue Parakeet: Rethinking How You Read the Bible*. Grand Rapids: Zondervan, 2008.

Meacham, Jon. "Rob Bell." *Time* 177, no. 17 (May 2, 2011): 75.

Meyers, Carol. *Discovering Eve: Ancient Israelite Women in Context*. New York: Oxford University Press, 1988.

———. "The Hebrew Bible." Pages 4–11 in *Women in Scripture*. Edited by Carol Meyers. Grand Rapids: Eerdmans, 2000.

———, ed. *Women in Scripture*. Grand Rapids: Eerdmans, 2000.

Middleton, J. Richard. *The Liberating Image: The* Imago Dei *in Genesis 1*. Grand Rapids: Brazos, 2005.

Middleton, J. Richard, and Brian J. Walsh. *Truth Is Stranger Than It Used to Be: Biblical Truth in a Postmodern Age*. Downers Grove, IL: InterVarsity, 1995.

Midgley, Mary. "Evolutionary Dramas." Pages 239–45 in *The Essential Mary Midgley*. Edited by David Midgley. New York: Routledge, 2005.

Milgrom, Jacob. "The Alien in Your Midst." *Biblical Research* 11, no. 6 (December 1995): 18, 48.

———. "Food and Faith: The Ethical Foundations of the Biblical Diet Laws." *Biblical Research* 8, no. 6 (December 1992): 5, 10.

———. "Jews Are Not Hunters: Biblical Kashrut as an Ethical System." *Reconstructionist* 25, no. 11 (October 1959): 27–30.

———. *Leviticus: A Book of Ritual and Ethics*. Continental Commentaries. Minneapolis: Fortress, 2004.

———. "The Rationale for Biblical Impurity." *Journal of the Ancient Near Eastern Society of Columbia University* 22 (1993): 107–11.

———. "Seeing the Ethical within the Ritual." *Biblical Research* 8, no. 4 (August 1992): 6, 13.

Miller, Patrick D., Jr. "Current Issues in Psalms Studies." *Word and World* 5 (1985): 132–43.

———. "God the Warrior: A Problem in Biblical Interpretation and Apologetics." *Interpretation* 19 (1965): 39–46.

———. *The Ten Commandments*. Interpretation: Resources for the Use of Scripture in the Church. Louisville: Westminster John Knox, 2009.

———. *They Cried to the Lord: The Form and Theology of Biblical Prayer*. Minneapolis: Fortress, 1994.

Milne, Pamela J. "The Patriarchal Stamp of Scripture: The Implications of Structuralist Analyses for Feminist Hermeneutics." *Journal of Feminist Studies in Religion* 5 (1989): 17–34.

Miłosz, Czesław. "Discreet Charm of Nihilism." *New York Review of Books*. November 19, 1998. http://www.nybooks.com/articles/archives/1998/nov/19/discreet-charm-of-nihilism.

Miner, Horace. "Body Ritual among the Nacirema." *American Anthropologist* 58 (1956): 503–7.

Miscall, Peter D. *1 Samuel*. Bloomington: Indiana University Press, 1986.

Moberly, Walter. "How Should One Read the Early Chapters of Genesis?" Pages 5–21 in *Reading Genesis after Darwin*. Edited by Stephen C. Barton and David Wilkinson. Oxford: Oxford University Press, 2009.

Moll, Sebastian. *The Arch-Heretic Marcion*. Tübingen: Mohr Siebeck, 2010.

Moltmann, Jürgen. *God in Creation: A New Theology of Creation and the Spirit of God*. Minneapolis: Fortress, 1993.

Moore, Russell D. "After Patriarchy, What? Why Egalitarians Are Winning the Gender Debate." *Journal of the Evangelical Theological Society* 49 (2006): 569–76.

Morgan, Thomas. *The Moral Philosopher*. 3 vols. Edited by Günter Gawlick. Stuttgart-Bad Cannstatt: Friedrich Frommann, 1969.

Morris, Leon. *The Gospel according to Matthew*. Grand Rapids: Eerdmans, 1992.

Murdoch, Iris. *An Accidental Man*. Reissue ed. New York: Penguin, 1988.

Murphy, Roland E. *The Gift of the Psalms*. Peabody, MA: Hendrickson, 2000.

Myers, Steven Lee, and Diana Jean Schemo. "After the Attacks: The Pentagon; Amid the Soot and Uncertainty, Officials Try to Portray Business as Usual." *New York Times*. September 13,

2001. http://www.nytimes.com/2001/09/13/us/after-attacks-pentagon-amid-soot-uncertainty
-officials-try-portray-business.html.

Neusner, Jacob, ed. *The Babylonian Talmud: A Translation and Commentary*. 22 vols. Peabody, MA: Hendrickson, 2005.

Newsom, Carol A. "Bakhtin, the Bible, and Dialogic Truth." *Journal of Religion* 76 (1996): 290–306.

———. "Spying Out the Land: A Report from Genology." Pages 19–30 in *Bakhtin and Genre Theory in Biblical Studies*. Atlanta: Society of Biblical Literature, 2007.

Newsom, Carol A., Sharon H. Ringe, and Jacqueline E. Lapsley, eds. *Women's Bible Commentary: Twentieth-Anniversary Edition*. Rev. and updated ed. Louisville: Westminster John Knox, 2012.

Niditch, Susan. *War in the Hebrew Bible: A Study in the Ethics of Nonviolence*. New York: Oxford University Press, 1993.

Nowak, Martin A., with Roger Highfield. *SuperCooperators: Altruism, Evolution, and Why We Need Each Other to Survive*. New York: Free Press, 2011.

Nussbaum, Martha. *The Fragility of Goodness: Luck and Ethics in Greek Tragedy and Philosophy*. Rev. ed. Cambridge: Cambridge University Press, 2001.

———. *Hiding from Humanity: Disgust, Shame, and the Law*. Princeton: Princeton University Press, 2004.

———. *Love's Knowledge: Essays on Philosophy and Literature*. New York: Oxford University Press, 1990.

———. *Poetic Justice: The Literary Imagination and Public Life*. Boston: Beacon, 1995.

OED Online. Oxford University Press: March 2013. www.oed.com.

Olson, Dennis T. "Biblical Theology as Provisional Monologization: A Dialogue with Childs, Brueggemann and Bakhtin." *Biblical Interpretation* 6 (1998): 162–80.

———. "Exodus." Pages 81–153 OT in *CEB Study Bible*. Nashville: Common English Bible, 2013.

———. "Untying the Knot? Masculinity, Violence, and the Creation-Fall Story of Genesis 2–4." Pages 73–86 in *Engaging the Bible in a Gendered World*. Edited by Linda Day and Carolyn Pressler. Louisville: Westminster John Knox, 2006.

Osteen, Joel. *Your Best Life Now*. New York: Faith Words, 2004.

Ostling, Richard N. "The Search for the Historical Adam." *Christianity Today* 55, no. 6. (June 2011): 22–27.

Otto, Eckart. *Theologische Ethik des alten Testaments*. Stuttgart: W. Kohlhammer, 1994.

Parry, Robin Allinson. *Lamentations*. Two Horizons. Grand Rapids: Eerdmans, 2010.

———. *Old Testament Story and Christian Ethics: The Rape of Dinah as a Case Study*. Milton Keynes, UK: Paternoster, 2004.

"Pat Robertson Net Worth." *Celebrity Net Worth*. 2013. http://www.celebritynetworth.com /richest-celebrities/pat-robertson-net-worth.

Patrick, Dale. *Old Testament Law*. Atlanta: John Knox, 1985.

Paul, Annie Murphy. "Your Brain on Fiction." *New York Times*. March 17, 2012. http://www .nytimes.com/2012/03/18/opinion/sunday/the-neuroscience-of-your-brain-on-fiction.html?_r =2&ref=general&src=me&pagewanted=print.

Pearl, Debi. *Created to Be His Help Meet: Discover How God Can Make Your Marriage Glorious.* Pleasantville, TN: No Greater Joy Ministries, 2004.

Perry, Ben Edwin, ed. *Babrius and Phaedrus: . . . Fables in the Aesopic Tradition.* Loeb Classical Library 436. Cambridge: Harvard University Press, 1965.

Petersen, David L., and Kent Harold Richards. *Interpreting Hebrew Poetry.* Old Testament Studies. Minneapolis: Fortress, 1992.

Pinnock, Clark H. "Climbing Out of a Swamp: The Evangelical Struggle to Understand the Creation Texts." *Interpretation* 43 (1989): 143–55.

Plummer, Robert L. *40 Questions about Interpreting the Bible.* Grand Rapids: Kregel, 2010.

Pope, Marvin H. *Job.* Anchor Bible 15. Garden City, NY: Doubleday, 1973.

Portier-Young, Anathea. *Apocalypse against Empire: Theologies of Resistance in Early Judaism.* Grand Rapids: Eerdmans, 2011.

———. "Drinking the Cup of Horror and Gnawing on Its Shards: Biblical Theology through Biblical Violence, Not around It." Pages 387–408 in *Beyond Biblical Theologies.* Edited by Heinrich Assel, Stefan Beyerle, and Christfried Böttrich. Tübingen: Mohr Siebeck, 2012.

Porton, Gary G. "Midrash." Pages 818–22 in vol. 4 of *Anchor Bible Dictionary.* Edited by D. N. Freedman. 6 vols. New York: Doubleday, 1992.

Postell, Seth D. *Adam as Israel: Genesis 1–3 as the Introduction to the Torah and Tanakh.* Eugene, OR: Pickwick Publications, 2011.

Pregeant, Russell. *Reading the Bible for All the Wrong Reasons.* Minneapolis: Fortress, 2011.

Price, Reynolds. *A Whole New Life: An Illness and a Healing.* New York: Atheneum, 1994.

Pritchard, James B., ed. *The Ancient Near East: An Anthology of Texts and Pictures.* Princeton: Princeton University Press, 1958.

Rad, Gerhard von. *Old Testament Theology.* Translated by D. M. G. Stalker. 2 vols. Louisville: Westminster John Knox, 1965.

Radday, Yehuda T. "The Four Rivers of Paradise." *Hebrew Studies* 24 (1982): 23–31.

Ratheiser, Gershom M. H. *Mitzvoth Ethics and the Jewish Bible: The End of Old Testament Theology.* New York: T&T Clark, 2007.

Ricoeur, Paul. *Oneself as Another.* Translated by Kathleen Blamey. Chicago: University of Chicago Press, 1992.

———. *The Symbolism of Evil.* Translated by Emerson Buchanan. New York: Harper & Row, 1967.

Rivera, Diego. "South Wall of a Mural Depicting Detroit Industry, 1932–33 (Fresco)." *Bridgeman.* http://tinyurl.com/chb43lj.

Roberts, J. J. M. "The Importance of the Old Testament for the Church." *Christian Studies* 21 (2005–6): 15–25.

Roberts, Robert C. "Narrative Ethics." Pages 473–80 in *A Companion to Philosophy of Religion.* Edited by Philip L. Quinn and Charles Taliaferro. Cambridge, MA: Blackwell, 1997.

Rodale, J. I. *The Synonym Finder.* Edited by Laurence Urdang and Nancy LaRoche. Emmaus, PA: Rodale, 1978.

Rodd, Cyril S. *Glimpses of a Strange Land: Studies in Old Testament Ethics.* Edinburgh: T&T Clark, 2001.

Rogerson, John. *According to the Scriptures? The Challenge of Using the Bible in Social, Moral and Political Questions*. London: Equinox, 2007.

———. *Theory and Practice in Old Testament Ethics*. Edited by M. Daniel Carroll R. New York: T&T Clark, 2004.

———. "What Difference Did Darwin Make? The Interpretation of Genesis in the Nineteenth Century." Pages 75–91 in *Reading Genesis after Darwin*. Edited by Stephen C. Barton and David Wilkinson. Oxford: Oxford University Press, 2009.

Roncace, Mark. *Raw Revelation: The Bible They Never Tell You About*. North Charleston, SC: CreateSpace, 2012.

Rose, Michael S. *Ugly as Sin: Why They Changed Our Churches from Sacred Places to Meeting Spaces—and How We Can Change Them Back Again*. Manchester, UK: Sophia Institute, 2001.

Rowlett, Lori L. *Joshua and the Rhetoric of Violence*. Journal for the Study of the Old Testament: Supplement Series 226. Sheffield: Sheffield Academic Press, 1996.

Rozin, Paul, Jonathan Haidt, and Clark R. McCauley. "Disgust." Pages 757–67 in *Handbook of Emotions*. Edited by Michael Lewis, Jeannette M. Haviland-Jones, and Lisa Feldman Barrett. 3rd ed. New York: Guilford, 2008.

Sakenfeld, Katharine Doob. *Just Wives? Stories of Power and Survival in the Old Testament and Today*. Louisville: Westminster John Knox, 2003.

Salzberg, Hugh W. *From Caveman to Chemist: Circumstances and Achievements*. Washington, DC: American Chemical Society, 1991.

Sanders, E. P. *Jewish Law from Jesus to the Mishnah: Five Studies*. London: SCM, 1990.

Santmire, H. Paul. "Partnership with Nature according to the Scriptures: Beyond the Theology of Stewardship." *Christian Scholar's Review* 32 (2003): 381–412.

Santucci, Peter John. "Telling Details: No Safe Parts in Scripture." *Christian Century*, September 8, 1999. http://www.christiancentury.org/article/2011-07/telling-details.

Schleiermacher, Friedrich. *The Christian Faith*. Edited by H. R. Mackintosh and J. S. Stewart. Edinburgh: T&T Clark, 1928.

Schlimm, Matthew Richard. "At Sin's Entryway: A Reply to C. L. Crouch." *Zeitschrift für die alttestamentliche Wissenschaft* 124 (2012): 409–15.

———. "Different Perspectives on Divine Pathos: An Examination of Hermeneutics in Biblical Theology." *Catholic Biblical Quarterly* 69, no. 4 (2007): 673–94.

———. *From Fratricide to Forgiveness: The Language and Ethics of Anger in Genesis*. Siphrut: Literature and Theology of the Hebrew Scriptures 7. Winona Lake, IN: Eisenbrauns, 2011.

———. "Prisoners of War." Pages 627–28 in *The Dictionary of Scripture and Ethics*. Edited by Joel Green. Grand Rapids: Baker Academic, 2011.

———. "Teaching the Hebrew Bible amid the Current Human Rights Crisis: The Pedagogical Opportunities Presented by Amos 1:3–2:3." *SBL Forum*. 2006. http://sbl-site.org/Article .aspx?ArticleId=478.

———. "Wrestling with Marduk: Old Testament Parallels and Prevenient Grace." *Wesleyan Theological Journal* 48, no. 2 (2013): 181–92.

Scholz, Susanne. *Introducing the Women's Hebrew Bible*. New York: T&T Clark, 2007.

———. "Was It Really Rape in Genesis 34? Biblical Scholarship as a Reflection of Cultural Assumptions." Pages 182–98 in *Escaping Eden: New Feminist Perspectives on the Bible*. Edited by Harold C. Washington, Susan Lochrie Graham, and Pamela Thimmes. Washington Square: New York University Press, 1999.

Seibert, Eric A. *Disturbing Divine Behavior: Troubling Old Testament Images of God*. Minneapolis: Fortress, 2009.

———. *The Violence of Scripture: Overcoming the Old Testament's Troubling Legacy*. Minneapolis: Fortress, 2012.

Seymour, Peter, ed. *The Treasure of Friendship*. Kansas City, MO: Hallmark, 1968.

Sharp, Carolyn J. *Irony and Meaning in the Hebrew Bible*. Bloomington: Indiana University Press, 2009.

Sheldon, Charles M. *In His Steps: What Would Jesus Do?* Chicago: Chicago Advance, 1896.

Smith, Christian. *The Bible Made Impossible*. Grand Rapids: Brazos, 2011.

Smith, Jonathan Z. *To Take Place: Toward Theory in Ritual*. Chicago: University of Chicago Press, 1987.

Smith, Mark S. *The Memoirs of God: History, Memory, and the Experience of the Divine in Ancient Israel*. Minneapolis: Fortress, 2004.

———. *The Priestly Vision of Genesis 1*. Minneapolis: Fortress, 2010.

Smith, Michael J. "The Role of the Pedagogue in Galatians." *Bibliotheca sacra* 163 (2006): 197–214.

Smith-Christopher, Daniel L. *A Biblical Theology of Exile*. Overtures to Biblical Theology. Minneapolis: Fortress, 2002.

———. *Jonah, Jesus, and Other Good Coyotes: Speaking Peace to Power in the Bible*. Nashville: Abingdon, 2007.

Sommer, Benjamin D. *The Bodies of God and the World of Ancient Israel*. Cambridge: Cambridge University Press, 2009.

Southern Baptist Convention. "The Family." Section 18 in *The Baptist Faith and Message*. http://www.sbc.net/bfm2000/bfm2000.asp.

Southwood, Katherine. "The Holy Seed: The Significance of Endogamous Boundaries and Their Transgression in Ezra 9–10." Pages 189–224 in *Judah and the Judeans in the Achaemenid Period*. Edited by Oded Lipschits, Gary N. Knoppers, and Manfred Oeming. Winona Lake, IN: Eisenbrauns, 2011.

Sparks, Kenton L. *Ancient Texts for the Study of the Hebrew Bible: A Guide to the Background Literature*. Peabody, MA: Hendrickson, 2005.

———. *God's Word in Human Words: An Evangelical Appropriation of Critical Biblical Scholarship*. Grand Rapids: Baker Academic, 2008.

———. *Sacred Word, Broken Word: Biblical Authority and the Dark Side of Scripture*. Grand Rapids: Eerdmans, 2012.

Speiser, E. A. *Genesis: A New Translation with Introduction and Commentary*. 3rd ed. Anchor Bible 1. New York: Doubleday, 1980.

Spong, John Shelby. *The Sins of Scripture: Exposing the Bible's Texts of Hate to Reveal the God of Love*. Kindle ed. New York: HarperCollins, 2005.

Stearns, Peter N. *American Cool: Constructing a Twentieth-Century Emotional Style*. New York: New York University Press, 1994.

Stone, Lawson. "Ethical and Apologetic Tendencies in the Redaction of the Book of Joshua." *Catholic Biblical Quarterly* 53 (1991): 25–35.

Stott, John R. W. *The Message of the Sermon on the Mount (Matthew 5–7): Christian Counter-Culture.* Leicester, UK: Inter-Varsity, 1978.

Strawn, Brent. "Evolution(ism) and Creation(ism), Canon and Creed." *Nazarenes Exploring Evolution.* http://exploringevolution.com/essays/2013/03/04/evolutionism-creationism-cannon-creed/#.Uaj4TEDFXTo.

———. "Genesis, Gilgamesh, and 'Gettin' Jiggy wit It': Ancient Near Eastern Parallels, Scripture, and Hip Hop Sampling." *Teaching Theology and Religion* 10, no. 2 (2007): 66–69.

———. "Teaching the Old Testament: When God Seems Unjust." *Circuit Rider* 36, no. 4 (August–October 2012): 7–9.

Talmon, Shemaryahu. "The 'Comparative Method' in Biblical Interpretation—Principles and Problems." Pages 320–55 in *Congress Volume.* Vol. 29. Leiden: E. J. Brill, 1978.

Tanner, Beth LaNeel. *The Psalms for Today.* Louisville: Westminster John Knox, 2008.

Tennyson, Alfred Lord. "XCVI." Pages 96–97 in *In Memoriam.* Edited by Eugene Parsons. New York: Thomas Y. Crowell, 1902.

Theological Dictionary of the New Testament. Edited by G. Kittel and G. Friedrich. Translated by G. W. Bromiley. 10 vols. Grand Rapids: Eerdmans, 1964–76.

Theological Dictionary of the Old Testament. Edited by G. J. Botterweck and H. Ringgren. Translated by J. T. Willis, G. W. Bromiley, and D. E. Green. 15 vols. Grand Rapids: Eerdmans, 1974–95.

Thomas Aquinas. *The Old Law (1a2æ. 98–105).* Translated and edited by David Bourke and Arthur Littledale. In *Summa theologica* 29. London: Blackfriars, 1969.

Thompson, John L. *Writing the Wrongs: Women of the Old Testament among Biblical Commentators from Philo through the Reformation.* Oxford: Oxford University Press, 2001.

Thorsen, Don, and Keith H. Reeves. *What Christians Believe about the Bible.* Grand Rapids: Baker Academic, 2012.

Trible, Phyllis. "Depatriarchalizing in Biblical Interpretation." *Journal of the American Academy of Religion* 41 (1973): 30–48.

———. *God and the Rhetoric of Sexuality.* Overtures to Biblical Theology. Philadelphia: Fortress, 1978.

———. "Take Back the Bible." *Review and Expositor* 97 (2000): 425–31.

———. *Texts of Terror: Literary-Feminist Readings of Biblical Narratives.* Overtures to Biblical Theology. Philadelphia: Fortress, 1984.

Turkle, Sherry. *Alone Together: Why We Expect More from Technology and Less from Each Other.* New York: Basic Books, 2011.

Tutu, Desmond. *God Is Not a Christian: And Other Provocations.* New York: HarperOne, 2011.

Verhey, Allen. *Remembering Jesus: Christian Community, Scripture, and the Moral Life.* Grand Rapids: Eerdmans, 2002.

Visotzky, Burton L. *The Genesis of Ethics.* New York: Crown, 1996.

Waltke, Bruce K. "The Literary Genre of Genesis, Chapter One." *Crux* 27, no. 7 (1991): 2–10.

Walton, John H. *Ancient Near Eastern Thought and the Old Testament: Introducing the Conceptual World of the Hebrew Bible.* Grand Rapids: Baker Academic, 2006.

———. *The Lost World of Genesis One*. Downers Grove: IVP Academic, 2009.

Walzer, Michael. *Exodus and Revolution*. New York: Basic Books, 1985.

Watterson, Bill. *There's Treasure Everywhere*. Kansas City, MO: Andrews McMeel, 1996.

Watts, James W. *Ritual and Rhetoric in Leviticus: From Sacrifice to Scripture*. Cambridge: Cambridge University Press, 2012.

Weems, Renita J. *Battered Love: Marriage, Sex, and Violence in the Hebrew Prophets*. Overtures to Biblical Theology. Minneapolis: Fortress, 1995.

Wenham, Gordon J. *Genesis 1–15*. Word Biblical Commentary 1. Nashville: Nelson, 1987.

———. *The Psalter Reclaimed: Praying and Praising with the Psalms*. Wheaton: Crossway, 2013.

———. *Story as Torah: Reading Old Testament Narrative Ethically*. Grand Rapids: Baker Academic, 2000.

Wenham, John W. *The Goodness of God*. Downers Grove, IL: InterVarsity, 1974.

Wesley, John. *Sermons*. 4 vols. Edited by Albert C. Outler. In *The Works of John Wesley*. Bicentennial ed. 34 vols. Nashville: Abingdon, 1976–.

West, Gerald O. Review of *Voices from the Margin: Interpreting the Bible in the Third World*, ed. R. S. Sugirtharajah, *Review of Biblical Literature*, 2007. http://www.bookreviews.org/pdf/5534_5829.pdf.

Westermann, Claus. "The Bible and the Life of Faith: A Personal Reflection." *Word and World* 13 (1993): 337–44.

———. *Genesis 1–11*. Translated by John J. Scullion. Continental Commentaries. Minneapolis: Fortress, 1994.

———. *Genesis 12–36*. Translated by John J. Scullion. Continental Commentaries. Minneapolis: Fortress, 1995.

———. *Lamentations: Issues and Interpretation*. Translated by Charles Muenchow. Edinburgh: T&T Clark, 1994.

———. *Praise and Lament in the Psalms*. Translated by Keith R. Crim and Richard N. Soulen. Atlanta: John Knox, 1981.

Wilde, Oscar. *The Importance of Being Earnest*. Pages 247–307 in *The Importance of Being Earnest and Other Plays*. Oxford: Oxford University Press, 2008.

Wilkinson, Bruce. *The Prayer of Jabez: Breaking Through to the Blessed Life*. Multnomah, OR: Sisters, 2000.

Wilkinson, David. *The Message of Creation: Encountering the Lord of the Universe*. Downers Grove, IL: InterVarsity, 2002.

Williams, Bernard. *Shame and Necessity*. Berkeley: University of California Press, 1993.

Wolde, Ellen van. *Reframing Biblical Studies: When Language and Text Meet Culture, Cognition, and Context*. Winona Lake, IN: Eisenbrauns, 2009.

Wolterstorff, Nicholas. *Lament for a Son*. Grand Rapids: Eerdmans, 1987.

———. "Reading Joshua." Pages 236–56 in *Divine Evil? The Moral Character of the God of Abraham*. Edited by Michael Bergmann, Michael J. Murray, and Michael C. Rea. Oxford: Oxford University Press, 2011.

Wright, Christopher J. H. *The God I Don't Understand: Reflections on Tough Questions of Faith*. Grand Rapids: Zondervan, 2008.

Wright, George Ernest. *God Who Acts: Biblical Theology as Recital*. London: SCM, 1952.

———. *The Old Testament and Theology*. New York: Harper & Row, 1969.

Wright, N. T. *The Climax of the Covenant: Christ and Law in Pauline Theology*. Minneapolis: Fortress, 1993.

Yancey, Philip. *The Bible Jesus Read*. Grand Rapids: Zondervan, 1999.

Yang, Seung Ai. "The Word of Creative Love, Peace, and Justice." Pages 132–40 in *Engaging Biblical Authority: Perspectives on the Bible as Scripture*. Edited by William P. Brown. Louisville: Westminster John Knox, 2007.

Yoder, Christine Roy. "The Objects of Our Affections: Emotions and the Moral Life in Proverbs 1–9." Pages 73–88 in *Shaking Heaven and Earth: Essays in Honor of Walter Brueggemann and Charles B. Cousar*. Edited by Christine Roy Yoder et al. Louisville: Westminster John Knox, 2005.

———. "The Shape and Shaping of Emotion." *@ This Point: Theological Investigations in Church and Culture* 6 (2011). http://www.atthispoint.net/professional-responses/the-shape-and-shaping-of-emotion/220.

Yoder, John Howard. *The Politics of Jesus*. 2nd ed. Grand Rapids: Eerdmans, 1994.

Zahnd, Brian (@BrianZahnd). Twitter. August 23, 2012. https://twitter.com/BrianZahnd/status/238791776381583361.

Zenger, Erich. *A God of Vengeance? Understanding the Psalms of Divine Wrath*. Translated by Linda M. Maloney. Louisville: Westminster John Knox, 1996.

Zuckerman, Phil. *Faith No More: Why People Reject Religion*. Oxford: Oxford University Press, 2012.

Author Index

Scripture Index

Subject Index